REFLECTIONS ON THE LOCH

REFLECTIONS ON THE LOCH

Tales, tactics and top flies for loch trout

Stan Headley

Coch-y-Bonddu Books
2019

REFLECTIONS ON THE LOCH
by Stan Headley

This book is based on articles published in *Trout & Salmon* magazine during a period of over ten years. Thanks to H Bauer Publishing Ltd for permission to reproduce them here.

First published by Coch-y-Bonddu Books Ltd, Machynlleth, 2019

ISBN 978 1 904784 91 3

Coch-y-Bonddu Books Ltd,
Machynlleth,
Powys, SY20 8DG

01654 702837

www.anglebooks.com

For my darling daughters, Catriona Alexandra and Nadine Margaret,
and my brother Marc, who has been a rock.

Contents

Acknowledgements

Where do I start?

Well, obviously top of the list must be Paul Morgan of Coch-y-Bonddu Books, and Andrew Flitcroft and the staff of *Trout & Salmon* magazine, without whose dedicated involvement this work would never have got off the ground.

Next on the list are the photographers – Stan Clementsmith, Peter Gathercole, Colin 'Puck' Kirkpatrick, Vivien Martin, Shane O'Reilly, Colin Riach and Glyn Satterley – whose brilliant and sumptuous photography was the visual making of the book. Not to forget designer Pete Mackenzie who has assembled the layout. Ever in your debt, guys.

Not to be forgotten are my very dear friends – Keith and Julie White, and Danijel and Sladana Vrbas – whose support and encouragement were invaluable. And of course, my oldest fishing pal, Norman Irvine, who unconsciously helped me become the fisherman I am today.

Paul Young, another dear old friend, whose Foreword gives me more praise than I'm due.

And lastly, to all those wonderful people and friends out there who work tirelessly to ensure that some sort of fishing will continue to exist despite all the industrial, ecological and environmental threats stacked against them, especially Colin Kirkpatrick, Eddie McCarthy, Ken Reid, Paul Smith, Don Staniford and Willie Wilson.

Anyone who feels they should have had a mention and can't find it here is very welcome to pop round and give me a swift kick in the fundament. Form an orderly line, please.

Stan Headley

The author's pal, Paul Young, in his element

Foreword

by Paul Young

I FIRST MET Stan Headley when we filmed an episode of the television series *Hooked on Scotland* on his native Orkney. We fished Loch of Harray on the mainland of Orkney for brown trout, and along the shores of Hoy for saltwater sea-trout. He was amusing, helpful and knowledgeable during the filming and we have remained friends ever since.

Stan has written two books: one, *The Trout and Salmon Flies of Scotland*, is an illustrated guide to trout and salmon flies. He is an accomplished and innovative fly-tyer, developing leggy Bumbles and giving us many successful new patterns such as the Doobry and the Sedgehog. The other is *The Loch Fisher's Bible* – an in-depth examination of all aspects of loch fishing. He is a regular contributor of thoughtful and interesting articles to *Trout & Salmon Magazine*, the journal for game anglers.

This collection of his excellent writings from *Trout & Salmon* covers many aspects of fishing for wild brown trout and, as a past Scottish National Flyfishing Champion, he writes from experience. He talks not only about the methods and practicality but touches on the philosophy involved in hunting brown trout, loch sea-trout and salmon. Stan believes that a thinking angler will be a successful angler and his writings are not just informative but also encourage the reader to consider all the different aspects of trout fishing.

He has fished extensively in Ireland and the Scottish mainland and islands, and when I read his articles I always find them pertinent and thought provoking. They are written by a man who knows his subject well and cares about and respects his quarry and the environment.

Even experienced fishers will find something to enjoy and ponder over in this book and I heartily recommend it to you.

Stan, thanks for being a pal and great fishing companion.

The author, doing what he does best

Preface

Loch-fishing, like all fishing, yields best results to the man who scorns the orthodox in method and puts his powers of observation and deduction against the mood of the fish.

Hamish Stewart, *The Book of the Sea Trout*, 1917

My dad's father was a very wealthy businessman in South America (British Guiana as it was then; Guyana as it is known now). A whole wall in our sitting room given over to aquaria, housing all shapes and sizes of tropical fish – quite a luxurious affectation in post-war Britain – was one of the manifestations of the wealth that my dad could access. As a child I would gaze in awe at these delicate, colourful fish moving with total grace amongst the weed fronds. They captivated me and, although we had a primeval television set, I would spend more time studying living fish than watching *Muffin the Mule* or *Noddy*.

And that was the very start of my love affair with fish. My fascination with all fish led me to fishing rather than vice-versa. When we moved to Orkney from Glenrothes in 1958, a whole new type of landscape was opened up to me. We lived in a coastal village in the south of the island group which was bordered by vast areas of reclaimed grasslands. My fish-love was very much a comprehensive, youthful passion – sticklebacks and eels in the burns; juvenile saithe off the piers. Being somewhat of a loner back then, wandering the ponds, burns and shorelines came naturally and, as a side-line, this passion developed into a desire to understand what was actually going on in the alien, aquatic environments.

Of course, my old man took my brother and me fishing on the Orkney lochs, but rather than be trapped in a boat waiting for a fish to join us, I preferred to wander the shorelines, peering under stones and watching insect life hovering amongst the wild flowers. Back in those far-off days I actually preferred sea fishing from the rocks and causeways – there was a greater range of species, both fish, invertebrates, and birdlife. A virtual smorgasbord of nature, and I could do my own thing without parental control.

All the other boys in school covered the outside of their jotters with WWII scenes. Tanks, fighter planes, guns and explosions, which was understandable given the proximity of those dreadful times and, of course, Scapa Flow. Every adult in the local community had first-hand memories of what seems now to be ancient history. I drew fish on my jotters.

In my very early teens I discovered that I could tie trout flies, and I used this talent to boost my pitiful pocket-money (my grandfather having had his business nationalised by his government, the external cash-flow had dried up). Tying flies inevitably drew me closer to trout fishing, and I was becoming physically fit enough to wield my dad's cast-off split cane rods for the bulk of the day afloat.

My first encounter with insight into the mechanics of flyfishing happened one day on Boardhouse when my brother and I accompanied my father. I was 'on the oars' and they were fishing when they both played fish at the same time. It turned out that both Paul's fly and my father's fly were in the single trout's mouth. While they argued as to who could claim the trout, I was more interested in how this could happen. So, I started watching what was going on. And then I noticed that my brother wasn't keeping up with his flies against the wind drift whilst my dad was. It occurred to me that the fish had engulfed Paul's fly on dead drift and then swam over and attacked my father's fly on a tight line. Paul had only connected with the fish because of its flight reaction to my dad's strike. A lesson learnt at an early age. Always fish your flies faster upwind than the boat is drifting downwind.

Eventually the bright lights and the music scene attracted me to London where I spent six years. No trout fishing was available, so I turned to coarse fishing. This was an eye-opener. I had come from a fishing environment where a nine-foot length of 9 lb b.s. nylon was used for ¾ lb fish, and absolutely no consideration of fish behaviour was ever factored into human fishing activities. Coarse fishing taught me to take a technical, quasi-scientific approach to trout fishing when I returned to Orkney in the '70s.

It's almost as if I had been born an observer, a sceptic and a seeker after reason. Accepted 'truth' was not for me unless I could verify it, and neither was rote learning (probably one of the reasons I was a such poor scholar). Answers had to come from logic and observation. Using human logic to analyse trout behaviour has many pit-falls, but some scientific reasoning reduced their number. Not a lot of my compatriots indulged in this type of thinking, and treated my theories with doubt at best, and scorn more often than not. Flyfishing was, back then, full of trite suppositions, feeble anthropomorphisms and half-baked theories. It's not an awful lot better today.

In the following chapters you may read propositions, concepts and theories that don't fit with your ideas of flyfishing. It matters not a jot. But what does matter is that the ideas I put forward may make you think or even, maybe, re-think. I don't, by any stretch of imagination, have all the answers. No-one does. But we, together, can make great leaps forward in the fundamentals in the great art of flyfishing.

Keep that mind open, and the lines tight.

A typical Scottish Highland wild brown trout

— 1 —

Real Trout

IF YOU ARE planning a trip to Scotland this year for some real trout fishing, there is a list of things worth bearing in mind.

- Every adult male is not called Jock.
- The staple diet is not haggis and porridge.
- Only eccentrics, wedding guests, and people from Edinburgh wear the kilt.
- Real wild trout don't behave like stocked trout of any species.

The principal difference between wild brown trout and rainbows, from an angling perspective, is that browns are largely territorial fish and rainbows like to shoal-up and wander. These basic behavioural differences make themselves known to anglers in a variety of different ways. Traditional boat fishing – drifting the shallows; working along a contour line; continually covering new 'ground' is a reflection of the territorial behaviour of wild trout. The modern-day tendency to anchor-up is a reaction to rainbow trout behaviour, which can be defined thus – find a place where they are, or have been, and they will turn up there repeatedly, throughout the day, until some extraneous factor changes their routine.

The latter method is hopeless for the large majority of wild trout populations, because once an area has been fished for a given amount of time, the trout within it are either caught or spooked, and the chances of further catches within the area are minimal because trout will not be moving into the cleared area in the foreseeable future. However, drift fishing for rainbows or wild browns can be very successful. Drift fishing allowing you to pass over new territory containing fresh brown trout, or through water through which shoals of rainbows are travelling.

And to continue this line of thought and action, the rainbow trout fishing technique of finding a bank location and staying put, covering a procession of fish wandering through a precise area, fails for brown trout for exactly the same reasons as those given above. It was always easy to spot southern anglers bank fishing a brown trout loch by their tendency to stay in any spot where they'd come into contact with a fish or two and being perplexed as to why continued fishing in that area had produced no further action.

To put meat on the bones of this insight, one must fully understand trout behaviour. Wild trout, being territorial, inhabit a given amount of water which can be defined as three-dimensional, reaching from loch bed to surface. Their hunting technique tends to be in a vertical direction, the fish lying deep and feeding above their position. Stocked fish, due to their shoaling behaviour – and this extends to tank-reared brown trout, whose basic territorial instinct has been compromised by artificially induced feeding within a tank environment over a long period – tend to feed in a horizontal direction, feeding at a given depth and continually moving throughout this horizontal plane in search of new food items.

These well-defined feeding practices can be easily seen in fishing experience by the differing ways we catch browns and rainbows. Rainbow trout anglers well appreciate the need for specific line densities, as the critical factor is 'find the depth' and presenting their flies within this horizontal feeding zone. Rainbows are pelagic feeders, much in the way that herring, mackerel, and other shoaling fish are. This tends to make them much more selective feeders than wild browns, as they will home in on specific shoaling food items trapped within, or moving through, precise bands of water, e.g. daphnia, midge pupae, fish fry. Pelagic feeders tend to show, by stomach content analysis, one specific item of prey with few opportunistic additions. Loch or lake wild brown trout spend their formative years in streams before taking up a stillwater habitation. This encourages them to adopt feeding behaviour based on the premise that their 'lie' is inviolate, and that the stream will bring their food to them and little active hunting is required. Their adult feeding mirrors this adaptation. They still feed primarily above their resting position and hold in their selected area expecting to be provided their nutritional requirements. Another truism is that wild trout tend to show variety of prey in stomach content analysis, unless a harvest of prey items – a hatch of insects – is available. Loch anglers, appreciating the territorial and vertical feeding nature of their prey, concern themselves less with depth of presentation and more with area location, and a water depth where bottom lying fish will be able to see their flies and respond in a positive nature. The illustration shows this better than words can explain.

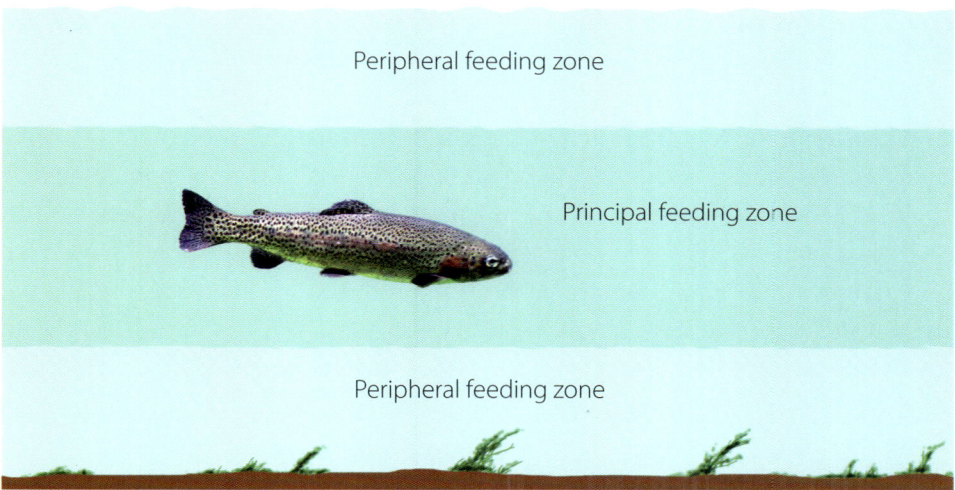

Trout feeding regimes: above, Rainbow Trout and below, Brown Trout

Furthermore, because rainbows have a pelagic, searching lifestyle, their feeding behaviour drives them towards a continuous feeding regime. Basically, they are 'protein hoovers,' always hunting, always feeding. Wild browns are opportunistic feeders; taking almost anything edible which strays into their territory, whether trapped in the surface film or venturing out from under a stone on the bottom. But they can, and do, undergo long periods of fasting brought about by the spasmodic production of food by their environment – bingeing when possible and becoming comatose to preserve stored energy when forced by circumstance.

Of course, in life nothing is quite as cut and dried as the above may tend to suggest. There are populations of wild trout which show pelagic behavioural predispositions. Famous waters such as Loch Leven and Lough Melvin have trout populations which have adapted their behaviour to suit the environment. Both of these waters produce large quantities of daphnia, and this has encouraged trout to adapt to suit. Melvin's sonaghan show the extreme end of such an ecological reaction, in that they have become a racially distinct subspecies, not interbreeding with other races of trout within the lough. Leven fish have not quite gone that far, probably because the factors impelling them towards a pelagic lifestyle have not been in operation for as long as those in Melvin.

Other lochs show a slightly watered-down version of these phenomena. Boardhouse, Watten, Calladail and Harray, and many others, seem to have split populations, with a substantial percentage of their resident trout betraying pelagic behaviour, shoaling in open water, whilst a significant number remain in shallow water and show classic territorial response. The behaviour of either is neither fixed nor firm, as the pelagic trout rarely exceed the 2 lb mark and the territorial fish tend, on average, to be heavier than their offshore brothers and sisters. This would indicate that there is movement between the populations, the smaller fish finding it easier to succeed through a pelagic lifestyle, the larger fish finding opportunistic feeding behaviour better suited to maintaining their girth and appetite.

Colouration also gives the game away. Pelagic feeding trout tend to have silvery bellies, few, if any, red spots and green/grey backs. This reflects camouflage requirements produced by a 'high in the water' location preference – they expect unwelcome predation to come from below. The colouration of territorial trout tends to mimic the tones of the bottom of the lake/loch – browns, black or, occasionally, green backs, golden bellies, with a rich spattering of different coloured spots on their flanks. Predators searching for such trout tend to attack from above. This colour pattern extends through most fish species of a similar bent – pike, carp and cod being either territorial or strictly bottom feeding are colourful fish, whilst high swimming pelagic feeders such as marine salmon, herring, roach, etc., tend to be silvery and less colourful.

One of the major criticisms of brown trout is that they don't fight as well as rainbows. Rainbows tend to streak off like a 'cut cat' whilst browns 'dog' around the boat and frequently end up being played 'out the back'. The rainbow trout in question has no definitive home and is simply trying to get as far away as possible from the source of danger. The brown trout, however, has been caught in his home and wants to stay where he feels safe. It is common for a brown trout to stay fighting in exactly the same place as he was hooked, and any perceived motion away is actually supplied by boat drift, which is why big browns are almost invariably played out of the back of a drifting boat.

So how does this affect angling practice? Well, it should be obvious from the above that tactics should be honed to suit the fish in question. Boats drifting the shallows, or step-and-cast wading, is by far the best means by which to locate and catch better than average sized wild trout. Staying put equates to catching sod all. Locating the feeding shoal of pelagic feeding trout will ensure sport, and staying within the area that the shoal prefers will see maximisation of catch.

Always remember that wild trout tend to be territorial, opportunistic feeders that feed in the area above them, and fish accordingly. Offer them variety in fly selection because this will mimic the natural diversity of food items entering their domain. Be aware that the bulk of natural feed is to be found in shallow water and concentrate your efforts in such areas – that's where the bulk of fish, and every glass case specimen, will be.

If you are on a wild trout loch where the locals fish over the open water, be assured that trout with a pelagic lifestyle are to be found there, and by all means use reservoir techniques to catch them. Depth will be critical, and a variety of line densities may have to be employed to correctly locate them. More than likely the fish will be feeding on daphnia, and appropriately coloured flies, in black, white, orange or lime-green will, more often than not, do the business. Don't expect to find such fish whilst wading or bank fishing, as they are open water fish and best targeted from a boat. So, if you are bank fishing, keep on the move.

And one last tip which may stand you in good stead whilst angling in the wild North – dry fly, in appropriate conditions, works better on wild, territorial trout than it does on rainbows. There is a false impression that dry fly tactics were invented on southern reservoirs and that said methods are for rainbows only. Nothing could be farther from the truth. I have books in my library, dating back to the early part of the last century, which have whole chapters dedicated to dry fly technique for loch-style wild trout fishing. A trip to the big Irish loughs will convince anyone willing to learn that dry fly techniques are essential tactics on those waters. Many years ago, when I first seriously employed dry fly tactics on Orkney wild trout, all the lochs I fished produced their best fish to dries. It is a most enjoyable and efficient way of selecting out big, territorial browns whose laziness and opportunism is perfectly addressed by insects trapped in the surface film, drifting over their domain.

So, there you have the fundamentals to ensure good wild trout fishing. They may not behave as your local pit, pond or reservoir fish do, so adapt to suit the local fish because the fish, as sure as hell, won't adapt to suit you.

– 2 –

Interior Lighting

A VERY IMPORTANT aspect of fly-tying is the art of imitation. Unfortunately, when we set our minds to imitating trout food, most of our tying time can be wasted. I've lost count of the number of guys (and gals) who have shown me patterns that they have devised as imitations of real-life bugs, that totally miss a fundamental point – what you see is not necessarily what you get! Or to put it another way; for trout, seeing is not always believing.

It's all to do with how we see things as opposed to how they appear to trout. I've said all this before, but it one of the most fundamental rules that an innovative fly tyer can learn – humans don't see things as trout see them. When we look at, say, a buzzer pupa with a view to imitating it, we will lay it on our palm or, perhaps, float it in a small dish of water, and the image we see is produced by reflective light – that is, light from the sky/sun shines on the subject and bounces back to our eyes, producing an image. We then take this image and replicate it at the tying bench. It looks good. In fact, the finished fly cannot be faulted; it's almost an identical copy of the real thing. Then why is it, more often than not, ignored when placed in front of a fish which is munching its way through a succession of identical naturals?

The world of trout rarely has much use for reflected light. Fish which have their eyes placed on the upper side of the skull (this includes all salmonids) are programmed to hunt and feed above their position. For a trout to look up it can remain in a horizontal position; for it to look down it has to manoeuvre its body into a virtually vertical state. That's why the occasional trout which is a habitual bottom feeder often has a rubbed and blistered nose. They are not intrinsically designed to feed below their horizontal position, hence the nose damage. We used to see this a lot on Swannay, in Orkney, where shrimp-feeders were often not content to hunt their prey in open water, they would root amongst the stones for

Stained glass via reflected light   *Stained glass via transmitted light*

them. It was relatively common to see tails emerging from shallow water as the trout up-ended as they hunted.

Right, with that out of the way, we can now look at light and how it is used by a fish which tends to look above for its tucker. We habitually use reflected light to examine things; trout habitually use transmitted light. Because they view items from below, said item will appear against a bright light source (the sky). If the item is opaque or the light is vastly reduced, the item will appear black. However, most aquatic invertebrates are translucent, and in normal conditions light will pass through their bodies and be altered by fluids and organ colour with their bodies. The bog-standard parallel I use to easily describe this phenomenon is the stained-glass window. From outside the building, using reflected light, a stained-glass window is dull and boring; from inside the building, using transmitted light, the window virtually explodes with colour. That dull, greyish bug in your hand, when immersed in water and viewed against a bright light source can become a living jewel. Beauty is in the eye of the beholder, but dependant on how the light gets there!

If we accept, as accept we must, the undisputable fact that most aquatic invertebrates are, to a greater or lesser degree, translucent, how do we factor that into our imitations? In days gone by tyers used lightly dubbed, well teased-out, animal furs, feather slips, and sparse hackling to achieve translucency. Whether the desire gave birth to the technique or it was a happy accident is beside the point – sufficient to say that dubbing and hackling developed in eras when hard opaque materials were predominantly used in imitative patterns. To the human eye, using reflected light, tinsel bodies, silk thread and floss silks produced passable imitations. Unfortunately, light refused to pass through these opaque mediums so their appearance under transmitted light failed the 'lifelike' test. It is no surprise that modern tying techniques have largely relegated these materials to the 'subs bench'. (It is indicative of how far we have come that the only floss silk that I use nowadays is black. In the 1970s I had the whole range of Pearsall's floss silks on my bench.) In the good old days, trout fishing in stillwater was largely for brown trout and the technique was pulling wet flies. A pulled wet fly can get away with the merest nod in the direction of translucency, because trout were rarely allowed to get a long, hard look at a fly, and the movement inherent within the pattern was enough to suggest life. Nowadays when stillwater fishing almost is defined by rainbow trout, we fish very much slower, and often the only way to lure a 'bow is to present your flies without any movement at all. If you invite a trout to have a good, long look at your flies, you'd better hope it 'ticks all the boxes'.

There is an inherent problem in insect-style translucency imitation. Light transmitting through an invertebrate body has its own fire. Light passing through the internal fluids and organs seems enhanced and augmented. The visible effect is similar to a 'living glow' from within. To imitate this effect requires subtlety, imagination and deftness of touch on the part of the tyer. Done well it produces patterns upon which you will come to rely.

I have been using holographic tinsel over-laid with Spanflex© for some years now, and having ironed out the wrinkles, I now use it for my best buzzer patterns. Duckfly patterns are legion, but most of them suffer from classic human eye/

reflected light syndrome. They look good in the hand but resemble what the human eye sees and ignore the fact that they glow with internal fire when viewed by a trout. Mind you, trout often are in such a feeding frenzy during the hatch that 'close enough is often good enough' with imitations. But the problem with feeding frenzies is that they are the 'icing on the cake' and should the trout get choosy then only the very good imitators work worth a damn.

Well-stretched Spanflex is translucent, even the black stuff. However, one needs to use the fine gauge or translucency is diminished. Holographic tinsel shatters light, producing a very lifelike spread across the spectrum. The effect I try to achieve is the internal fire of haemoglobin (red holographic tinsel) shining through the slightly opaque chitin skin (Spanflex) of the natural. It looks so good it bolsters confidence, and over the past three years this has become my *numero uno* buzzer pattern, out-fishing its competitors by a massive factor. Whether on wild browns on Corrib, or in the far north of Scotland, or on Midlands reservoir rainbows, it stands on its own.

To those who may not appreciate the finer points of buzzer fishing, let me just say that though it is simplicity itself, it is also one of the most exciting forms of flyfishing. The takes are very often compared to hooking a fast-moving train. Not only are most takes almost unmissable, but they have a tendency to come from better than average fish, not to mention the sort of specimens you were unaware of in your 'weel-kent' water. There must be something about static presentation that lures big fish. I've also noted that the other static presentation – dry fly – also tend to weed out small fish. And if you haven't enjoyed the joys of buzzer fishing, whether for browns or 'bows, I strongly advise you to get out there and give it a go. I caught my first Harray trout on static buzzer some twenty-five years ago, plus or minus, and it took me hours to get the look of pleasure and surprise off my face.

– 3 –

The Dalnaha Time Machine

THEY SAY IT is better to travel hopefully than to arrive. And there is little doubt that the trail to Dalnaha cottage will fill the heart with hope and anticipation. However, arrival at this sublime outpost contains its own joys and the balm of spiritual healing.

In this age of technology and materialism, the human soul is, for the majority, denied peace. Our requirement for the tranquillity inherent in wilderness grows as the opportunity diminishes. Life was designed to be simpler. Our need for interaction between ourselves and nature, whilst being actively denied by those environmentalists who, in their hearts, should know better, is a real and living thing.

Fishing in the wild, or trekking the moorland with gun and dog, is a therapy not found in hands-off country pursuits. You will never sleep so soundly or live so well than when indulging in a life nature intended for us. We cannot deny our inheritance no matter how strenuously the 21st century plastic world would ask us. Almost every physical and social ill we suffer stems from this profound imbalance.

I well remember standing on the track leading to Altnabreac and looking southwards into the Flow Country. It was a 'road to Damascus' moment for me. My eyes were opened to a blinding truth – wilderness exists despite us, and while we chip away at its edges with every passing day, it ignores our existence. As I looked over the miles of seeming emptiness it was as if I could hear the strong beating heart of our nation. Don't look for it on Prince's Street or seek its pulse in Sauchiehall Street. It has been obliterated by the bustle of humanity and traffic noise. But in the sigh of the breeze through heather, the call of the stonechat, the imperative demand of the startled grouse, or the roar of the stag, it is there for the beleaguered soul.

To witness the dawn or dusk over the river; to drift the wide expanses of Loch More; to launch a boat on the Duck Loch; all these things are available to fly fishermen. In fact, there is almost too much fishing to be tackled in one short week. And, the quality of it all is unsurpassed. There are vast distances to roam with rod or gun, mile upon mile of wilderness bearing no sign of the hand of man.

Dalnaha Cottage does bow to modern trends in its comfort and facilities, a quality that even the most ardent hunter/gatherer amongst us demands, and its setting in the midst of the Flow Country, on the shores of Loch More, is idyllic. The good men of the region have worked with Mother Nature to create a paradise on Earth.

Come, stay, and, for a blessed time, heal all the hurts, the cuts and stresses that modern society inflicts.

I wrote this following my first visit to Dalnaha Cottage. I felt inspired by the location and feel it is the perfect place for those who grow weary of our modern regimented life and are looking for a less formalised way of experiencing the other, more satisfying, alternative world, and, of course, the surrounding lochs.

LOCH MORE & GLUTT WATER

At the top of the river Thurso lies Loch More. In the 19th century this was the focus of the most prolific, successful salmon fishing on the river. In those days, the Thurso was a spate river and the loch was fished from boats. It was reckoned to be one of the best loch spring-salmon fisheries in Scotland and was immensely popular.

At the end of the 19th century a plan was put in place to control water flow from the system and improve the river as a fishery. In 1908 a dam was designed by P D Malloch for the loch which would reduce the spate flows and allow a steady flow in the river. A very similar plan was realised on the river Helmsdale at roughly the same time. River salmon fishing held a greater attraction at that time than loch fishing, and it was envisaged that creating a larger number of river beats would raise the value of the fishings as opposed to a very limited number of boat places on Loch More. The idea that spate water could be held back by the dam at Loch

More and allowed to swell the river when rainfall couldn't, was, unfortunately, only partially successful on the Thurso.

Back then, circa 1910, Loch More was stripped of its boats and became a safe haven for the salmon which had made it up into the loch. Well, perhaps not a totally safe refuge, for anglers on any river beat could fish Loch More from the shore should they wish. Few took advantage of that option because, unless the loch was extremely low (probably down to its historic level), salmon were very rarely encountered.

That was the historical context. When Lord Thurso relinquished the main river to other proprietors and set up Ulbster Estates (Sporting) Ltd, he retained some parts of the system, notably the Private Beat and the loch and river above the dam on Loch More. The fishing on these locations is strictly preserved for the occupants of Dalnaha Cottage, and there is a boat and outboard available on the loch.

The river above Loch More – the Glutt Water – is stuffed with trout and rising water levels will pull salmon up from the loch. There is some very attractive fly water up there, but the going can be quite rigorous; no manicured lawns in the Flow Country. The waters above the dam are primarily trout fishing locations so great restraint is requested from fishers when it comes to encountering salmon. Trout fishermen will chance upon salmon more often than not, but this area of water is still considered to be a reserve for them, vital to the health of the main river, so catch and release of salmon is an imperative.

Hugo Ross, Brian Thomson and I had the privilege of taking the second boat out on Loch More in a century and caught browns up to 2 lb, although the bulk were shy of this weight. Surprisingly, given the number of salmon that must have been in there, we never raised one although we saw plenty jumping. Loch More is virtually a new fishing venue with a whole lot of questions unanswered.

THE DUCK LOCH

Jamie and Ben McCarthy took me up to fish the Duck Loch one July day this year. I had heard much about it; the quality of the trout; their willingness to come to a well-presented fly; and that only a floating line was ever required. The latter truth was made very evident to me on that day.

As with almost every loch in this region, the Duck Loch requires a walk in from the dirt track road over some quaky bogs and tussocky outgrowths. Nothing life threatening, you understand, but the occasional stumble can be expected. I must admit, to my embarrassment, that I measured my length in the heather a couple of times to the great amusement of my compatriots.

It was a fine morning with high cloud pushing in front of a westerly breeze. Midges were out in good strength but they didn't follow us out onto the loch, thank heavens. I can't say that my first view of the Duck Loch had my soul singing. Flow country lochs are not known for their spectacular scenery, the land being flat and open, but I was reassured that the fishing would well make up for any lack of visual aesthetics.

And so it proved to be, in spades. I had noticed some buzzers, sedges and mayfly on the surface film and was tempted to go 'dry', but decided to give the wets an initial trial, as did Jamie. I plumped for a Leggy Golden-Olive Bumble on the top dropper with a couple of Snatchers down below on a short midge-tip line. The 'Leggy' is a good, vaguely-imitative pattern for hatching mayfly in Scotland, as long as the dubbing is truly golden olive. Many commercial examples have too much of a yellow cast for me … and the trout.

It was only a few minutes into the session when Jamie scored with a fine pound-and-a-half trout to an olive hopper that led him a merry dance. Jamie was getting more trout response than I was, which I put down to fly choice, but later proved to be line choice. The full floater was simply 'pulling' more fish as I discovered when I changed to one. A succession of 'pea in the pod' fish around the 1½ pounds mark paid brief visits to the boat before being released, every one coming to the top dropper fly whether on Jamie's or my rod.

I finally decided to give the dries a trot out and selected a couple of my favourite Irish patterns – Patsy Deery's Roll-Over May and a Mosely May. I could see what I thought were rises to natural mayfly and there was a regular trickle of the duns hatching out. In short order another 1½ pounder engulfed the Roll-Over, and that was my last fish of the day. The wind had swung to the east, rain was pelting down, all insect life disappeared, and the trout said, "Sod this!", and went back to bed. Ben was ill-prepared for the rain and was getting a real good soaking, so we called it a day.

That there are bigger trout in the Duck Loch I have no doubt, and on a breezier day I'd love to give them a good going over with some Hogs. One for the future, if I'm 'speared', as they say in Caithness.

LOCH NAM FEAR

In the past fifty years I've fished all over Scotland and largely given up hope of a truly new experience, something akin to my earliest fishing days when everything was a new adventure. Have you ever dreamed of stepping into a time machine with your modern-day fishing tackle and techniques and travelling back to a time when everything was as nature intended? I often do, but time-machines don't exist, so this would always remain but a dream, right? Wrong.

After our excursion on the Duck Loch, we were next scheduled to fish Loch nam Fear, a remote loch that had not had a boat on it for nigh on thirty years. Not only is it remote but it is a proper bugger to get to, the approach route being marshy and boggy in the extreme. We had a quad bike to make the journey feasible, and I had as much excitement and adventure just getting to the loch edge as I would expect from a day's fishing – grit your teeth, relax your body, hang on and everything will be just fine. That was the mantra I repeated continually to myself as Jamie's driving skills bounced, slithered and sloughed us to the loch's edge. Jamie returned to the road to gather up Ben and his camera gear, and whist he did so I gathered myself together, rigged up my gear and had a long look round. I was going to boat-fish a loch that hadn't been so approached in a couple of generations. To say I was excited was a gross understatement.

Nam Fear is a pretty loch, or as pretty as a Flow Country loch can be given the flatness of the landscape. Bordered by a Forestry Commission plantation to the north and east it was well-sheltered, and there was plenty of fish sign, rises all over the loch but mostly along the rocky western shoreline. Small and shallow, nam Fear was a delight to fish even though the breeze was very light and variable all day.

Given all the fish sign that we were seeing, I had no compunction in dispatching the first fish to come to hand. A loch that hasn't been fished for nigh on thirty years is a blank sheet of paper and I felt an overwhelming desire to fill in the blanks. The marrow spoon showed a good diet of midge pupae, pea mussels and a scattering of unidentifiable to the naked eye insects and nymphs. That there were mysterious bugs in there was of little surprise. This was a unique, unexplored environment. I wouldn't be at all surprised to learn that there were new-to-science invertebrates jumbled in the mix.

The trout were some of the most beautiful specimens I have ever seen. The quality of their feeding was borne out by the almost total lack of red spots, flanks were of a steel-grey colouration and small heads and strong shoulders helped them fight like athletes. We never saw a fish under a pound and the best we caught was just under 2 lbs. Jamie caught on a Golden-Olive Bumble and I got mine on a small Kate McLaren Snatcher. That's not to say it was easy fishing, as the near flat calm conditions weren't really in our favour. We could hardly blame over-fishing for the reluctance of the trout to accept our offerings. During our short visit, we hooked and lost quite a few, netted five, and every one was a picture, the epitome of wild trout. A stunning loch with superb trout. I defy you to resist the temptation.

Another unique experience was granted to us that day. A golden eagle flew low over the coniferous plantation and its population of ravens went ballistic, screaming at the interloper. A wilderness delight and a unique experience for me, but just part and parcel of day-to-day experience in the wilds that time forgot.

– 4 –

A Funny Thing Happened To Me
on the Way to the Loch

THE GREATEST REDEEMING feature of fishermen, of whatever stamp, is that they all enjoy a good, earthy laugh – the muckier the joke, the more we like it. Of course, our daily activity is packed with potential for true stories which can be infinitely funnier than the made-up gag.

Some years back, Norm and I were out fishing on the Swannay Loch in early May. It was one of the most glorious spring mornings you could possibly imagine, and the 'dicky-birds' were 'giving it laldy' from the margins. We drifted gently, a mere cast-length from the shoreline, luxuriating in the peaceful ambience of nature in its finest form.

The only sounds to break the all-enshrouding peace were the gentle 'lip-lap' of the wavelets kissing the planks of the boat, the soft susurration of fly rod and line, and the aforementioned bird song. The world was ours, and we, barely uttering a word, fitted in perfectly.

Suddenly we were aware of a figure advancing along the shoreline, singing at the top of his voice. My first thought was that this poor sod had been 'released back into the community' and it was our rotten luck that the community in question was ours. As we drifted towards him, he tackled up and entered into a very bizarre, loud, one-sided conversation, which went something like this:

"Hello, boys. A fine day is it no'?"

[Grunt from Norman.]

"Aye, there's nothing better than a day's fushin'! I've got me flask an' a couple of sarnies, and I'm set for the day."

[Grunt from me.]

"Got onny fush yet? Ach, you boys look like you know whit's whit. Ye'll have a few, eh?"

[Grunt from Norman.]

"Me, I dinna care much if I get onny or no'. It's jist great to be awa' fae the boss, and the phone… and the wife, for that matter, wi' a whole day's fishin' in front o' me. My, is it no' just grand and peacefu'?"

["It certainly used to be!" from Norman.]

By this time, we were right alongside the blithering idiot and there was little point in pretending he didn't exist. All we could hope for was that, as we drifted past, he would get the message and leave us to our peaceful idyll. Some hope!

"I see yer on the floating line lads. Ah'm an intermediate man, me. Only ever fish twa flees – an Alexandria an' a Grouse 'n Carrot. Ye'll have boxes fu' o' flees, I suppose?"

[Grunt from me.]

"I dinna like the boat! Much prefer wadin'. Canna be bothered wi' hivin' to make conversation a' day. But each to his own, eh? A'll jist have a wee wade doon this shore here, an' hope the wind disna change."

By this time, he had to shout to maintain his one-sided conversation, and we were, mercifully, drifting out of ear-shot.

"Ah'll nae doubt see ye later, boys. Guid talkin' tae ye, and guid fushin'."

I was beginning to wonder whether a trip to the far side of the loch was in order when I heard a muffled grunt behind us. Looking round I was greeted by the weird sight of a pair of wading boots protruding from the depths – nothing else, just the boots. The poor sod had stepped into one of the many drop-offs along the loch shore and gone right under, his feet being the first to surface. I had only just managed to say to Norm "Have a look at this. You'll no' believe it!", when he erupted out of the water, arms flailing, water ejecting out of every orifice, desperately trying to get solid ground under his feet. His attempts to retrieve his rod and hat, which had sailed jauntily down the breeze, gave us a few moments more gob-smacked amusement, and then he announced, in his cheerful, irrepressible style, "Ach, weel, ah think ah'll awa' hame and get dried oot. See ye again sometime!" And off he set, whistling a wee tune as if no other outcome to his extremely short day's fishing was imaginable or preferable.

Some years later I was guiding an English angler who was looking for a trophy trout. I had decided that the guy was dedicated enough to stand a trip to Sanday's Loch Bea where the chance of a fish was low, but if one came along it was more than likely to be the fish of a lifetime. To get to Sanday involved a trip on a North Isles ferry, whose travelling clientele was invariably comprised of couthy islanders – farmers going to or returning from the mart, old age pensioners visiting relatives, wives, old and young, to or from 'the toon' for some shopping, with the odd trout angler topping off the mix.

Islander folk are simple, straightforward people who have a simplistic and very moral outlook on life. Not for them the racy hustle and bustle of town life with clubs and pubs. A church social or coffee morning is considered racy, and a wedding is bordering on debauchery. So, you can imagine the scene. As the ferry puffed its way between the islands, muted conversations in the passenger lounge were all about Maggie's hens going off the lay, the twin-headed calf born last month, the up-and-coming sports day at the school, the price of butcher meat – you get the idea. All this time, as some sort of soporific background, the PA system relayed a radio programme – Radio Scotland or Radio 4 – something innocuous and bland. My mind was on plans to beat the odds and get Mark a 'muckle troot', and he seemed to be half-dozing in the gentle and benign atmosphere.

Through my mental peregrinations concerning big fish and their frustrating ways, a female voice on the radio cut through, clearly stating "There is now incontrovertible evidence to suggest that for a woman to achieve orgasm, some form of clitoral stimulation is required!", immediately followed by the PA system shutting off.

When a couple of dozen people go quiet, the silence is deafening. I will never forget, to my dying day, the efforts made to avoid eye contact by all and sundry. I almost ruptured myself trying not to laugh, and Mark and I had to leave the lounge or make a spectacle of ourselves. The mental picture of the skipper, predicting the course of conversation on the radio and desperately trying to reach the on/off switch for the public address system before the fateful moment arrived, is one that brings a smile to my lips to this day. Oh, by the way, Mark got his fish. It weighed seven pounds.

Out in South Uist there was a ghillie called John Beaton. A wonderful guy, loved like a brother by everyone who ever met him. John sadly passed away at the early age of 47 in a tragic accident, but memories of him are full of light and laughter and he is sadly missed.

John had one all-encompassing weakness, he liked a 'wee drap'. Okay, to be one hundred percent honest, he liked a very big 'drap' indeed, and it was par for the course to see him in the morning suffering the sort of hangover that would kill a lesser mortal, but still rarin' to go for another day on the oars. I well remember coming into the bar of the Lochboisdale Hotel where the rods and ghillies would meet to plan the day, and seeing John holding on to the bar like a cowboy on a bucking bronco. He looked like death cooled down and a testament to the punishment that the body could endure on a day to day basis. Keith Richards, eat your heart out! Approaching the swaying John, whose eyes never left the bar in case it did something unexpected, I asked, somewhat fatuously, "How you doin', John?", expecting a long list of aches, pains and assorted misery as reply. He looked up, focussed his eyes on me and stated, coherently and optimistically, "A-1 okay!" That was John in a nutshell – hung-over past understanding, he was ready for the worst the day could throw at him. God, I loved that guy.

There is another little tale about John that tickles me to this day. All his clients were warned by the management not to take a surfeit of alcohol with them because John would inevitably track it down and consume it. After that happened anything was possible, to the risk of life and limb. On one fateful day, his clients ignored this advice and set off 'likkered up' for an enjoyably 'wet' day's fishing. John, of course, drank most of it, a lethal mixture of whisky and canned beer. Miserably sober, his clients decided to pack in early as John, in his sublimely pissed state, was no more capable of ghillieing his punters than climbing the Matterhorn. Under instruction, John set off rowing towards the mooring point, the aforementioned punters giving course directions. On arrival the guests stepped out of the boat, pulled it clear of the water, collected their gear, and set off for their car. John, when last seen, was still rowing the boat like a good 'un, even though it was high and dry and securely tied to the hitching post.

John, wherever you are, I hope the drams are enormous and hangovers non-existent. God bless you.

– 5 –

South Uist: Grogarry and West Ollay

SOMETIMES YOU GET so close to dream fulfilment that you can almost taste it. But flyfishing has always had an element of tease.

As we approached the machair edge on the extreme western shore of West Ollay, and the flies, following up the Di-3 sinking line, emerged from the depths, I saw a large grey shape following them up. This is always a quandary-filled moment. If you can resist the temptation to act rashly or freeze, one must decide on the course of action in the immediate future to ensure a positive outcome, and there's not much time to deliberate.

Assuming that it's a good idea to continue whatever attracted the fish in the first place I tend to keep doing whatever has lured the trout. So it was in this case. But – and it's a big but – I was fishing the sinking line because I had come to the conclusion that fish were reluctant to come right up into the surface layers because of wind-chill. How far up should I bring the flies before the following fish lost interest?

This was a big trout, possibly the largest trout I had ever come across in South Uist, and I didn't wish to wave it goodbye without a fight. As the bob fly – a WOIGO Kate Muddler (WOIGO = West of Ireland golden olive) – approached the surface, the trout turned away from the flies and showed me a very deep flank. I estimated, by length and depth, that the fish was in excess of 8 lbs. I wasn't about to let it depart without so much as a 'by your leave', so I flicked the flies ahead of the departing fish. I gave the line a couple of short pulls and then, glory hallelujah, I felt the line draw tight. A big fish, pulled up, that doesn't take will often stay 'up' in the water and may be susceptible to re-presentation of flies. I thought I was well in, again on the WOIGO Kate – but the fish gave a shake of its head... and was gone. I was disappointed, but not to the extent of losing the plot. Any encounter with a fish of this class leaves an indelible memory in the mind, often more so than a big fish caught. Strange but true.

As intimated previously, we were on West Loch Ollay in the machair lands of South Uist; one of the Scottish big trout lochs which can justifiably be classed as dour. But then all big trout lochs are dour. There are universal reasons why this should be so. Big fish lochs are always low on trout destiny which allows the available food to be shared by a few fish which grow quickly on a rich diet, so encountering one needs an element of luck or perseverance. Also, because they are well-fed their drive to be opportunistic – taking artificial flies willingly – is reduced.

Many anglers avoid such lochs because their need for 'sport' overcomes their willingness to optimistically endure the many inactive periods between fish. I have, over the years, accepted that fishing such lochs requires diligence and long, sometimes boring, stretches of time. It's a price I am more than happy to pay for the chance of nailing a monster.

Growth rate and ultimate size in trout is perplexing. There seem to be two different types of trout, dictated by environmental conditions. Trout in poor nutritional habitats grow slowly and small fish can be incredibly old. But, given a rich food source (char for example), great size can be achieved. There is low correlation between size and age. In highly fertile environments growth rate can be spectacular, but there is a downside. Fast-growing trout will not have the same long life-expectancy of trout from nutritionally poor lochs, thus limiting their potential size. So, while a trout from rich eutrophic waters rarely, if ever, reach the mid-teens in poundage, ferox regularly exceed 20 lbs, and 30 lbs+ individuals exist in some deep oligotrophic Scottish lochs.

Another thing that differentiates big fish lochs from those with large populations of average sized specimens regardless of fertility or food production, is lack of spawning facilities. Nature's intention is to produce large numbers of fish in a habitat in order to increase the genetic variation and as protection against natural (or unnatural) disasters. This intent is often stymied by poor spawning facilities which inevitably reduces natural recruitment to trout populations. Every rich environment producing low numbers of big fish that I have knowledge of has very poor spawning facilities.

Bornish and West Loch Ollay are classic examples of both manifestations of what happens when spawning opportunities are good or poor. Bornish is connected to all her neighbouring lochs and will receive stock top-ups from all of them. West

Kate Muddler

Hook: Standard wet fly
Thread: Black
Butt: 2 turns flat silver tinsel
Tail: Golden pheasant crest
Rib: Medium silver oval or wire
Body: Black seal's fur
Body Hackle: Black cock
Head: Deer hair (dyed West of Ireland
              golden-olive)

Ollay has one connection to its sister loch, Mid Ollay, which has one connection to East Ollay, providing scant or poor stock recruitment. West Ollay is a loch you visit hoping for quality so continual action is not on the agenda; Bornish hopefully provides quantity but very few trophies.

So, with this in mind, on my fourth day scheduled for Bornish I expected a bit of sport, but the prevailing easterly wind had been a bit of a problem in this regard and the machair trout were sulky in the extreme. As expected the wind was from the east when we arrived at Bornish, but good cloud cover added an element of optimism. However, looking out over the Atlantic there was a clear distinction between a grey sky and a blue one. Sunshine was on the way.

After a slow start with the odd fish showing some unenthusiastic and unproductive interest in my flies, a strange thing happened. Reaching the top of the drift in the far north-eastern corner of the loch I attempted to get line out and only succeeded in throwing a loop around the top eye. My normal procedure is to slip the butt of the rod over the back of the boat so I can reach the rod tip. While I was doing this, with the leader in my hand, I felt the line draw tight, so I struck with my hand and not the rod. I dropped the leader and hefted the rod back into the boat, and I was into a very energetic and determined trout somewhere between 1½ and 1¾ pounds. Bizarre. You fish properly with little result, then do something from left-field and you get a positive take. There's nowt as queer as trout. This trout was typical machair fish – firm, fat and beautiful – and had taken a fly I had lashed together primarily for this trip, a March Brown snatcher with an element of yellow seal's fur under the hare's mask fur which gives it a unique olive cast. Knowing how important gammarid shrimp are to the South Uist trout I expected big things of this pattern. Sitting patiently on the sub's bench I had tried it out when up in Durness – again a place where freshwater shrimp are important – and it had performed reasonably well. Maybe it showed a lack of total confidence that I had located it in the middle of the three-fly cast (never the best position for any fly), but it had scored in strange circumstances.

Unfortunately, this fish was destined for the table as it was un-returnable, so I had the opportunity to spoon it. It's not often I am stumped by the contents of a marrow spoon, but I was this time. There were easily recognisable items such as snails, shrimp and cased caddis, but the bulk of items were small, black items which I couldn't recognise. I had to assume that they were mites or, at a stretch, the thoraxes of caenis. As there was little evidence of a caenis hatch – they usually leave corpses all over the boat from the previous evening/morning – so, mites it must be. Very hard to imitate those little sods.

But things were slow. Blue sky was building from the west, and when the wind changed with the advancing weather front it showed from the south-east. This is usually indicative of an approaching low-pressure system and, depending on the depth of the low, can be good or bad news. If the low is deep there will be a sharp decline in atmospheric pressure which is rarely, if ever, good. If the approaching low is shallow I generally find that fishing improves. Rapid drops or rises in atmospheric pressure seem to have an adverse effect on fish swim-bladders which no fish welcomes. Unfortunately, this was a 'dartboard' low, deep with closely packed isobars which was to give me problems for the next few days.

In mid-afternoon I spotted some cattle in a field directly upwind of the loch and wondered if there might be some terrestrials coming off the disturbed pasture. As nothing was happening elsewhere we popped over for a look, and I immediately saw a good natural rise to something 'on the top'. The likelihood was that the fly in question would be a cow-dung, so I stuck on a Golden-Olive Bumble snatcher on the top dropper. Having been raised in Orkney, an area famous for cattle-rearing, I was well acquainted with cow-dung fly coming down on the lochs and the alacrity with which the fish greeted them. The surprising thing about these events is that, almost uniquely, trout will accept wet fly representations almost as well as dry imitators.

With a thin veil of cloud moving in front of a moderate wind, which had now turned westerly, I was optimistic. It took no time to hook and land a fine trout on the Golden Olive Bumble snatcher, of similar size to that first unlucky fish of the morning session. When we returned to the head of the drift, the cattle were gone, presumably moved by the crofter. And so were the fly and the fish. Everything returned to the disappointing norm. Still we hunted on. We tried here, there and everywhere with only the slightest encouragement in the form of aborted offers.

There was nothing for it but to keep our powder dry for the morrow. At the very least I had the Borrodale Hotel chef's very excellent seafood to look forward to, and some of that excellent Harris gin to cut the tar out of the back of my throat. There's always an up-side. You just have to look for it.

Out on Loch Lochy, under the forbidding presence of Ben Nevis

– 6 –

The Wild Ones

AMONGST THOSE WHO have never done it, fishing for wild loch trout is perceived to be relatively easy. The flawed reasoning goes something like this: many lochs are rarely fished so the trout in them must be remarkably unsophisticated; lochs are short on trout-food, so all the trout in them come complete with a kamikaze headband and as much concern for their own welfare as a suicide bomber on roller skates.

Let's get a few things straight. That which is generally perceived to be starvation is actually opportunism and competition. Competition is intense in waters where the fish population is comprised of many small specimens. The achievement of even a slightly larger size than normal status is much to be desired as this leads to – prime territory attainment (which means more food); the ability to bully its peers (which leads to more food); and the ability to feed on a wider range of items, many of which may be too large for smaller fish (which leads to more food). Larger size is the aim, and this comes from better utilisation of the larder. Averaged-sized fish haven't quite worked out that fishermen's flies will curtail rather than enhance their life, so they tend to tuck into them with gay abandon. If you couple all this with the fact that at any given time artificial flies chucked into the water are in range of a large number of very competitive fish, this leads us to believe that the little blighters are starving.

Any self-sustaining loch will strive to support just as many fish as it is able. This gross tonnage (or poundage) will have adapted to available food and their expectancy will match the availability. Unproductive oligotrophic waters will support a lower volume of fish-mass than highly productive ones, based on freely obtainable food. In such lochs this gross volume will either be divided into many small fish or a few very large fish, or a combination of both. Ferox waters are a prime example. In highly fertile lowland waters the same governing principles apply, but the gross tonnage will be higher on an acreage basis, again based on fish-food availability. Fish in neither environment type will face starvation, all things being equal and no unnatural events taking place; the lives of individual fish being geared around nutrition, fertile waters producing fast growing fish, oligotrophic waters producing, on the whole, slow maturing fish.

That's all fairly logical if somewhat simplistic. In reality all lochs are different, having varying levels or fertility right across the scale. If one divides Scotland down a fairly central line, north and south, it is common to find the fertile waters in the east and the less fertile ones in the west. There are of course striking contrary examples. The machair lochs of the Western Isles are very fertile, as are the limestone lochs of the far West Coast; and the eastern lochs of Ross-shire and the hill lochs of Angus are more like the upland, low fertility, lochs of the Highlands.

Now, does any of this matter to the loch fisherman? It most certainly does because it means that every single loch is likely to be totally different from any other. To try and use experience gained on one loch to specifically tackle another is a flawed tactic and liable to fail.

However, on the brighter side, there are constant factors which can be used to good effect. For instance, feeding behaviours are relatively unvarying. Trout are all carnivorous so knowledge of food items likely to occur will point to the best direction of approach. Trout are primarily shallow water feeders, and water less than three metres deep tends to be favoured. Trout are largely diurnal (daylight) feeders, but almost all populations have a dislike for very bright conditions (although there are exceptions), and are likely to retreat to the deeper extent of their preferred range in such conditions. Periods of day when trout are more inclined to feed are remarkably constant also, the best being very early morning before the sun's light touches the water; between 10 a.m. and midday; between 4 p.m. and 7 p.m. (which might extend until true darkness, dependant upon latitude).

Regional variations can be marked. The further north one travels the more likelihood that anything resembling an 'evening rise' is unlikely. By an evening rise, I of course refer to that phenomenon which occurs about an hour before sunset when fish are likely to come right up into the surface layers and react very aggressively to any hatch of insects, regardless of how meagre. To offset this lack, trout activity between 4 p.m. and 7 p.m. is more marked in the northern regions.

A hatchery-reared fish and a wild one from Loch Leven, back in the day

Another regional variation across the latitudes is that trout reaction to weather can differ. Wild, windy days in the north can be a lot more productive than such conditions in the far south and, conversely, flat calms are generally more productive the farther south one fishes.

Fly pattern choice can be dictated to by region. I made the claim in my *Trout & Salmon Flies of Scotland* that I can decipher where a Scottish angler does most of his flyfishing by the style and colouration of his fly patterns. I still stand by this statement. The following differentiations are generalisations but tenuously hold a solid truth – flies get more heavily dressed the farther north one travels; tinsel bodies, pale colours and sparse hackling in the south, dubbed bodies, bold colours and bumble-style hackling in the north; silver ribs in the west, gold ribs in the east and far north. All these factors are controlled by water 'colour', chemical composition and clarity, climatic effects, regional variations in aquatic invertebrate types and some other minor features.

I spent forty-odd years fishing the Orkney lochs and can tell you that each of the five major ones has distinct preferences when it comes to pattern style and colour. Harray – relatively small and lightly dressed patterns in olives, browns, gold, chartreuse and black; Boardhouse – big, heavily dressed wingless patterns in green, blue, yellow, white and claret with 'Sedgehog' style wings; Swannay – relatively small but heavily dressed patterns in black, claret, and silver and bronze mallard wings; Hundland – along the same lines as Boardhouse but even brighter colours and teal wings; Stenness – small, lightly dressed and as bright and garish as the imagination will allow. This generalisation again points to a basic truth and covers a group of lochs no farther apart than ten miles from a central point.

Let's have a look at tackle. A basic reservoir outfit will do just fine – a ten-foot rod of anything from #4 – #7 will suffice. Lines are more subjective but without a floater, a slow and a fast intermediate, and something with a sink rate of about 4″ per second, I would feel under gunned. Flies are, of course, even more subjective, and I would strongly advise a visit to the local tackle shop or a phone call some days before arrival. A wading net that can be hung from a belt or D-ring will prove useful, and chest waders can turn a 'blown-off' day into a success.

If you are in the situation of having to fish an unknown loch without local help, here are a few tips that will get you up the first few rungs of the ladder:

1. Stick to shallow water until you discover different (which won't be often!). Generally speaking, you will find shallow water where the land is low, and deep water under cliffs, steep banks and hillsides. Lochs surrounded by high hills are rarely shallow; lochs surrounded by low lying land are rarely deep.

2. Select an area where there is a decent breeze. This will most likely be productive, masking your approach from wary fish. If you are in a boat, a steady breeze will take you over a constant 'stream' of fish. If you are wading (bank fishing) select an area where the breeze runs parallel to the shoreline, and step-and-cast your way down the shoreline.

3. Remember wild brown trout are territorial, so standing in one spot won't work. You've got to keep on the move to cover new territories.

4. In the early part of the season the calm water at the head of the wind is likely to be most productive, because, when the weather is cold, there is less wind-chill where the wind first meets the water. In mid – late season search the tail of the wind, not because, as many of us erroneously believe, all the food is there, but because the water at the tail of the wind contains more oxygen.

5. Be aware that specific insects, invertebrates and others may have times when they are more likely to be preyed on by trout. Finding insect shucks on the

water at midday may mean you've missed the hatch which took place in the early morning. If the marrow spoon shows fry remains in the morning, the likelihood is that the fry were 'bumped off' in the hours of darkness. Late evening and early morning are best for caenis, sedge and midge; midday for olives and mayfly. Terrestrials don't necessarily need strong wind to bring them to the water. In fact in high winds most terrestrials 'hunker down' in the vegetation and wait for less wind before taking to the wing.

6. Don't rush onto the water without even a backward glance. Have a good look round. Check the surrounding topography as it will tell you about water depth and likely areas to concentrate on. Check in the margins for signs of insect activity – the likes of buzzer or pupal shucks can point to likely pattern choice and/or technique. Also, the presence of snail shells, shrimp, cased caddis, etc., point to fertility; lack of same points to infertility. Oh, and by the way, peaty water is not necessarily an indication of infertility, no more than clear water is a fertility sign. I know of a few very peaty lochs which are stunningly fertile and productive; in some of the most infertile waters I have come across you could read the small print on a beer can sunk in 20 feet of water!

7. Be aware that weather may have a profound impact on the fishing. In bright weather consider doing something other than baking in a boat, as results may be better as the sun sets in the evening. In a prolonged spell of hot, bright weather give some thought to turning the clock around and turning night into day, as the most productive times will be after the sun sets and just before it rises.

General knowledge of this kind is a vital key in unlocking the secrets of basic approach and tactics. Unfortunately acquiring such knowledge can take months, or more likely, years. The shortcut to this highly desirable state is local knowledge and advice, to which personal day-to-day experience supplies the finished product. I can't stress highly enough the need for visiting or holidaying anglers to gain local knowledge. If there is a local tackle shop – and God knows they become rarer with each passing season – get in there and ask about. That should provide not only key advice like the where, when and how, but also provide a range of locally popular fly patterns. The local tackle shop should also be able to provide you with, at a price, the services of trustworthy guides or ghillies, and where boat hire can be had.

Fly fishermen are a funny lot. They are generally loath to hire help, considering such to be a negative reflection on their ability. I've fished all over the UK and Ireland and never turn down local help. I use local experience to augment my own ability and knowledge, such as it is, to avoid unproductive learning time. I like to be in amongst fish from the word go, and the only way to do so is to be put in the right place, fishing in a locally acceptable manner. This is not a 'coward's way out', it is just plain common sense. Fishing holidays are not cheap and to spend those valuable days going to all the wrong spots and fishing in an unproductive manner is simply foolish. The hiring of a local guide or ghillie for a day or two is worth fish in the boat, and it is just conceivable you may end up with a friend for life. And if you are going to hire help, for the sake of all that's merciful, listen to and act on the advice given. If you don't, you may find that the 'well of experience' suddenly dries up and, what you are paying hard cash for no longer exists.

Invest in the experience and you will find that wild trout fishing holds all the joys and rewards that have captivated generations of fly fishermen since Noah was a boy.

– 7 –

House of Cards

THE CREATION OF a fishery which maintains an ecological balance but also addresses the requirements of anglers is well-nigh impossible task. Self-sustaining waters with indigenous trout populations severely resent human manipulation. And human manipulation seems necessary to achieve what human anglers want – lots of big fish, relatively easy to catch regardless of all other considerations.

To become a 'perfect' fishery plenty of attractive, healthy trout must be available to be caught on any given day. In other words, man must create a well-balanced dynamic system which has all the positives of a wild fishery with none of the negatives. What are the negatives of a wild water? In a naturally occurring trout habitat the fish biomass can be split into lots of small individuals (boring) or a few large specimens (frustrating); the fishing can be easy (shortage of natural food) or extremely difficult (too much natural forage leading to selectively feeding trout); logistical difficulties – involving hiking boots, etc. – may deter anglers; the list is endless. Manipulated wild/stocked fisheries attempt to square the circle by creating perfect fisheries where none of the above applies. In doing so, they come up against the laws of dynamics as they apply to ecological principles.

The precise, definitive reasons may be hard to establish, but the working principle is easily identified. All natural environments are dynamic systems and even the slightest disturbance to a dynamic system will create reactions which can be wildly out of proportion to the cause.

Let me give you an example. Back in my old stomping grounds of Orkney there is a loch called Swannay. The history of this loch as a trout fishery is long, varied and highly interesting. In the early parts of the last century, Swannay was a typical moorland, peat-water loch which provided lots and lots of what a local referred to as 'herring sized' trout. Good sport and plenty of it. The Orkney Trout Fishing Association, with best intentions imaginable, started to manipulate the stock in order to increase its attraction to fly fishermen. It is easy for us to look back with 20-20 hindsight and criticise their programme of improvements, but they endeavoured to construct, through human agency, a perfect fishery. Not satisfied with the naturally occurring and self-sustaining population of 'herring-sized' trout, their intent was to replace them with bigger (and therefore better) trout. Fry, raised in their hatchery from fertilised eggs gathered from lochs where the average-sized trout was higher than in Swannay, had a progressive result, and indeed the average size of Swannay trout increased dramatically.

I never knew the Swannay of old. As far as I was concerned, Swannay was a dour, difficult loch where monsters swam and were occasionally caught. Forty years ago, my father and I shared a basket of three fish which weighed 12½ pounds, and in that same year, through hard graft and dedication, I captured thirteen fish of over three-pounds. This was the product of 'salting' the spawning burn with fry which hopefully contained fast-growth genetic material.

Human nature being what it is the OTFA was not satisfied with this result, the feeling being that Swannay was not achieving its true potential. A policy was devised which attempted to create a fishery in Swannay which still produced big fish, only more of them. This led to a plan which involved discontinuing the planting of fry in the burns and replacing it with the release of grown-on, hatchery produced fish directly into the loch. On the face of it, this addressed a number of concerns associated with the original stocking policy, namely wastage of fry through disease, predation, etc., better control of stock numbers in the loch, and the introduction of ready-to-catch-fish for the hungry anglers. In practice it was an unmitigated disaster.

Within a season or two Swannay was deserted by the anglers, who found that the native, indigenous trout of old had simply disappeared from the catch statistics and the only fish available to the anglers seemed to be the grown-on stocked trout. In the following two winters large numbers of fish, covered with fungal infections, were washed up dead on the shores and the spawning burn seemed remarkably devoid of breeding fish in the Autumn. In retrospect we now accept that the dead fish were individuals from the grown-on stocked fish populations.

The OTFA then wisely decided to implement a moratorium on stock introduction on Swannay, and nature was allowed to reassert itself without human interference.

Nature will always have its way despite human interference, and Swannay now has reverted to its ancient blueprint, producing plenty of trout of modest size.

Obviously, there are lessons to be learnt here. Amongst the most interesting are:

1. The amount of time trout spend in hatchery conditions is in indirect proportion to their ability to blend with wild stock;
2. Grown-on stocked fish disrupt the natural balance/ecology of an already self-sustaining fishery to the detriment of the indigenous stock;
3. Human interference with stock dynamics on self-sustaining waters should be done as a last resort. It should also be done in a manner which closely imitates natural processes, or the result will likely end in chaos.
4. Interfere with a dynamic system at your peril. It's the easiest thing in the world to get the toothpaste out of a tube but it's a slightly different matter getting it back in.

What is a dynamic system? Imagine a delicately balanced house of cards, with each individual card relying on the balance of every other card to maintain its own position and stability. Then envisage a card being added to, or subtracted from, the construction. At the very least, the structure will no longer bear any resemblance to its original form. For every action there is an equal and opposite reaction. Dynamic systems in nature exist as they are because of the participation of every indigenous living organism. Should the interaction of one of these participating organisms be increased or reduced the whole dynamic system will change to adapt to the modification. Some life-forms will flourish to the detriment of others. Dynamic systems do not occur by chance, they develop over time due to the balance between, and interaction of, participating life-forms. Human interference with such delicate arrangements *always* causes some form of upheaval because tampering with one aspect of a dynamic system will inevitably affect all the other factors.

What has happened on Loch Leven over the past decade and a half is a classic example: this world-famous wild trout fishery has been on the receiving end of the economic effects of trying to manipulate a self-sustaining dynamic system. The boat fleet at 'The Loch', as it is widely known hereabouts, has been reduced by 75%, and the management have been forced by economic pressures to return the loch to its own natural devices. The fish-farm deliveries are now a thing of the past, and management policy is no longer to try and augment the wild stock from a grown-on population from its own hatchery. What has been the initial impact of these changes? It is probably too early to be sure, but it is safe to say that the dynamic system that is Leven was seriously 'knocked off line' by management stocking policies in the past. The mass introduction of rainbow trout saw wild trout populations declining dramatically as part of the seasonal catch. There is reason to believe that the wild fish population did not collapse, as was widely rumoured, but that it retreated to the depths and became dedicated to collecting nutrition from the bed of the loch.

For a major section of the biomass to completely change its behaviour has to have had a profound impact on the dynamic processes with the loch as a whole. I find it interesting that after the termination of rainbow trout stocking, brown trout have been much more willing to be present high in the water column, and that the 'evening rise' is back with attitude, if not quite vengeance. Is it a coincidence that in 2007, and again in 2011, we have witnessed the best hatches of 'curly-bums' (the large, deep-water midge of Leven) for many a long year, after most of us had come to look upon them as a thing of the past? I expect in the next few years we will see other evidence of the traditional dynamic attempting to re-assert itself.

It has to be said that a major part of the Leven catch this year has been made up of acclimatised stock browns from last year's stocking, but there is significant evidence of true wild fish re-appearing in greater numbers as the season progressed. Willie Simpson, fishery manager, tells me that shoals of undersized trout were noted in late August. Given that there has been no stocking of any form on Leven during 2007, these fish must be recruits from the spawning burns which one would expect to show at this time.

The pressures on wild trout have never been greater as 21st century attitudes of supply and demand harden. There are many anglers out there who think indigenous wild trout are a mere irrelevance and the catching of a limit bag as being the sole purpose of a day's fishing. Fishery management must react to consumer demand or go out of business. Leven's bold step to buck the trend hasn't been universally welcomed and, even though the quality of fishing there has improved, many of its most dedicated adherents of past years have been noticeable by their absence. But we anglers have to be aware that our demands as consumers are having a degrading and destructive effect on our sport. We can't go on burying our heads in the sand trying to ignore the likely consequences of rampant stocking of self-sustaining trout lochs. The mathematics will defeat us. Two stocked fish added to two wild fish will ultimately restrict us to two stocked fish, with waters which have been so ecologically damaged that they may take generations to return to biologically dynamic systems.

Loch Dionard, the Hall of the Mountain King

− 8 −

In The Hall of the Mountain King

THEY SAY YOU can never go back; that you never cross the same river twice. Loch Dionard must then be trapped in a time-warp, because every time I return it is totally unchanged.

We sat at the breakfast table in the Gaulin Lodge. Peter Grubb, my host, and I were destined to fish Loch Dionard (pronounced *Gin-ard)* that very day, and I can state, with due humility, that I was excited. I was moved to say, in front of the whole ensemble that I had never visited the loch without taking at least one fish, generally salmon and occasionally a big sea-trout. There was much sucking of teeth, and many warding gestures, salt thrown over left shoulders and mumbled spells to thwart the 'evil eye'. Was I worried? Not a jot. In anything more than a flat calm, I was confident that the gods of fishing and the beneficent loch would provide.

Dionard sits in a fold of the Sutherland hills, lorded over by towering Foinaven and Arkle. It is, without doubt, one of the most spectacular pieces of scenery Scotland has to offer, and every time I return I stand in awe as millions of years of the convolutions of the Earth's crust are laid out before my very eyes. It must have been somewhere like this that stimulated Edvard Greig (originally of Scottish crofter descent) to pen *In the Hall of the Mountain King.*

If I was a Buddhist, I could sit for days studying the folds and twists of the rock strata that make up the western side of Loch Dionard and see in them the very essence of immutability and the futility of mankind. It is a sobering, spiritual and elemental experience to hunt fish on Dionard. Mind you, the midges are quite sobering and very elemental. That's the price you pay to sit in the hall of the Mountain King.

And the fishing? In my opinion Loch Dionard is the most reliable loch for salmon and sea-trout in the UK, and that's going some! In *The Salmon Rivers of Scotland* by Derek Mills and Neil Graesser, the authors have this to say about it:

The loch [Dionard] itself has a very high reputation as a sea-trout fishery and many people consider it to be as good as, if not better than, Loch Stack for size and numbers of sea-trout and salmon.

This was in the days before the cataclysmic and virtually universal sea-trout decline in the North and West of Scotland. Nowadays, sea-trout are an endangered species in Stack and many other waters, but although average size has declined very reasonable numbers of sea-trout are caught on Dionard every year. A possible sign of better days ahead was recorded on the loch in mid-summer when a 13lb sea-trout was caught and released.

The Bible tells us that it is a long and troublesome road to Paradise. Whoever wrote that must have travelled to Loch Dionard in the bad old days, when no track existed and the journey in and out took six hours. It's no longer like that; a buggy drops off the anglers and, after they have spent a hopefully happy and productive day, picks them up again in time for an evening meal. However, there is always an alternative. A well-appointed bothy sits at the edge of the loch where enthusiastic anglers can spend the night, allowing them an evening on the loch and a wee morning jaunt out before the buggy arrives. But take my advice and don't even think about popping out after dark, in the 'skud', for a call of nature. I did it once, the midges swarmed all over me and I ended up looking like a well-used dartboard. I got bitten in places where I didn't know I had places!

Dionard is, by any measure, small, and the number of fish which pack into it during the summer months means they must be stacked like cordwood in the favoured areas. When they are really 'on' it is possible to be moving a fish almost every other cast, but like salmon and sea-trout anywhere they can be 'tricksy' and temperamental. When Peter, Henry the ghillie and I arrived at the loch it was bright with a light breeze. We had confidence that the conditions would improve later in the day, but there was hope for the odd fish in the less than perfect conditions. We 'laid on' just outside the downstream river mouth and set about exploring the first little mini-bay on the north-east shore. We moved a handful of fish in an area the size of a decent domestic dining room, but never felt the weight of any of them. In any other location you would be forgiven for tearing your hair out, perhaps thinking that all your chances had been blown in the first half-hour. But on Dionard you merely think "We'll have another go at them later, when they're properly on!" and move to fresh drifts.

Peter and I were both fishing midge-tips to allow the flies to 'dig-in' a bit in the light breeze, but I was growing a bit dissatisfied with this technique and opted for an Airflo Fast-Glass to take the flies away from the sun's glare. I had on my long-term Loch Dionard cast – Peter Ross on the point, and a Clan Chief variant on the bob. In a loch where large numbers of fish can inhabit restricted areas it is probably unwise to fish a three-fly cast when the possibility of trailing flies towed by a hooked fish can prove irresistible to others. A fish in the hand is worth a lot more than two pulling in opposite directions on the same leader.

At first, no benefit came from this change. At the back of my mind lurked the negative thought that the intermediate was not the best for salmon, but it would probably suit the sea-trout better, *if* they would play. So far, we had seen no definitive signs of sea-trout 'on the prod', but salmon sign was all about us. Peter stuck to his virtual floater and I to my intermediate, so we had all the bases covered.

The first fish slammed into my Clan Chief on the north side of the permanent weed bed in the big bay between the islands and the burn mouth. The way it kept pulling the rod tip down to the water surface certainly had me convinced it was a quality customer, but when it jumped I realised it was fighting twice its weight, which was a modest 1½ pound. Not sea-liced, but bright as a penny and as fit as a butcher's dog!

Shortly after, a rather tentative take exploded into action as I rather hesitantly jabbed the hook home. The first fish had been a boy-racer, determined to get as far from me as possible, this sea-trout however performed an aerial display worthy of the Red Arrows. When you've been away from sea-trout for awhile, you tend to forget just how spectacularly they fight. In my experience, pound for pound they'll outfight anything that swims in the UK.

By lunchtime the wind had picked up and another sea-trout, slightly bigger than the previous two, had been caught and returned. We still hadn't had a salmon but things, wind-wise, were looking up for the afternoon. I prefer a 'howler' for salmon, but a steady breeze for sea-trout, and I've not met anyone who disagrees with this view. Henry manfully fought the boat back to the bothy under oar-power and reflected that his decision to by-pass the outboard had been a tad optimistic. We had a damned fine lunch, but it was obvious that even Henry was itching to get back out on the loch and find out what the afternoon had in store. So, we strapped the outboard to the back of the boat and set out full of crisps, pies and optimism.

We felt we had to re-try that first wee bay on the north-east shore, but surprisingly, given the action we had seen in it on the first drift, we failed to elicit any response whatsoever. That's always the way with migratory fish – they're on, they're off and then, hopefully, they're back on again, and there seems no decipherable rhyme or reason to it. It's always wise to remember that these fish, be they salmon or sea-trout, aren't feeding fish. They, particularly sea-trout, may eat the odd item, but this action isn't a nutritional requirement, simply an instinctive reaction.

The cloud built, and the wind freshened, and we decided to give the west shore a good going over. I have always thought of the west shore of Dionard as the 'salmon' side; the east shore being preferred by sea-trout. A minor adjustment to this thinking was required because we had seen a lot of salmon sign on the east shore, but as we meandered down the west side we encountered a few salmon, all of which were a tad 'sniffy'. I had a bizarre experience down this shoreline. We had arrived at a deeply indented bay into which the wind seemed reluctant to enter. Taking this opportunity to attend to a few matters of importance, I reeled in most of my line and chucked a short line over the back of the boat for a few moments. Chores attended to, I raised the rod tip... and I was into a very strong fish, which ripped line off the reel. Way behind the boat, a double figure salmon cart-wheeled across the waves, and my line and leader rocketed back and draped themselves around my neck and shoulders. It wasn't just that this normally very cagey fish should take the fly, virtually static, in the shadow of the boat, but also, upon inspection, the leader was found to be frayed a good four inches above where the missing fly should have been. I can only assume that the fish had totally swallowed the fly (a #8 Peter Ross) and the leader had come in contact with the vomerine teeth (located on the tongue) which reduced it to strands. It was a pity because, despite the somewhat 'novel' means of hooking, it was a damned fine fish and I would have liked the encounter to have had a longer duration.

Peter, on the other hand, was having a fine time amongst the salmon. He had his favoured big muddler on the top dropper and it was bringing fish up regularly enough that I was cursing, having inadvertently left my muddler box securely at home on my tying bench. Generally, and in the past, the Clan Chief has served me well enough for Dionard salmon, but on this day only the sea-trout had any respect for it. I can only repeat that salmon and sea-trout in freshwater (and particularly on lochs) are tricksy beasts and you simply *must* pander to their whims. You've got to bow your head and eat crow if you want success. To emphasise this point, Henry regularly commented on the fact that almost every fish was showing well out from the shoreline, but Peter and I kept encouraging him into the wave-swept shallows where we expected to find salmon. It wasn't until we gave Henry his head and ventured out a cast-length from the shore that salmon were hooked.

Apart from that strange fish which disappeared with my Peter Ross, I never felt the weight of a salmon, all for lack of a big muddler. Still I had had my sea-trout and was not disconsolate. In this day and age, a loch-caught sea-trout is a pearl above value, and I had brought three to the boat. Peter had two salmon and a sea-trout in the afternoon and was well chuffed, and when we returned to the bothy at 5.00 pm, we all reflected on a job well done – Peter and I had our fish and Henry had kept us in the best fishing water.

There is nowhere like Loch Dionard and return I will, with the blessing of the Mountain King.

A massive fish re-enters the water after admiring the Loch Hope scenery

– 9 –

Twenty Top Tips for Boat Anglers

WEATHER

1. In the first few months of the season it is generally better to stick to top-of-wind drifts (where the wind first touches the water) to avoid the effects of wind-chill. Cold winds blowing in the early months of the season will create a situation where the surface layers rapidly become colder than the deeper layers. Within broad parameters, early-season trout will become used to the average water temperatures and avoid cold layers. This is often marked by fish 'coming short' to flies. Although brown trout are a cold-water species, being quite comfortable in water temperatures which are only just above the freezing point, they dislike sudden change in any external conditions.

2. Brown trout generally like a good wave; rainbow trout generally dislike windy conditions. However, the belief that the higher the wind-speed the better for brown trout can be erroneous. It is not unusual to find very rough water at the tail of a very strong wind deserted by fish, and fishing effort in these regions unproductive.

3. Wind, and its associated wave, isn't necessarily uniform. Some winds can produce a 'lifting' wave and others a 'flattening' wave. A 'lifting' wave is one with a defined crest; a 'flattening' wave can either be a series of short, 'jabbly', chaotic forms or the dreaded 'scud' – very small, dark ripples driven in front of a squall. A 'lifting' wave generally produces good fishing conditions; a 'flattening' wave, more often than not, spells disaster. The best wave of all for wild trout fishing is a rolling, oily, crest-less wave which often appears after a good blow, and as the wind decreases the waves maintain their vigour but lose their crest and increase the distance from peak to peak.

4. Is rain good or bad for fishing? Well, yes and no. It isn't rain or any other form of precipitation that is the problem; it is what it heralds or has caused it. Rain is

generally a product of changing weather patterns and is frequently the visible manifestation of invisible atmospheric pressure change. Light rain is generally a result of slight atmospheric pressure change, and as such isn't normally much of a problem. Heavy rain and showers are almost always a product of dramatic pressure drop whether frontal or caused by localised thunder clouds and will have a profound and negative effect on trout behaviour. Heavy rain is arguably worse than heavy showers because the effects will last longer and be slower to improve as the front passes. Heavy showers, being temporary and localised, involve a very sharp drop in air pressure and a sharp return to normal immediately after. Spectacular increases in fish activity can frequently occur immediately after a thunder shower. Strangely, in the early months of the season, the onset of snow can often change a fishing day for the better. This is probably because the sudden increase in ambient temperature associated with snow in cold weather greatly offsets any atmospheric pressure change.

5. The old saying regarding wind direction and the feeding habits of fish is, on balance, reliable. West winds tend to be a product of stable atmospheric pressure; north and east winds can often be associated with unseasonably low temperature and falling atmospheric pressure; south winds herald an increasing air pressure and, more often than not, improving temperatures. Personally, I have no great antipathy to east or north winds and have found them as liable to produce sport as to destroy it. West has never been my favourite direction of wind for varying reasons – the geography of Scotland has a tendency to have a south-east, north-west alignment and, given that, west winds very often cut across lochs providing few attractive drifts; also, west and north-west winds are often accompanied by bright skies.

FLIES AND PATTERN COLOUR

6. Much as I dislike the concept, it seems irrefutable that almost every loch has a pattern, or selection of patterns, which work wonders on them, and are virtually useless elsewhere. There are, no doubt, reasons for this conundrum, some logical, others shrouded in mystery. Therefore, it is always wise to make serious enquiries about popular fly patterns when visiting strange waters.

But one thing I have found which almost contradicts the above is that the patterns you are employing with success on your local waters can often work surprisingly well many miles from home.

7. Nothing is as valuable as local information and the best way to acquire it is to hire a local guide or ghillie. On the reverse side of this coin, treat any comments that use the terms 'never' and 'always' with suspicion. I remember taking out an English chap on an Orkney loch who, in desperation attached a #8 long shank White Lure to his cast and asked whether I concurred with his decision. I confidently stated that he was more likely to have a meaningful relationship with Cleopatra than catching even one trout on the 'dead seagull'! Do I need to say more? It was a lesson hard learnt by an overconfident guide.

8. Size of fly is an interesting subject for study. It is a slightly flawed truism that the bigger the water the bigger the fly required. The trout in some big lochs respond better to small flies, however, to select large (#10) patterns on a new big water is a justifiable starting point. The response of trout to a fly size can point the way to better size selection. Trout that come short to a large fly will often respond positively to the same pattern in a smaller size. Occasionally I have seen a succession of trout jump over a specific fly, and when this rare event happens a change 'up' in size has led to success. But it is more common for trout to ignore a fly which is right in pattern but too big or small.

9. Some patterns work best in specific sizes. I have a few patterns in my collection which will work only in small sizes and never in a large form, and vice versa. The patterns in question are not necessarily imitative flies, when one or other of the sizes does not replicate the size of the item imitated.

10. One of my best pieces of advice for colour choice in pattern is to open the fly box and, with a glance, select the pattern which attracts the eye. I often use this tactic when I am stumped for choice, and when no scientific or logical solutions are available. It is amazing how often this works and, when we appreciate that scientists are convinced that the general construction of the eye of a fish is remarkably similar to that of a human eye, it becomes a logical step.

11. Dark flies should be a first-choice selection for dark or peat-stained water. It is also a truism that strong colours will tend to out-fish tones and subtle colours in similar scenarios. Very dark, even black, patterns will work anywhere and at

anytime, regardless of the water colour. Gut content analysis of *feeding* fish will almost always contain a black item or two, regardless of the main colouration of the favoured food item. Black items seem to have general acceptance, all other things being equal.

12. The old saying "bright day; bright fly" is virtually useless to a trout angler. I suspect that we have borrowed this tip from salmon fishing, but even in that field of endeavour I would harbour strong doubts. In very bright conditions on a trout loch I would *always* fish a black fly on the cast; not dark, but black. However, I have a strong fondness for orange and gold in similar light conditions.

FISHING PRACTICE

13. If at all possible, try to draw your flies away from the sun. If for example the sun is over your right shoulder, endeavour to pull your flies from right to left, and vice versa. This simple piece of advice is based on the concept that trout see a fly better when it is not back-dropped by the brightest sky. This is one of the reasons why two anglers, sitting side by side and fishing in identical manner, can have totally different results.

14. If repeating a successful drift always, if possible, take a wide detour to avoid disturbing the fish you wish to catch. This may seem a simple and obvious piece of advice, but it never fails to amaze me how many anglers believe that they can motor over fish and expect them to ignore it. This advice is essential for surface active trout, marginally less so for fish feeding at depth.

15. Fish seen to be active on the surface are not necessarily best tackled with a floating line, just as rising fish are not always susceptible to a dry fly. Quite often when trout are capturing an item of prey at the surface they have 'locked on' to it below the surface. This happens often with olives and sedges and is a strong feature of fry bashers. In such a situation a slow sinker or intermediate line is best.

16. It is very good practice when fishing for brown trout to hold the rod at a short distance above the water surface. This allows a slack curve of line to exist below the rod tip which will help hook a fish as it turns down with the fly. Brown trout generally take in a vertical movement and require a small amount of slack line

to allow them to turn down with the fly. Pointing the rod at the surface will result in many abortive takes as the fly will be pulled out of the fish's mouth before it has properly engulfed it. Rainbow trout tend to take in a horizontal manner and a tight-ish line is required for successful hook-ups.

17. 'Bobbing', or 'dibbling' (an anglicised version of the same), has many adherents. I am not one of them. Too many fishermen do it out of habit, regardless of their success or lack of it. When fly hatches were more prolific it most certainly had its uses, but now that most trout food is sub-aquatic it has lost much of its relevance. By all means give it a go, but if it doesn't work and all trout are coming on 'the pull', try to assess just how much fishing time you are losing while the top dropper fly is bouncing about ineffectively on the surface. I prefer the 'lift & hang' method, even with a floating line. It is much more natural for a fly to pause just in or under the surface film than performing the Fandango across the surface.

18. Some anglers like to pull their flies across the wind direction in the belief that this will expose their flies to more fish. Apart from the fact that two anglers in a boat both attempting to cast across the wind is a vision of Hell, it doesn't tend to work in practice. It can make a difference in relation to the position of the sun (see above), but not because there are more trout 'covered'. I have a theory that aquatic invertebrates that can swim, like trout, prefer to do so into the wind. Flies chucked down the wind and retrieved into it simply appear more normal.

19. Leader construction can be a bone of contention amongst fly fishermen. My default wet-fly leader is 18′ two-dropper cast, fishing three flies. I generally fish a 14′ one-dropper cast when fishing dries. For a 'washing-line' set-up, in the first half of the season I prefer an 18′ three-dropper cast, but revert to a two-dropper cast when the fish 'have seen it all'. A 15′ two-dropper cast is fine for migratory fish in a good wave, but I'll drop it down to one dropper in calm conditions. I don't like to fill up a leader with flies, but like a good distance between them. Short leaders are fine in a good wave, but the over-the-counter 9′ two-dropper leader is badly out of date.

20. Loch fishing for migratory species, an esoteric branch of flyfishing, hardly varies at all from traditional trout fishing. For salmon I like a full floating line;

sea-trout, in some places, seem to respond better to an intermediate. For both I like a muddler on the top, a good, bushy palmer in the middle and, quite often, another muddler on the point. Strangely, salmon, a fish which lives much of its life in the wide expanses of the ocean, prefers very shallow water in lochs; sea-trout, a creature of the inter-tidal zone, loves deep water in lochs. Bizarre but true.

– 10 –

Lough Mask

AFTER A NICE lunch on Inisgleastai, Declan Gibbons and I were quite keen to get back out amongst the Mask fish. Late morning and early afternoon had been very productive, and we hoped the trout were still 'on the prod'.

Declan got to the bow of the boat and I stepped into the water to pull on the gunnel. Well – spank my bum and call me Mary – the next I knew I was lying in a couple of feet of water staring up at the sky. Those Mask rocks can be a bit slippery, and this was not the sort of Mask action I was happy to experience... nor, indeed, the raucous laughter of my companions. Water is a sine qua non from an angling perspective – without water there are no fish, and without fish... But I was suddenly experiencing a whole lot more water than I was comfortable dealing with. All this in the late spring of 2016 when I and many others experienced wall-to-wall sunshine and little hope for good fishing conditions, or rain for that matter.

But I'm getting ahead of myself. On our first day, pickings were slim and we were blighted by harsh sunlight, so I was well chuffed to pick up a nice trout in Caher Bay on a dry mayfly pattern. Moving on to the side of Saint's Island we saw enough hatching mayfly and associated rising fish to stir the blood. Declan and I in one boat, and Peter Gathercole and Kevin Crowley in another, were hunting the lower reaches of Mask in search of good fishing, launching at Cushlough. We tended to hunt in a pack as Peter's photographic input was essential to record our successes, should they occur. The opportunity to split up looking for action was not really available to us. After a rather tough day, we returned to our moorings. Cushlough Bay had the look of a buzzer habitat but the coolness of that first evening put paid to that idea so, with a promise to return on the next day, we retired bruised but not defeated.

Whilst not having the superb quality of trout of her sister-water Corrib, it is impossible to view Mask without a sense of awe and excitement. Mask is a majestic lake, sitting as it does bordered by high hills to the north and north-west. Prior to May 2016, I had only fished her twice before. Once in late-March and again in late-summer. The spring visit with Gerry Dixon took place amongst the indents and bays of the southern reaches, and wet flies and lures fished off a wet-cel 2 took some very bonny trout up to 4 lb +. Later that year I was out searching for daphnia feeders with Mike Keady on the main lake, and it was all it was cracked-up to be. Very visually exciting with lots of fishy action.

This trip occurred in late May 2016, and mayfly were top of the trout's menu. When most of the opportunities are likely to come from a mayfly hatch, early daytime fishing can be a bit slow. Mayfly tend to start hatching about mid to late-morning. So, we elected to give Cushlough Bay that promised going over with epoxy buzzers. Cushlough Bay fairly reeks of fish and I did wonder how many launching boats ignored its potential whilst roaring away in search of pastures new and distant. Peter got a couple of knocks to his buzzer rig and I managed a very decent trout before pressure from the Irish component had us away, heading for Saint's Island. As mentioned above, we had seen a reasonable hatch of mays there the day before and Declan was optimistic about our chances. Having spent previous days on Corrib and Sheelin where trout were less than enthusiastic about 'coming on the rise' to desultory mayfly hatches I had my doubts, which I thought were best kept to myself.

One of the major problems with fly hatches is being totally confident in what is actually happening. Trout will generally, almost always, concentrate their feeding regime on one stage of the hatching process. As we are talking mayfly, let's focus on them. During the hatch the pupae will swim rapidly to the surface and, in a very short time, emerge from the pupal shuck. After that they will either float happily sitting on the surface film or fly away to begin the final process which is to enter the imago, or sexually mature, phase. In a calm or light breeze, they often sit on the water for a fairly long period. In a fresh breeze their rest will be cut short. All of these factors affect trout feeding behaviour. I suspect that in meagre hatches nymphs are taken readily subsurface as they ascend. The emerging phase I believe is the least popular for trout interest as it happens so quickly. In a prolific hatch on a calm day trout will tend to concentrate their attention on the post-emergent duns as they offer an easy target.

Drifting behind Inisgleastai. Classic wet fly water

So, what are the fishing tactic options? In meagre hatches when there's some wind I would always go for wets on a subsurface line. In similar conditions in flat calm I would try nymphs and/or dry fly. In a good hatch with calm conditions it has to be dries; and with a breeze I'd hope to fish dries but would be quick to change to wets on a midge tip or floater.

It all seems so easy when laid down like that in black and white. On the water I frequently ignore my own advice and end up wondering "Why am I doing this when experience tells me it's all wrong?"

When we got to Saint's Island there were the usual mini-flotilla of boats working the popular drifts, so we tucked in behind and followed them through. It seemed as though not too much was happening with rods or hatching fly, and in a lazy manner I just kept chucking dries in front of the boat instead of trying wets on a medium sink line. However, Peter and Kevin both managed a fish – one each on wets and dries – during our stay, but we never saw another rod bent though the number of duns on the water or in the air slowly grew.

Declan suggested a drift in behind the islands and I jumped at the chance. The breeze was a light northerly and perfect to run the contour lines behind Inisgleastai. Arriving, after a very short run, behind the island, we saw a few duns about but both Declan and I believed we would be better with wets, and so it proved to be. I stuck with vague mayfly imitators such as French Partridge straddlebugs and that old Orkney favourite, the White-Hackled Invicta, whilst Declan went the more locally popular route with Dabblers, Cock Robin and Lough Arrow Mayfly variants. We were into good fish almost straight away. Nothing monstrous but excellent quality fish approaching the 2 lb mark.

This was easy fishing, the sort I grew up with, and instantly recognisable. Cloud had drifted in from the south-west and slightly more than a corduroy ripple was running the length of the drift, a good 200-yard stretch of rock-infested water. I was fishing a midge-tip and Declan was alternating between an intermediate and a midge-tip, and as we approached the western bank we were picking up fish right to the shore. Great fun and most enjoyable. Dry fly is undoubtedly my favourite technique for wild fish – when they will co-operate (and it does tend to select out bigger than average trout) – but wets in this format is extraordinarily exciting, the sort a magnificent lake like Mask can provide.

And so, after a half-dozen plus fish, it was time for a long-delayed lunch. As the guys were getting the Kelly kettle fired up I decided to walk down to the tail-end of Inisgleastai for a chuck of buzzers in the calm water just off the shore. My first cast nailed a measuring fish, but the word must have gone out pretty damned quickly as I never got another offer and seeing a pillar of smoke coming from the lunch site, I happily re-joined the guys.

Lunch devoured and gagging to get back out amongst the action, I was keen to help Declan relaunch. And that's when I took an involuntary trip subsurface to examine the aquatic flora and fauna of Mask water. It wasn't a cold day but when you get soaked to the veritable unmentionables you chill down pretty damned fast. Declan took me back to Cushlough as fast as he could, and I returned to the comforting embrace of the Angler's Rest in Headford where a hot bath was soon run and enjoyed. Dry clothing on and dinner gobbled down, I raced back to Cushlough for an evening's foray in the bay. I returned to the launch site to discover that the rest of the afternoon hadn't been particularly fruitful for the chaps. There's

The high quality of Mask trout is indisputable

no doubt in my mind that a break away from fishing can spoil the day, and that is why I prefer to eat packed lunch 'on the hoof', so to speak. I have experienced that scenario so often – you get back in the boat, return to the area of activity, use the successful flies of the morning, and something has changed. I suppose the events governing fish activity and behaviour are like a chain, connected links, and as the day progresses, as one link changes to another, it's possible to keep up but if a few links are missed it's almost impossible to stay with the game.

As the guys complimented me on my freshly-laundered look, I ignored the banter and set up some hatching buzzer patterns for the evening session. It was looking good. The breeze had dropped to a gentle whisper, the daytime temperature hadn't dropped much at all, and good cloud cover looked as if it would trap in the warmth and give us a really good chance of a buzzer hatch and associated trout activity. But the Law of Sod will get you every time. Just when you think things couldn't be better it doesn't take much to turn the day on its head.

We set up our drifts with high expectations... and almost immediately a fine drizzle drifted across the bay, the temperature dropped like a brick and that was our evening over, from a fishing perspective at least. Reading these lines, it would almost appear as if our time on Mask had been one step forward and two steps back, but no-one can control the weather, and these are the punches that fly fishermen have to take on the chin. However, the spell of wet flyfishing at the back of Inisgleastai that Declan and I enjoyed was fabulous and will live with me through the long winter days. And the low point? Well, there really wasn't one. A day's fishing with so much variety – wet fly, dry fly and buzzers, each having some success – would be hard to replicate anywhere. My graceful immersion in the wetness? Another punch to the chin gratefully received, and a very small price to pay for a most enjoyable day's fishing on mighty Mask.

– 11 –

Less is Often Best

SINCE NORMAN IRVINE devised the Half Hog, a significant variant of the Hedgehog, in the '90s, this style of dressing has developed a small but loyal and dedicated following.

It is little wonder. The Half Hog is one of the most versatile patterns available. It can be fished as a wet fly, nymph or dry (emerger). And it works just as well for rainbow trout as for browns.

Fishing Half Hogs is a delicate style of fishing which is very cathartic. You can fish them successfully off fast-sinking lines if you so desire but, primarily, they suit low-density lines much better. And the dressings are semi-imitative, so they can stand close inspection by fish, thus slow and static retrieve-styles won't jeopardise your catch returns. But best of all, they are a doddle to tie as long as you obey a few important rules.

Norman's original dressing had no hackle, but I always felt that this style of fly was boosted by a light fringe of hackle fibres, especially in the un-dubbed patterns.

One of the best ways of fishing Half Hogs is to lightly grease-up the hair wing, then fish them as dry flies for a short period before a slow figure-of-eight brings them back. When fish are high in the water, and you get pattern/colour selection of Half Hogs just right, the sport can be fast and furious.

In a situation where you can't quite work out whether the fish are taking surface items or sub-surface items this technique is usually the answer. Hatching olive and midge often create this scenario. Often, during an olive hatch, it looks as though trout are taking the dun when they are in fact attacking pre-emergent nymphs. That they are doing this amongst a litter of post-emergent duns leads to confusion and poor catches. Hatching midge can be just as confusing, as trout will take the bug in all states of emergence and working out just what stage attracts them most is critical.

They also make a very good addition to a wet-fly combo, especially in the early months of the season. Slim patterns come to the fore then because most trout food is slim in profile during the intense feeding cycle of late spring – early summer.

HALF HOG HOPPERS

Sticking knotted legs on a Half Hog seemed entirely logical and doing so added somewhat of an extra dimension to an already very effective style of fly.

Legged patterns are, in my opinion, best accompanied with a seal's fur dubbed body. I suppose this is because I generally use them as dry patterns, but as a pulled wet they can be very successful too.

In the early years of this century there was an attempt to hijack the Half Hog Hopper by substituting the deer hair for cdc and calling it a Harry Potter. This substitution seems like a good idea at first, but deer hair is much easier to revitalise after continual immersion than cdc.

Whilst I tend to think of the Half Hog as an early-season fly, I start thinking about the hopper version later on. As a durable, semi-drowned imitator it can cover a pretty wide range of terrestrial flies. I tend to only treat the hair wing with floatant especially in a light ripple but am often a bit more extravagant in the brisk breezes of autumn.

It is almost mandatory, when using knotted pheasant-tail fibres, that the tyer uses three each side. However, for the Half Hog Hopper series I prefer a pair each side. Somehow the extra legs only seem to confuse the issue and are not necessary. The whole idea is a light touch and sparseness.

PATTERNS

Olive Quill Half Hog

Hook:	Fulling Mill All Purpose Medium, #12
Thread:	Black
Body:	Yellow dyed peacock eye quill, stripped of herl and varnished
1st Wing tuft:	Light roe deer hair
Dubbing:	Olive seal's fur mixed with hare's ear
2nd Wing tuft:	As 1st wing tuft
Cheeks:	Yellow dyed jungle cock splits
Hackle:	Olive hen, 2 turns

A very positive general-purpose pattern that crosses the borders of many invertebrate food items of trout – shrimp, olive nymphs, olive buzzers, etc., etc.

Quill Half Hog

Hook:	Fulling Mill All Purpose Medium, #12
Thread:	Black
Body:	Natural peacock eye quill, stripped of herl and varnished
1st Wing tuft:	Dark roe deer hair
Dubbing:	Peacock herl
2nd Wing tuft:	As 1st wing tuft
Hackle:	Dark furnace hen, 2 turns

A general-usage pattern, particularly effective for Duck Fly or any other dark midge hatches.

The material forming the thorax between the wing tufts is down to the tyer's preferences. I have used peacock herl, but a brighter 'trigger point' is an option.

Hutch's Half Hog

Hook:	Fulling Mill All Purpose Medium, #12
Thread:	Black
Body:	Tying thread
Rib:	Fine red holographic tinsel
1st Wing tuft:	Dark roe deer hair
Dubbing:	Black seal's fur
2nd Wing tuft:	White roe deer hair
Cheeks:	Jungle cock splits, or small eyes

This version was heavily influenced by Ian Hutcheon's pattern, Hutch's Pennell, with its white and black hackle configuration at the head.

A great rainbow trout pattern; its mix of black, red and white ticks a lot of boxes, especially early in the season.

I have dispensed with a head hackle for this pattern. It doesn't need one, and such an addition would only lessen the impact of the wing.

Heather Half Hog Hopper

Hook:	Fulling Mill All Purpose Medium, #12 & #10
Thread:	Black
Butt:	Flat red holo tinsel
Rib:	Medium red wire
Body:	Black seal's fur
1st Wing tuft:	Dark roe deer hair
Dubbing:	Black seal's fur
2nd Wing tuft:	As 1st wing tuft
Legs:	2 pairs knotted scarlet-dyed cock pheasant tail fibres
Hackle:	Black hen, 2 turns

A seriously good back-end pattern when the heather fly are about. Also an excellent general-use pattern.

Hare's Ear Half Hog Hopper

Hook:	Fulling Mill All Purpose Medium, #12 & #10
Thread:	Black
Butt:	Flat Mirage pearl tinsel
Rib:	Butt material, twisted
Body:	Hare's mask fur
1st Wing tuft:	Light roe deer hair
Dubbing:	As body
2nd Wing tuft:	As 1st wing tuft
Legs:	2 pairs knotted cock pheasant tail fibres
Hackle:	Golden olive hen, 2 turns
Cheeks:	Yellow Jungle Cock splits

There's always a need for hare's ear patterns in any trout fly selection, and the Half Hog Hopper covers a multitude of jobs. It functions well as a corixa imitator, and also for pale midge and sedge, on the far northern lochs and the Midlands reservoirs.

Hot-Red Half Hog Hopper

Hook:	Fulling Mill All Purpose Medium, #12 & #10
Thread:	Red
Rib:	Fine red wire
Body:	Fluorescent red seal's fur
1st Wing tuft:	Light roe deer hair
Dubbing:	As body
2nd Wing tuft:	As 1st wing tuft
Legs:	2 pairs knotted cock pheasant tail fibres
Hackle:	Ginger hen, 2 turns

This is a recent addition to my Half Hog Hopper range. A friend from the south showed me a sedge pattern of his which included the fluo red dubbing and which he claimed to be his *numero uno* dry pattern on Midlands ressies. We were on the Lake of Mentieth and we had one helluva time using his red sedges on the local 'bows. Naturally, this variation screamed out to be an addition to my dry fly box.

Preparing for a day out on Loch Lochy

− 12 −

Ferox on Fly

MARK AND I were drifting quietly down the south shore of Loch Arkaig. During my three-day stay the wind had proved a continual disappointment, either blowing off the shores we wanted to fish, or just not puffin' enough!

As we chatted, joked and laughed, our flies flying forward, swimming and flying again, neither of us contemplated the near impossibility of our task – trying to locate a fish in 2,6573 million cubic feet of water. Never mind Mark's photos of unbelievably big trout, I had seen it done. My guide and mentor had caught and released a fish estimated at between six and seven pounds on the previous evening.

We were approaching a rare feature on the otherwise featureless shoreline. "Nearly always a fish here!" quipped Mark. I raised my top dropper onto the bob, hung it for a second or two, and swung the rod back to make the next cast. Only the flies refused to leave the water. Something irresistible was holding on fast. Suddenly, explosively, the water erupted, and a massive trout threw itself sideways out of the water to land an impressive five feet away. Two thoughts rapidly flashed across my mind; "This could be my heaviest trout ever!" and "A whole new world of flyfishing has just opened up for me!"

There is something about big wild brown trout that hits me right where I live. I don't get anything remotely like this thrill with big salmon. Any salmon, no matter how big, is extremely unlikely to be more than five years old. Compared to a big wild trout, that is still 'pulling pig-tails, sucking sweets' territory.

I had heard a rumour that big trout were regularly coming from some unlikely locations over on the west coast of Scotland, and by 'big' I mean well into double figures. Trout up to 14 lb were being taken on a regular basis by Mark Hirst and friends. I was gob-smacked, but accompanying photos proved the validity of the claims. The lochs in question were Arkaig and Lochy.

Now a whole lot of you will be scratching your heads because neither of these two lochs is synonymous with quality trout fishing. They are both what are referred to as 'ribbon lochs' which to the layman means glacial, deep, dark and menacing. The Highlands of Scotland, particularly in the west and north, are full of them, and they had always been of peripheral interest to fly fishermen because they are commonly thought to be home to varying numbers of 'four to the pound' tiddlers, charr and fly-despising ferox. My (minimal) experience of these waters only served to confirm this widespread belief and I've spent forty-odd years avoiding going anywhere near them.

So, sucker as I am for big trout, I swallowed my disbelief and did some homework. Arkaig is 12 miles long and up to 360′ deep; Lochy is a mind-blowing 530′ deep but shorter, at 10 miles long. These are classic 'wet deserts'; unproductive, low-nutrient environments where small fish just about get by and big trout eat them. From a fisherman's perspective they are fascinating habitats for fish, and the food chain is simple and effective. In the open waters forage fish, such as char and small browns, live on zooplankton (such as daphnia) and in the shallow loch edges small browns make an uncertain and poor living on a paucity of aquatic invertebrates and terrestrial falls. Hovering around these small succulent fish are varying numbers of predators; sometimes alien pike, but, more interestingly, environmentally-adapted trout generally referred to as ferox. Ferox are capable of extremely fast growth on this high protein diet and the current UK record is a mouth-watering 31 lb 12 ozs.

I am not about to get involved in the current debate about ferox v. piscivorous brown trout. From a non-scientific perspective it really doesn't matter what these fish are called, only that they exist in larger numbers, are more widespread than the layman is likely to believe. Ferox- and char-fanatic/expert, Ron Greer, is quite happy to declare that any trout from such an environment exceeding 3 lb is a ferox, because the ability of a trout over that weight to survive and grow in these lochs requires an almost totally fish-based diet. That's certainly good enough for me. I hope its good enough for you.

I had made the relatively short journey from the civilised east coast of Scotland to the wild, west wilderness that is Highland Scotland. Turning off the main Fort William-Inverness route and having a quick glance at the Commando Monument just east of Spean Bridge, it occurred to me that commandos, towering hills, bottomless lochs and ferox trout all made some kind of visceral sense. Everything was extreme, tough, rugged and larger than life. In this kind of country anything, no matter how challenging, was possible.

I couldn't stay in Simon Laird's purpose-built self-catering accommodation by the loch-side because it was a few weeks short of completion, but he had very kindly offered me the use of his own hunting lodge a few yards away. It was sumptuous and comfortable to the nth degree, and the self-catering cottage is a facsimile of it, just in a smaller scale. I got a preview, and as I wandered round it, stepping over the power cables and workman's tools, I thought "I'm going to be very comfortable here when I return."

Mark and I fished a lot in the three days, but as he explained to me, the good fish will come all through the day in the early and late summer months, but in July and August nothing generally happens until the evening. This matches up with what the deep trollers find; their poorest time for catches is around the height of summer. Mark also told me that these fish are ready and waiting in Loch Arkaig from opening day, and in the late summer are boosted by an upstream migration of similar fish from Loch Lochy.

We spent a fruitless day on Loch Lochy, but the loch was a good two feet above normal summer level and would appear not to produce in these circumstances. The fact that the cloud-level was down to the loch surface for most of the day didn't help either. For years I've driven up and down the road skirting Lochy and never considered it a serious venue for flyfishing, but Mark said that on its day it will produce more and bigger fish than Arkaig. This is all hard for me to get my head round. After all, it has been a tenet of loch-fishers that trying to catch ferox on fly is like trying to get toothpaste back in the tube – don't even bother trying.

Well, there I was by the side of Loch Arkaig cuddling seven-pounds-plus of toothy beauty. Okay, not my biggest ever wild trout, but damned close. I was thinking "It really doesn't get much better than this!"

So how do you catch the fish of a lifetime? Well, I'm no expert – how many people are? – but this is what Mark taught me. First of all, if you like continual action and lots of fish, this is not for you. This is about the fish of a lifetime and they don't come easy. You've got to pick the right water, and that involves someone with pretty comprehensive local knowledge – I got lucky. The right flies for the water are important (see opposite). If you are bouncing your flies off the dry stones at the loch edge you are only going to catch tiddlers, so we spent almost all our time a good cast-length-plus from the water's edge in about 15 feet of water, give or take. The line density seems crucial too and Mark advised, rather surprisingly, a slow intermediate, or when the fish are really 'up', a floater. Breaking strain of nylon in 8–10 lb b.s. is appropriate. And some sort of wind is critical to success. Later in the evening, after I had nailed my fish, it went glassy calm and although the odd fish was moving, we couldn't get a cast near them. They simply sidled away from even the most cautious approach.

On the other hand, on the evening when Mark hooked his fish, we were surrounded by massive trout cavorting about in a light ripple for about three-quarters of an hour. I once witnessed something similar one late evening on Loch Borralaidh, but nowhere near the numbers. I have rarely seen anything so exciting or unsettling as that evening on Arkaig. Trying to extrapolate the possible stock of massive fish in the loch by what we saw in a couple of hundred yards just about blew my neural circuits.

I've been fishing Scottish waters for about 50 years and I thought I'd done it all. I've caught very big trout from fertile waters and sea-trout from the sea. I've seen the best of UK rainbow trout and possibly the worst, caught salmon on lochs, and some 'stonking' trout on dry fly from rivers. I thought my last years of flyfishing would be a case of re-doing what I had already done. It's a joy, and somewhat of a relief, to realise that in the wild places in Scotland there are more, bigger, tougher and better challenges still waiting.

Next year I'm going to return and catch a 15 lb wild trout on fly! What do you think of them apples?

FLIES

Mark Hirst states that there are only three flies for Arkaig and Lochy trout. I may have introduced a level of doubt about that statement and added another.

Tail fly – *Silver Invicta* variant (Hirst)

Hook:	Double #10
Thread:	Black
Tail:	Golden pheasant crest
Body:	Flat silver
Rib:	Medium oval silver
Body hackle:	Medium red game cock
Throat:	Blue jay
Wing:	Sparse red squirrel tail hair

Middle dropper – *Clan Chief*

Hook:	Standard wet fly, #8
Thread:	Black
Butt:	Flat silver
Tag:	No. 4 GloBrite floss (red) over No. 10 GloBrite floss (yellow)
Body:	Black seal's fur
Rib:	Medium oval silver
Body hackles:	Paired scarlet and black cock hackles
Head hackle:	Black hen, tied long

Bob fly – *Stone Goat* (Hirst)

Hook:	Standard wet fly, #8
Thread:	Black
Tail:	Golden pheasant crest
Body:	Dark claret seal's fur
Rib:	Medium oval gold
Body hackles:	Paired magenta and black cock
Head hackle:	Dyed blue grizzle or guinea fowl, tied long

Alternative Point Fly – *Worm Fly*

Hooks:	Fulling Mill Competition Heavyweights, #10
Jointing:	Short length of nylon braid
Thread:	Black
Tag:	Fire-red fluorescent wool
Body:	Peacock herl
Rib:	Fine oval gold or wire
Hackle:	Medium red game hen

− 13 −

Hoggin' It

MANY YEARS AGO, somewhere about the mid-nineties, a revolution occurred. Sandy (Nic) Nicolson, one of the greats of Orkney flyfishing, introduced to the local scene a fly called a Hedgehog. He told me he'd picked up the original idea from some obscure fishing article. I've always expected this original creator to come forward to claim his place in the flyfishing hierarchy, but as the years pass this hope fades.

Hogs are all about deer hair, in varying quantities. Hedgehogs and Sedgehogs have full, matuka-style wings of hair, Half Hogs and Half Hog Hoppers truncated wings. And it is the creation of these composite wings that give Hogs of any description their killing power.

Deer hair, or specifically roe deer hair, is the essential material for creating Hog wings. Winter-culled roe deer hair has all the qualities required to produce top-quality wings. Hair from summer roe bucks is pretty-much useless, as it is not hollow and has none of the floating properties of winter hair. Some commentators advise the use of coastal deer hair, muntjac, and sika, but I have yet to use any material that surpasses winter roe deer hair for this purpose, and it is cheap, and readily available.

The handling of roe deer hair, or any deer hair, can bewilder inexperienced tyers to the extent that a) their flies don't work properly, or b) they avoid the effort. The purpose of this piece is to make available my twenty-plus years of Hog tying experience to eliminate the pit-falls, to set to rights much of the bad tying practice that is being promulgated by so-called experts, and, inasmuch as a short article can, give pertinent advice on how to turn an ordinary pattern into a miracle worker.

The principle problem with tying deer hair in as a bunch in a corporate wing is that it has a unique propensity to flare, and instead of forming an upright tuft tends to fan out in a semi-circular or circular shape. This is the central technique in muddler head construction, but one which *must be avoided* in hog-wing construction. The flare is caused by the fact that each individual hair fibre is a hollow tube and has a tendency to move haphazardly when crushed by thread. In muddler head construction the retaining loops of tying thread are tied in loose and gradually tightened; in hog-wing construction a tight pinch and loop is used to locate the deer hair tuft and the tips are held tightly by the fingers until enough tight turns of thread are in place to locate and secure the hair tuft. These tight retaining turns will form a base for the application of dubbing, and as such should be reduced to a minimum.

One thing I find virtually impossible to do is create a good hog wing without dubbing. Dubbing is essential for what I consider to be the best hog wings because it has the unique propensity to control the shape and position of the hair tufts. When the tufts are tied in, and bound down, there will always be some residual flare left in the fibres, but by bringing dubbed fur onto the fibre roots and, by stroking it back up the stalks, the angle and flare of the hair can be controlled. This is the ultimate secret to good hog wings; master that and you will have the hogs you've always wanted.

There are guides to hog tying out there that will leave you with the distinct impression that hog wings are all about cramming as much deer hair into the wing as is humanly possible. This is a direct contravention of the most basic fly-tying principle. Good fly-tying technique has always been about using as little material as will get the job done. A perfect hog wing is *not* about two or three big, opaque tufts of deer hair, but more to do with multiple sparse, translucent bunches to build up a wing. Always think 'matuka' when tying hogs and you won't go far wrong.

I've talked about dubbing and deer hair fibres as being integral to hog wings, but there is another essential required to make a hog work perfectly, and that is a good silcicone floatant. I will describe the unique fishing styles of hogs shortly but let me tell you how I prepare a hog straight out of the vice. Firstly, I give the patterns a good drenching in 'Dry Fly Silicone Mucilin' or equivalent liquid preparation, preferably overnight. Then I leave them a day to dry off before lodging them in the fly box. On selection for the leader the individual fly will be anointed a smear of 'Gink' or similar which is worked well into the dubbing and hair fibres. This treatment will render the fly unsinkable even under the most extreme of circumstances. A wee wring-out with amadou every now and again will bring the hog bobbing to the surface like a cork.

And it is this 'bobbing to the surface like cork' which raises hog patterns from the ordinary to the exquisite. Hogs, primarily Hedgehogs and Sedgehogs, when treated properly with floatant have a strong ability to stay above the water surface. Of course, line density will have a say in the matter, but when pulled in a traditional wet-fly way, they will scurry across the water surface or, even better, dip and dive in the most seductive of ways. Even when tethered by a couple of standard wet flies below, hogs will break loose of the water surface to 'emerge' in a most lifelike manner. A manner which trout find almost irresistible.

And it is this dipping and diving which I tend to concentrate on, the 'scurrying' I find less effective. So, I prefer a midge tip line for best results. The slight penetration of the water surface given by the short sinking component of a sinking tip allows for the hog to dip below the surface and easily pop up back to the surface. This technique will work in almost any weather condition except a glass-flat calm, as long as the trout are in that sort of mood – which they aren't always. The dictum we always used up in the isles was "If it ain't worked in a half-hour, it isn't going to work at all!" It's a basket-filler or, on the other hand, best avoided. There doesn't seem to be a half-way house. Of course, pattern can be important, and I have a half-dozen or so I keep handy just in case. But the fly line choice is much more important. I have known Hogs to work on a fast-sinking line, but that was probably a one-off situation and not a standard technique. My favourite line is, as stated above, varying lengths of midge tip, but in a big wind a floater can be extremely effective also. Medium or fast intermediates can produce fish on hogs, but I prefer to locate them on the point position rather than on the bob with floaters and sink tips. A sunk hog will catch fish, but it is on or in the surface film where they do their best work.

Another use for hogs is as the business end of a washing-line setup when fish are getting bored with boobies. And while we are on the subject, Hogs are not just for Scottish brown trout, rainbows can become suicidal on the things if the mood takes them. I also use Sedgehogs as dry flies, the hackle exaggerating the 'footprint'.

I'll be out there this year 'poppin' my hogs' the length and breadth of the country. If traditional fly-fishing styles appeal to you, 'ye cannae whack a hog!'

Bibio Sedgehog

Hook: Fulling Mill All Purpose medium, #12 & #10
Thread: Black
Tail: Slim bunch of roe deer hair
Body: Sparse dubbing of black seal's fur over deer hair roots, with one dub of scarlet seal's fur as a thorax
Wing: Slim bunches (4 or 5) deer hair, tied Matuka-style up the length of the body
Hackle: Black hen

Claret Sedgehog

Hook: Fulling Mill All Purpose medium, #12 & #10
Thread: Black
Tail: Slim bunch of roe deer hair
Body: Sparse dubbing of claret seal's fur over deer hair roots
Wing: Slim bunches (4 or 5) deer hair, tied Matuka-style up the length of the body
Hackle: Claret hen

Hare's-Ear Sedgehog

Hook: Fulling Mill All Purpose medium, #12 & #10
Thread: Rust
Tail: Slim bunch of roe deer hair
Body: Sparse dubbing of Orkney peach seal's fur over tail deer hair roots, finished with dubbed hare's mask fur
Wing: Slim bunches (4 or 5) deer hair, tied Matuka-style up the length of the body
Hackle: Light furnace hen

Olive Sedgehog

Hook: Fulling Mill All Purpose medium, #12 & #10
Thread: Olive
Tail: Slim bunch of roe deer hair
Body: Sparse dubbing of olive seal's fur over deer
           hair roots
Wing: Slim bunches (4 or 5) deer hair, tied Matuka-
           style up the length of the body
Hackle: Black hen

Orange Sedgehog

Hook: Fulling Mill All Purpose medium, #12 & #10
Thread: Orange or red
Tail: Slim bunch of roe deer hair
Body: Sparse dubbing of hot-orange seal's fur over
           tail deer hair roots
Wing: Slim bunches (4 or 5) deer hair, tied Matuka-
           style up the length of the body
Hackle: Hot-orange hen

Peach Sedgehog

Hook: Fulling Mill All Purpose medium, #12 & #10
Thread: Orange or red
Tail: Slim bunch of roe deer hair
Body: Sparse dubbing of Orkney peach seal's fur
           over tail deer hair roots
Wing: Slim bunches (4 or 5) deer hair, tied Matuka-
           style up the length of the body
Hackle: Orkney peach

Red-arsed Green Peter Sedgehog

Hook: Fulling Mill All Purpose medium, #12 & #10
Thread: Black
Tail: Slim bunch of roe deer hair
Body: Sparse dubbing of scarlet seal's fur over tail deer hair roots, finished with dubbed green highlander seal's fur
Wing: Slim bunches (4 or 5) deer hair, tied Matuka-style up the length of the body
Hackle: Light furnace hen

– 14 –

Loch Ailsh

BEFORE I VISIT a destination I have never seen I always build a picture in my mind of what it looks like. This is not a voluntary mind-game, it is a subconscious imperative. I suppose everyone does it.

My mental picture of Loch Ailsh was almost 100% perfect except that in my mind it was bigger and surrounded by broadleaf trees. It is, in fact, quite small and surrounded by Forestry Commission plantations. I dislike the uniformity of such plantations and their effect upon wildlife diversity in their confines. Pine needles do not provide the natural benefits bestowed by the annual fall of deciduous leaves. There is little doubt in my mind that trout and salmon lochs that have fir plantations in their catchment would benefit greatly by their replacement with indigenous trees.

Still, Ailsh has some magnificent vistas and, plantations aside, is a delight to the eye. To the north rise some spectacular hills/mountains amongst which are born the spawning reaches employed by the silver tourists which venture into the loch every summer and autumn. These fish run the famous River Oykel, a mightily productive river which exits into the Kyle of Sutherland at Bonar Bridge, and whilst all Oykel fish won't run into Ailsh, a significant proportion do.

Another misconception I had was that Ailsh would be primarily a salmon water. I had come to this flawed conclusion using simplistic logic, always a mistake when it comes to matters fishy. In most cases salmon like to get as far up a river system as possible and sea-trout are naturally lazy and will leave the main river as soon as possible. Considering just how many salmon run the Oykel – arguably every flood tide bestowing fish into the system – Ailsh, from mid-summer onwards, should be stuffed with them. But a loch-caught Ailsh salmon is hard to come by, strange as that may seem.

Lochs reluctant to give up their salmon to the fly are not unusual. Lochs Tay, Ness and Awe are classic examples where flyfishing rarely works and trolling seems the only way to nail a fish. Why this should be is a puzzle. I had always assumed that this was due to the length of time it took salmon to reach the loch, but this does not bear close scrutiny. A more likely solution to this conundrum is that big, massive, deep lochs are just not suitable for flyfishing because of many factors including that fish are spread out too thinly. But Ailsh, as already stated, is a small, shallow loch with a good head of fish. As in all fishing matters, especially when it concerns migratory fish, there are more questions than answers.

Prior to getting there, I was unaware of the simple fact that catching a salmon would be the exception rather than the rule, and that I should concentrate my efforts on sea-trout. In most lochs of this type one should fish close in for salmon and in more open water for sea-trout, but Ailsh is a very shallow loch so it would be fair to assume that both species could be expected from similar depths.

I wouldn't go so far as to say that I have differing tactics and techniques for either species, but what I will say is that if I am targeting salmon I fish muddlers on a floating line with a medium paced retrieve. For sea-trout on the other hand, I have been known to fish an intermediate with good effect, loaded with bushy palmers/bumbles, with a faster retrieve.

However, whilst following these guidelines I sometimes find that the fish don't necessarily follow the same rules and a salmon will fall for flies presented on an intermediate and sea-trout can't stop themselves from savaging muddlers, on occasion. Middle flies on a two-dropper cast can be drearily ineffective. I tend to spice up the middle fly with a dash of floatant. In that moment before the retrieve kicks-in I have known good sea-trout to take a treated middle fly as if it was a dry fly. Given that sea-trout fishing can be highly unproductive at the best of times, every little helps.

Ghillies are a prime requisite for this type of fishing. Too much time can be spent in unproductive areas and productive areas are not always discernible to the inexperienced eye. Also, many visitors in search of loch silver come with background of stillwater techniques which can be counterproductive to this style of flyfishing, such as fishing with the rod tip low to the water, and desperately slow retrieve rates. A good ghillie will have these faults ironed out in a trice – indeed a good ghillie makes the difference between abject failure and success. A downside of this is that ghillies can often have closed minds and stick to the percentage

Small, but pretty Loch Ailsh sea-trout

game. The most exciting ghillies to go out with are the younger generation who, perhaps more than their elder associates, realise that there is much more to learn in this discipline.

A highly competent young ghillie, who I class as a good friend, is Peter O'Neil. He works out of the Oykel Bridge Hotel and, though mainly a river man, his fascination with the whole art of flyfishing made him indispensable on my visit to Ailsh. It was Peter who put me right on the loch's salmon. In all his visits to Ailsh he had never caught one, although a friend of his on brief visits had caught two, which I guessed got right up Peter's nose.

Peter, Glyn Satterley (a photographer and Yorkshireman with a deep and abiding love of the Highlands) and I arrived at Ailsh bright and early. The weather was encouraging – large fluffy clouds being pushed eastwards on a freshening westerly breeze – and we felt blessed. Ailsh isn't fished much – only two boats are allowed out at any given time, and when the estate owners are in residence access is strictly limited – so reports were few and basic. That there were sea-trout to be caught was never in doubt, but would they play?

Sea-trout in lochs can be exceptionally moody beasts. They have strict timetables of activity, spend most of their time ignoring the best efforts of the angler, then, for no apparent reason, switch on for a brief period and for no apparent reason. You can be in absolutely the right place, doing everything perfectly with no result whatsoever for great tracts of the day, and then – wallop – everything goes crazy and every sea-trout is wearing a kamikaze headband. Then, suddenly, you are back to square one and you'd be forgiven for thinking there wasn't a fish in the loch.

What information I had gleaned on Ailsh told me that the river-mouth at the north end of the loch was a hotspot, and the associated sandbar which stretched a long way into the loch was worthy of dedicated exploration. Apart from that all was mystery. From an earlier foray for brown trout I knew that the southern end was very shallow and heavily weeded, so I had largely written it off as a source of fish. I was slightly surprised when Peter confidently suggested that this was where we should start.

There were gaps in the weed but, strangely enough, it was in amongst the denser stuff that the fish were lying. Salmon love to lie on the fringes of weed beds as I discovered one glorious day on Loch Scourst. And sea-trout can be found in reed beds in Lower Kildonan, but I had never encountered them lying amongst dense potamageton type weed-growth. Mind you, I would probably have avoided such places like the plague in the past because a fish hooked on a multiple dropper cast, in a weed bed, doesn't have to do much to depart unseen with or without the offending fly. The best fish of the day – around about 2 lb – was hooked and lost in this manner as we approached the exit burn on Ailsh, and I was left wondering if I'd blown it for the day. Glyn was left wondering if he'd laid a jinx on us by whipping out his camera for an action shot just as the fish gave us the two-fingered salute.

Not wanting a re-run of that, Peter took us up to the river mouth where weed growth was minimal, and we got some action almost immediately, although most of it lacked a successful outcome for me. Peter hooked and landed a couple of fish while we drifted the sandbar, one of them a nice fish of about 1¾lb, but I was only

The stunning scenery of Loch Ailsh. One of the few East Coast migratory fish lochs

attracting the attention of 'suckers' (I mentioned these before in an article on Loch Naver – fish giving the flies a pull but being absent when you respond by tightening into them. I put this down to the fish being not quite on and not quite off, although fly-size just might have something to do with it!).

We drifted hither and yon on the small loch, taking in the relative deeps, the shallows and the promontories, picking up the odd small sea-trout and hoping for that surging boil that would herald that much sought after rarity, an Ailsh salmon. We had amassed six sea-trout, nothing bigger than Peter's first fish. He assured me that a record breaker was never going to come from the loch, the greater bulk of the fish being in the one to two pounds mark, and a real monster only achieving four or five pounds. I assumed that the bigger fish probably stayed in the river.

But it was fast becoming apparent that the loch was quietening down as the afternoon progressed. One of the things about this game that I find regrettable is that I always seem to be operating out of hotels and the like when fishing salmon and sea-trout lochs. They like you home, done and dusted, in time for an evening meal, with a couple of hours spare to buy expensive drinky-poos at the bar. Thus evening fishing is often curtailed and fishing into darkness impossible. Of course, if employing a ghillie, with the best will in the world, one can't expect him to be out there from dawn to dusk. So, evening fishing for loch salmon and sea-trout is pretty much virgin territory for me. I remember being out one evening on Voshimid with Ian (Jonesy) Jones and Michael Wilson from Loch Leven. We had good sport while the light remained, but as it faded and trout seemed to rise everywhere, none of us could do a damned thing with them. Pure lack of experience in a new environment, and a decided lack of time for experimentation.

So, with eyes on watches, we squeezed in a few drifts down at the south end where the weeds had stripped me of a good sea-trout earlier in the day. We were getting enough encouragement from jumping fish and tentative offers to run the clock down, when with the last cast of the day, I hooked a bonny fish from amongst the weed beds. No way was this re-run going to end up the same. I wasn't interested in being kind and forgiving. I bent the rod into him and didn't give an inch, up, down or sideways. Himself was less than pleased by my rough tactics and he thrashed the water to a foam under the gunnels of the boat, but it worked. The net was slipped under him by Peter, with Glynn snapping away like a good 'un. No weedy escape for that chap. At just under two pounds, he was my best of the day, and a fitting way to call it a day. I slid him back with a fond farewell, as we had done with all the rest. No monster, but very, very welcome for all that.

And, yes, we were late for dinner, but some soft words, crawling and fluttered eyelashes got us a bite to eat. I'll be back.

– 15 –

The Trout Fisherman's Holy Grail

THE AVERAGE WET fly box contains flies of every possible shape and size. The average angler generally doesn't have a system of selection other than "This was working well last year, here and at this time," or "This is my favourite, and I never have it off the cast."

Now, I'm not criticising these selection methods. They are ubiquitous, and work for you, me, and all Jock Tamson's bairns. But there is a way of adding a dash of science to them. Well, maybe not science *per se*, perhaps a better description of my way of quelling chaos with a helping of order is cognitive thought.

I was never happy to accept that we can't understand why a trout, or a succession of them, happily pick a fly they like and ignore a handful of others which they don't. Trout are not thinking or reasoning creatures. They don't add two-plus-two and get four. Trout are essentially motivated by instinct, immediate responses to observed stimuli. This works very well for creatures which don't have thinking, reasoning brains. Their response to anything entering their close environment is 'Can I eat it? Can I fight it? Should I run away from it? Or can I ignore it?' Apart from some basic reproductive responses, which don't or shouldn't involve anglers, that's about it.

It follows that the acceptance of an artificial fly as food means that it has triggered an instinctive urge. It also follows that the refusal to accept a different fly has done likewise. The responses are not the same, but they are equal, with no recognisable pattern. The artificial fly that a host of trout accepted with relish yesterday may well be totally ignored tomorrow. Most anglers, when faced with this scenario, tend to shake their heads and move on, or refuse to accept the glaring truth and persevere, hoping that 'a daft yin' will eventually turn up and make everything alright. My response is to wonder, try to inject some logic into what is, to a human mind illogical – a fundamental, instinctive response – and learn from it.

So far, my cerebral investigations into this conundrum have convinced me that external pressures dictate fly pattern acceptability. Light quality, atmospheric conditions, basic weather conditions, temperature, and the presence, or lack thereof, of natural food items are the major influences on fly pattern acceptability. Accepting these variants as fundamental allows us fly fishermen to use cognitive reasoning to help us to success.

Let us take salmon flyfishing as an example, and I will, here and now, ask all salmon anglers to forgive me for over-simplification. Salmon fishermen accept that there are times when it is nigh on impossible to get a fish to accept any fly, and that there are times when their chances are optimised. When conditions are perfect, they know by experience and understanding that specific patterns will offer the best chances of success. Big water, large fly; dark water, bright fly; clear water, black or muted patterns; thin water, small fly; and so on. How much of this example can we inject into trout fishing? Some of it, but not all. Whilst in freshwater mature salmon have a different set of agendas, for example the feeding impulse is muted and the aggressive, territorial, impulses raised. Because salmon have less behavioural factors impinging on them in freshwater, it has become relatively easy for anglers to break the code and find a suitable pattern list to cover most eventualities. That a similar break-through in trout fishing hasn't occurred is manifestly obvious when one considers the proliferation of new or varied trout patterns appearing almost every day.

But it does prove that logic can help solve pattern selection problems in fish. As I progressed through my trout fishing apprenticeship, insights into fly selection trickled into my consciousness. As I mentioned above, the influence of light, atmospheric conditions, etc., made a profound impact, and it became obvious that trout react very strongly to factors to which we humans have become oblivious. To the average man/woman, a cloud passing in front of the sun may be a minor irritant; to a trout it can trigger total behavioural change. Out on Loch Leven the angler can work away diligently under a bright sun with no reward, and then a rogue cloud can sweep over to dull the light, producing a brace of trout for the industrious, but overjoyed, angler.

Many years ago, as I was refurbishing my fly box ahead of a new season, I became aware of one of these rare insights into trout behaviour. Comparing the

Almost all of the early-season trout food items have a slim profile

early-season patterns with those favoured for mid-season onwards I was struck by the basic difference in aspect. Early-season patterns were slim and skimpy; late summer patterns were bushy and bulky. These differences had evolved from that basic human investigative technique – suck it and see. You keep what works and you throw away what doesn't.

But why should basic successful fly conformity alter so fundamentally through a season? The answers are both easy and complicated. Let's deal with the easy answers first. To understand what I'm going to describe one must accept that there are two different feeding periods in the year of the trout. First, there is the feeding season which extends from early spring to mid summer, during which all trout within a system will be feeding hard in preparation for an energy-sapping winter. This is the main period of hatch, emergence and bloom. Trout, being very much in tune with their environment, instinctively respond to this. The major part of any trout's feeding regime will take place in the first four months of the season. Almost all of the early-season trout food items have a slim profile – midge pupae, shrimp, insect larvae and nymphs, even fish fry, and these creatures will make up the bulk of trout food in any given year. There is a hard-wired recognition of these creatures and their basic appearance in a trout's simple mind. The second (remaining) period of the season sees the trout population split in two. There will be a proportion of trout which will be becoming sexually mature. These fish will start to lose their appetite and, while they still eat, their desire to feed is reduced. Eating is like us having a sweet or a biscuit; feeding is like a 'three square meals a day' regime. In effect, sexually mature trout behave like salmon in freshwater, for exactly the same reasons.

The other portion of the trout population which are not becoming sexually mature will continue to feed, just like their high-seas salmon compatriots. All marine salmon do not return to freshwater every year, only those approaching sexual maturity do. Similarly, not all trout in any environment spawn every winter, only those approaching sexual maturity will. Therefore, the behaviour of either portion of the trout population will respond to external influences in different ways. Given this, why do artificial fly preferences change so dramatically in the latter part of the season?

If we return to the behaviour of sexually mature salmon which, because of their metabolic imperatives, are in freshwater, we find that there are three on-going theories why these non-feeding fish will accept an artificial fly. 1) They are responding to some dim memories of feeding in freshwater as parr and smolts; 2) they are driven by aggression and territorial imperatives; and 3) they are not consciously aware that their sexual maturity prevents them from actively feeding so they will eat something which attracts or stimulates some form of memory.

Whilst all the above theories have their merits, I prefer option 3 because it tends to mirror sexually mature trout behaviour. Non-feeding trout will eat; non-feeding salmon will take a fly. And as we all know salmon flies are non-imitative but depend upon colour and form to lure salmon into striking the fly. This being the case it is hardly surprising that back-end trout flies tend not to be imitative either and are more brashly coloured and 'noticeable' than the flies we favour in the early months of the year.

One of the old adages about fly pattern construction is 'that which gets noticed gets eaten'. This is why, even in imitative patterns, tyers like to add the odd hot-spot or hint of flash – make it noticeable, get the fly to stand out from the crowd. This is classic salmon and back-end trout fly-tying technique.

It also occurs to me that our selection of dry flies during the season is similarly affected by trout metabolism. During hatches in the early months we certainly pick out imitative patterns and they work best – neat, skimpy flies which sit well down in the surface film. But as the season progresses, and the water-borne hatches subside, bigger, brasher patterns with a 'footprint' like a sasquatch become more appealing. It may be tempting to believe that the natural occurrence of terrestrials may have a lot to do with pattern conformity at the time of year and, while I wouldn't discount it altogether, I suspect that a big, tempting pattern sending out loud and clear signals of its presence is just the sort of 'tit-bit' to lure a non-feeding fish.

But, I hear you ask, what about the portion of the trout population that are not gaining sexual maturity? Experience suggests that these fish will continue to respond to imitative patterns and will certainly be on the hunt for any seasonal hatch or emergence. But what must be remembered is that the early-season glut of food will allow these fish to be very circumspect about their feeding activity. The cold-blooded nature of fish allows them to basically shut down, or slow down, their metabolism when it becomes necessary so that periods of low food availability will have little or no effect upon their lives. If this is so, it perhaps goes a long way to proving that our preferred target fish in the back-end are the non-feeders which are susceptible to a luring snack.

So, if you are still with me after that somewhat dry discussion on trout behaviour and feeding regime, what have we learnt that can make profound changes in our seasonal fishing tactics? Well, perhaps we can, once and for all, disassociate ourselves from age-old fallacies, typical of which is the often heard "they've got to get hungry sometime!" If after reading the above you still think that trout feeding activities in any way mirror those of humans, then I'm sorry to say that you are most likely deluding yourself. Fish and human behaviour are so basically dissimilar that fish might as well come from another planet. If we adopt fishing tactics that take into consideration the lifestyle of our target species we can expect improved results and fewer times when we feel like banging our heads on the gunnels out of pure frustration and incomprehension.

ESSENTIAL EARLY-SEASON PATTERNS

Red Arrow (variant)

Hook:	Fulling Mill All-purpose Medium, #12 & #10
Thread:	Black
Tail:	Golden pheasant tippets
Rib:	Fine silver oval or wire
Body:	Seal's fur in three parts: rear third, scarlet; mid third, claret; fore third, black
Cheeks:	Jungle cock splits
Hackle:	Dark furnace hen, two turns

I love this pattern during early-season midge hatches, and it provides a traditional way of semi-imitating buzzer pupae. Tied slim and sparse, it is reliable and capable of fishing anywhere on the cast and on a wide variety of line densities.

Hutch's Pennell Muddler

Hook:	Fulling Mill All-purpose Medium, #12 & #10
Thread:	Black
Butt:	Two turns of flat silver
Tail:	Golden pheasant tippets
Rib:	Fine silver oval or wire
Body:	Very fine peacock herl
Hackle:	Black hen, two turns
Head:	White deer hair, spun and clipped

Muddlers can make exceptional semi-imitative patterns, and needn't be bulky. Above is an adaptation of Hutch's Pennell, a great early to mid-season semi-imitative pattern for trout everywhere. It is highly effective fished slowly, high in the water during midge hatches.

ESSENTIAL LATE-SEASON PATTERNS

Leggy Claret Bumble

Hook: Fulling Mill Competition Heavy-weight, #12 & #10

Thread: Black or red

Butt: Two turns of flat silver

Tail: Golden pheasant tippets, dyed hot-orange

Rib: Medium gold oval

Body: Dark claret seal's fur

Body hackle: Black and claret cock, wound together

Shoulder hackle: Peacock body hackle

Collar: Blue jay

Nothing says back-end trout like a bumble pattern. This variation on Kingsmill-Moore's famous prototype is dressed to accentuate big, bold and brash factors which work so well when imitation is irrelevant and pattern style is the secret.

Clan Chief Muddler

Hook: Fulling Mill All-Purpose Medium, #12 & #10

Thread: Black

Butt: Two turns of flat silver

Tail: Fluorescent floss in two parts: under, yellow; above, scarlet

Rib: Medium silver oval

Body: Black seal's fur

Hackle: Black & scarlet cock, wound together

Head: Black deer hair, spun and clipped

If we compare this pattern with that of the Hutch's Pennell Muddler, they are like chalk and cheese. The Clan Chief makes no pretence of imitating anything and has all the bold features of a 'lure'. Very much a pattern for the back-end of the season.

The Irish like to disembark at lunchtime and fire up the Kelly kettle. Damned fine idea!

– 16 –

These Things I've Learnt

A SIXTIETH BIRTHDAY has a way of making one very introspective. Questions which occur to a slightly crumbling mind are – who is that old fart staring at me from my shaving mirror?; why is it impossible to get into or out of an armchair without sounding like a wounded warthog?; why is it that the with every passing year your trouser belt inches ever closer to your nipples, and hair sprouts everywhere but upon your head?; and why is limb stiffness so selective?

Ah well, life – in a somewhat altered state – goes on! On the brighter side, however, the slide towards senility has focussed my failing faculties on lessons learnt in a lifetime of fishing. Flyfishing has always been a search for understanding of the imponderable. The open mind has the ability to amass information and experience over the years, and the crucial part of that statement is the term 'open mind'! I often wonder whether it is possible to learn from others or whether first-hand experience is essential. An open mind certainly helps, but lessons learnt the hard way stick longer and impress profoundly.

Much of the flyfishing debate of the past fifty years has centred around the relationship between anglers and fish. In a deteriorating environment much concern centres round the viability of stock, be it wild or introduced. I have made no secret about the fact that I have grave misgivings about mandatory, blanket, catch and release policies. When I first wielded rod and line it was a given that a fish caught was a fish killed and eaten. Things have changed dramatically. Game fish are no longer viewed as an essential part of human fare, and as the clock moves on more and more people view them as a source of human entertainment rather than food items. Half a century ago the human menu was bland and repetitive, and the addition of highly nutritious and tasty alternative was most welcome in almost every household. Nowadays the wide and varied food products of the world call out to us from every stand in the supermarket, and a bland diet is a distant and fading memory. Therefore, the necessity or justifiable need to kill fish is diminished.

What worries me about this state of affairs is that as we now regard fish as playthings. We have lost the respect and love – the awe – which is a normal and functioning part of the hunter-prey relationship. I appreciate that, to many, the act of returning fish appears laudable, and very often it is, but to return a toy to its box so that we can play with it again tomorrow becomes an unfortunate allegory when applied to living organisms. Familiarity breeds contempt. If catch and release becomes the sole tenet or aim of fishing, then the whole sport becomes debased. To catch and release perfectly edible fish all day and then queue up for cod and chips on the way home seems the height of hypocrisy.

Anyone involved in the psychology of sport will tell you that performance is ultimately controlled by the mind of the participant. In games such as tennis, golf or football it is relatively easy to understand how confidence, or the lack of it, can affect the sportsman's ability to achieve success or succumb to failure. For the fisherman this scenario is complicated by the addition of a third-party, namely the fish. You can venture forth with all the ability and confidence in the world and still fail if the fish refuse to co-operate. But, if all things are equal, the fisherman who feels in control of the situation rather than a pawn of fate will do well. It still strikes me as strange that fish can respond well to the confident angler and be scornful of the efforts of the doubt-filled mind, but it is fact of life. This is one of the reasons I strongly advise fly fisherman to strongly reject flies which don't stimulate confidence, why some patterns have almost miraculous powers, and also why the sure-fire 'killer pattern' of last season can fail to replicate its charms in this one. Confidence catches fish; doubts lead to dismal failure.

Further to the above, the single best way to catch fish is to relax, take it easy and push catching of fish to the back of your mind. One of my most memorable days trout fishing occurred when catching fish was the last thing on my mind. I was due to fish a very important match on Leven. My second daughter, Nadine, was due but she was taking her good time. I had given up hope of making the match, but her sudden arrival meant that it was just feasible, and knowing that she and her mother were safe in the maternity unit, and convinced by the urging of the new mother, I grabbed my gear and hurtled down to the ferry. Arriving just in time for the match, I set out from the boat dock on the fateful day and the only thing on my mind were my beautiful new daughter and her mum, and how much I'd rather be there than here. I won the match by a country mile.

A corollary to this was my introduction to sea-trout fishing in the sea around the coasts of Orkney. My father was a devotee of this obscure branch of the sport and as a young teenager I would tag along hoping to catch one of nature's most beautiful creations – trout so white and silvery that there are almost translucent. I would stand close to my father in the salty water and watch him hook and land fish after fish, but I couldn't get a sniff. It drove me mad. I tried everything, to no effect. This went on season after season, and I was damned if I was going to let them beat me. After about four years of famine I was beginning to think I was hexed – cursed by some fishing deity. Then one day, whilst sea fishing from one of the historically famous Churchill Barriers which were constructed to deny German u-boats access to Scapa Flow, I tackled down and set off for home. As I passed by the Italian Chapel, I glanced at the sandy bay below it and thought I'd have a few casts for an improbable sea-trout. This wasn't a particularly good mark – it lacked the essential features to make it popular with the fish, but on occasion it had thrown up the odd one and, as is often said in Orkney, sea-trout are where you find them. My first cast – wonder heaped upon wonder – brought me my first salty sea-trout. I did a wee war dance in celebration, and my second cast brought an even bigger fish hurtling into the mini-surf at my feet before grabbing the lure and racing off with it. I ended up with five before the shoal spooked, never to return. After that sea-trout fishing in the sea lost its 'bogey' status for me. It never became easy – you could fish all day and never see a spotty fin – but I got my share, plus a few more. It was a very strange experience simply not being able to catch one even when the sea seemed very badly over-stocked with the wee beggars, and then suddenly the jinx was broken, and I was back in control. Similar things have happened with specific flies or techniques – you try and try, and fail, and then, suddenly, everything comes good and you're off to a flyer. Baffling!

This brings us smartly to one of flyfishing's imponderable questions – does fly pattern make a whole lot of difference? I have to declare an interest here, being an innovator of fly patterns, I have to answer a resounding "yes." Over the decades I have seen enough to know that, on occasion, the number of turns of rib or a precise shade of dubbing can make the difference between great success and dismal failure. It shouldn't make a lot of difference to a creature which has the brain size of a split lentil and the rapacious appetite of a hungry shark whether an artificial fly has cheeks of yellow or orange, but I'm sure it does. Well-tied flies catch fish; poorly tied ones don't catch as many. There are a million and one trout patterns out there. It is logical to assume that they only exist because there is a demand for them. And wild browns are choosier than any other fish I've come in contact with. Those who hunt rainbow trout can, during the close season, quite happily rattle up a series of flies which will take 80+% of their fish in the following season. They know this because the most successful patterns are standard and have been for a number of years. A brown trout fisher will find that, season after season, most of his/her most successful patterns will be tied as the season unfolds. You simply can't rely on last seasons 'killers' to do the business this season, and if you think they can you will have some very disappointing days. Pattern matters!

Fishermen seem to carry more than their fair share of testosterone. This manifests itself most notably in their attitude towards help and advice. Many, if not most, anglers have an ill-founded belief in their own innate ability to succeed in any given circumstance without help in any form. I have always believed that local help and advice is worth fish in the boat and that those venturing to pastures new can spend a whole lot of valuable time getting to know venues and the foibles of local fish populations. If you really want to spend half your valuable fishing holiday floundering about in fruitless effort, by all means don't accept help, but if you want to get off to a flying start hire a guide or ghillie for at least a day or two. "I did it my way!" should become the anthem of all those who returned, disgruntled, from a fishing holiday in far off places, vowing never to return.

Does the best gear catch more fish? Most definitely not, but it does make catching nothing more pleasurable – until, of course, you think about how much money you spent in the vain hope that it guarantees more fish. There is, also, no such thing as a 'perfect for everyone' rod or reel. Tackle choice is very subjective; if you like it, it's good; if you hate it, it's bad. Simple as that, really. However, having said that, by and large, in flyfishing tackle you get what you pay for. If you want to out-cast everyone else to reach those fish which seem to know, to the inch, the casting range of the average angler, its going to cost money in the rod and line department. A rod costing less than a hundred quid and a mill-end fly line is unlikely to get you 'placed' in a casting tournament. However, some product manufacturers do add a few bucks simply for the name emblazoned on their gear, so the rod that requires a second mortgage and a divorce may just be out-classed by the one which only makes your spouse weep.

So, the next time you are being winched out of a boat by a crane whilst contemplating the passage of years, be assured that the great number of years spanning your flyfishing career will have taken you from the depths of valleys to the tops of mountains; you will have seen the best of the world, and the worst of weather; some of the finest chaps and some pretty dismal accommodation. You will also have a fund of memories and experiences, which may get you referred to as a blithering old idiot, but they will keep you company through the dark days of the close season.

And last, but by no means least, enjoy your fishing. Forget everyone else and how they've done. The guy parading through the car-park displaying to all and sundry a bulging sack isn't Santa Claus, he's a rather sad individual whose pleasure comes not from flyfishing but from showing the world that he's 'the best'. He's also the guy who sneaks off quietly before everyone else is ashore when he's had a tough day. Enjoy your pain and your gain, revel in the success of others, slap a few backs, and be quick to say, "Well done, you lucky b@st@rd!" and the world and his brother will recognise you as a good chap and a true brother of the angle.

An Arkaig ferox: Gathering the vital statistics ... and being safely returned

– 17 –

Trout, on the Other Hand…

ITS AN AGE thing. Increasingly, I only want to fish places that suit me, and for the trout I love. Recently, I have fallen deeply in love with the massive, deep lochs of the far north-west, lochs that in times gone by I erroneously thought of as the home of stunted brown trout and unreachable char and ferox.

It is also an age thing that, as time passes, the skills and powers of your youth fade and wane. I well remember taking my ageing dad out fishing for the last time. I had to help him in and out of the boat, make up his leader and select flies, and remind him of the names of such unforgettable standards such as the Zulu and Kingfisher Butcher. I remember thinking "That'll be me in 30 or 40 years!"

I had arranged a wee trip up to fish Loch Lochy with my old mucker, Colin Riach. It had been fishing well and throwing out the odd very large trout. The fishing is classic wet fly – an intermediate line, a team of bumbly patterns, a delivery system which goes 'chuck, pull, pull, pull, lift and hold, and then back out again', a style of fishing which is both relaxing and hypnotic – and the fish being mostly in the 12 to 20 ounce bracket, feisty, aggressive and acrobatic, and plenty of them. There is also a chance of the fish of a lifetime. Double-figure browns roam close to the shoreline, accept trout flies regularly, also, regularly, frighten the 'bejasus' out of an incautious angler out for a few for the pan.

So, I was looking forward to it with relish when a small blip appeared on the scene to put a small dampener on the festivities. The age thing previously mentioned returned to haunt me in the form of reduced sense of balance, and as I attempted to rise from my armchair I tripped and shoved my left hand into a glowing coal fire. I can remember thinking, as I dragged my poor, maimed, mitt from the coals "What's that white stuff dripping from my hand?" That was skin.

Now, it could have been worse – I can think of other parts of my anatomy that would fare worse from a baptism of fire… such as feet or face. (What did you think

I meant?) So, though I was due on the road in 36 hours, postponing the trip was the last thing on my mind. I popped down to the nurse next morning and got it all bandaged up. Unfortunately, it never occurred to me, during said bandaging, that I would need my fingertips uncovered so that I could grasp the line, manufacture leaders, and tie and re-tie flies whilst fishing. A brief interlude with a pair of fly-tying scissors got that sorted out, though.

Surprisingly, given the extent of bared, seared flesh, there was very little pain, so when I jumped into Colin's car and headed north, I was very optimistic about being able to perform.

We arrived at Achnacarry, on the north-west shore of Loch Lochy, at about midday to be greeted by Mark Hirst and a polished loch. It is a very sad fact of life that you are never, ever going to get the best out of a highland loch in a flat calm. It may not be the worst thing to happen on a fertile lowland water, but on an oligotrophic upland water it is a death sentence. Better too much than too little. It is possible to find some shelter in a gale; in a flat calm the best you can hope for is that you chase 'mirage' ripple all day. Getting credible weather forecasting for wind speed and direction for this area is also a nightmare, and totally unreliable for a variety of reasons. The principal one being that the forecaster will provide a general weather forecast which may be suitable for the tops of mountains but fails to take into consideration that the folding and elevation of the landscape means that wind speed and direction are impossible to second guess from hour to hour, never mind day to day. And what might prove correct in one glen is totally incorrect in the next. Lochs Lochy and Arkaig are less than a mile apart, and I've seen one a raging sea whilst the other is becalmed. It is crazy but true.

Whilst the wind, or lack of it, played silly buggers with us, Colin asked Mark if he could guide us to some amadou. Every dry fly fisherman knows that for prepping flies that are sodden with slime and water, amadou is the dog's spheroids. The bracket fungus from which amadou can be derived is found on dead or dying birch trees, and the Achnacarry area is a virtual birch forest. Young fungus provides the best, most easily processed amadou, so we rejected a few and came away with a couple of prime pieces. You don't need a lot, and a good piece will last for years. I've been needing a replacement piece for years, so I was chuffed to bits

Back at the moorings, the wind was still non-existent, but, as said, wind direction and speed can change rapidly and, as we left the moorings, a breeze sprang up from the south-west which is about as good as it gets on Lochy. The skies were bright and virtually cloudless, but the strengthening wind gave us hope. Mark reassured us by claiming that sunshine, in the early months of the year, doesn't pose as many problems as it would later in the year. My standard rig for these lochs is a Hairwing Silver Invicta on the point, a Stone Goat on the bob and whatever grabs my fancy in the middle. However, over the years I have come to the conclusion that the small number of fish taken on a middle fly (and almost never a big 'un) means that it can be left out. A two-dropper cast on a six-metre leader is a lot less delicate presentation than a one-dropper leader on a 5-metre cast. I may well be wrong, but in less than perfect conditions tipping the odds in your favour by the application of finesse seems logical. I started with the Silver Invicta, but I am not a great fan of silver in bright conditions, so I soon swopped it for a Baby Gold Sparkler on a #12 double. And we were into fish from the get-go!

The importance of Mark's presence was that he would take us from one unproductive stretch of shoreline to an apparently identical spot that was 'hoatching' with fish. The inexpert eye could see no obvious difference between the two locations, but it was all to do with contour lines under the water surface, and one moment we would be fishing within feet of the shoreline, and the next many yards off.

One of the features of these massive and deep lochs which fascinates me is the diverse strains of trout present. It is all to do with niche exploitation, and adaptation of differing trout strains to environmental options. Loch Lochy is 8 square miles in area; 10 miles long, 1¼ wide at is greatest width, with an average depth of 70 metres (greatest depth approx. 250 metres). A gigantic, flooded glaciated valley, the loch is a remarkably stable environment, and average depths and temperature ranges vary very little from season to season. This stability allows inherited developments within the brown trout species to develop towards conclusion over thousands of years. It is evolution in action. In my opinion, there are three strains of brown trout in Lochy. There are the margins haunting brown trout that we all know and love; the open water plankton-harvesters which resemble sea-trout, being silvery with black fins; and the pinnacle of the food chain predatory, piscivorous trout which some refer to as ferox or simply as 'bloody big troot'.

There are logical problems with this differentiation. Brown trout are brown trout, so no problem there. The open water plankton-harvesters are referred to as sea-trout smolts by the locals, but I 'hae ma doots' – in all my travels I've never seen immature sea-trout with anything other than yellow belly fins, and the Lochy fish have very dark fins indeed. They seem to me to be classic pelagics, just like the sonaghan of Melvin (a very similar habitat), and it is noticeable that the larger specimens tend to be found in deeper water than the classic browns. Anecdotal stories exist about fish seen rising way out in the featureless waters mid-loch – classic 'pelagic' hunting territory, although without species identification, these fish could just about be char.

One of the great arguments that rage throughout all loch/lough fishing is the correct identification of ferox. This discussion has been compromised in Scotland by the negative effects of smolt-rearing cages in many classic ferox habitats. It is commonly known that in lochs where there is very scant record of large trout the intrusion of aqua-cultural cages and their associated pellet feeding regimes can produce very large brown trout as a by-product of waste pellets. That these 'grown-on' wild browns are not ferox is universally accepted. But in waters where ferox are an historical fact, what effect will cages have on these top-of-the-food-chain predators, and can we distinguish between 'cage trout' and true ferox?

To get back to Lochy, there are small/medium sized 'brown' trout, there are similarly sized silvery trout, and there are massive trout up to 20 lb+ (with no known upper limit in size), all swimming about with no overt fishing pressure on them – to see a couple of other boats out means it is crowded – and they are all more than happy to take wet flies of a size and construction recognizable to any wild trout fisherman.

I remember, about 10 years ago, long before I'd cast a fly into its water, parking at the northern end of Lochy to 'empty the dog'. I wandered down to the loch edge and, as I almost always do, puttered about in the shallows turning stones to check out the invertebrate life. I saw not a living creature and decided that the loch was one giant desert of no discernible interest to a fly fisherman. It later turned out that I could not have been more wrong. As Martin, Colin and I drifted down the south-western shoreline fish after fish hammered into our flies. It's interesting fishing but not complicated. An intermediate line, a bog-standard loch-style retrieve, nothing too fast, and fish come out of nowhere. You won't see many, if any, rising trout, but they are there in surprisingly large numbers. Stay tight to the shoreline and brown trout make up the catch, nothing big, ranging from 'titchy' to somewhere under two pounds. Wander away to a point where the stony bottom is not quite discernible through the gin-clear, sparkling water and you start seeing the odd similarly sized 'pelagic' brown trout, and, if your numbers come up, a real monster. Trout in the middle teens of pounds are far from uncommon, but you need everything going your way – weather, wave, and a whole host of intangibles – to be that lucky. So far, my dream fish has eluded me. I've moved a few leviathans and been smashed to pieces on occasion, and witnessed Mark and others take some fabulous fish, but as regards specimen sized trout I'm beginning to look upon Lochy as my bogey loch. Not to worry, my time will come I have no doubt.

I suppose the slight 'fly in the ointment' with these ribbon lakes is that they are invariably long, narrow, and steep sided, and they channel wind like you wouldn't believe. A slight breeze on a weather chart can become a howling gale at ground zero. On the plus side there are a number of lochs in the area with a wide variety of length axes which mean that if the wind is unsuitable on one it can be perfect in the neighbouring glen. For instance, on our second day we launched on Lochy in the morning into a beautiful, benign south-westerly. By mid-day the wind had swung easterly which provides no bankside drifting, so we hauled out, and popped over to Loch Arkaig, a modest mile away, and had perfect wind conditions to continue our day.

In my many years of wandering the wilder side of Scotland, hunting down the finest fishing, I have rarely found a better location for the complete fly-fishing experience. Lochy and its sister lochs offer everything, quantity and quality, the perfect wild brown trout experience. We were out in mid-May in Mediterranean weather, and the snow-covered slopes of Ben Nevis loomed over us reflecting the spring sunshine in a Disney-esque manner. Fairy tale fishing with wild browns cavorting on the end of our leaders. It doesn't get any better than that.

My hand? I can't say I noticed it that much. Colin's excellent bramble whisky may have had something to do with that, but I think I was too busy catching trout.

Traditional hand-lining works best for wild trout

– 18 –

The Mechanics of Retrieval

TROUT ARE VISION hunters, in that their principle method of identifying potential prey is via their eyesight. To the simple consciousness of a trout this triggers a thought process which goes like this – if it moves then it is alive; if it is alive it is, to a greater or lesser degree, edible; if it is edible then it is worth investigating, which can only be done with eyes and mouth.

This then underlies the very basis of flyfishing. Our flies must be made to trigger this fundamental aspect of fish behaviour. And to do this, for most of the time, we impart motion to our flies. The river fisherman largely uses water flow to impart motion to his flies. The stillwater angler must use a retrieve mechanism. There are external factors which will affect choice of retrieve, and I will hope to identify these whilst delving into the mechanics of fly retrieval.

In my earlier days of flyfishing I received a few lessons which showed me that wet fly fishing wasn't necessarily just 'chuck it out; haul it back'. Often when wet fly fishing I, and others, would notice that fish would only take during the first few seconds after a fly alighted on the water, with the actual retrieve being a waste of time.

A classic example of this happened during a late summer day on Harray. We were fishing away, largely unproductively, using the traditional chuck it out, haul it back regime and failing to elicit any response from the trout. It was late afternoon, I was bored, cold and getting pretty fed up after exploring all the hot-spots and now being reduced to checking out less productive areas. I chucked the flies out, sighed – I couldn't even muster the energy to raise the rod – and turned to my boat partner and said "For the love of gawd, let's get the f…!" The sentence was never completed. As the flies sank undisturbed, a trout slammed into #10 Black Zulu, and nearly wrenched the rod out of my hands. It weighed approximately three and a half pounds; a very notable Harray fish at that time.

Another indication that method of retrieve was critical was when an uninterrupted retrieve would bring a fish or two when standard retrieves were failing. This would occur when winding in or when a minor adjustment to boat position, with line still in the water, caused a long, steady, continuous fly movement. Nowadays, knowing what I know now, I would probably adopt a figure-of-eight or a roly-poly style retrieve to target fish, but that was then and this is now.

There are, to my mind at least, six major methods of retrieve: figure-of-eight; induced take; strip; roly-poly; mixed; and negative retrieve.

1. FIGURE-OF-EIGHT

This method of retrieve involves a simple recovery of fly line, involving a simple pinch (to trap the line) and a roll of the fingers (to recover the line). The amount of line retrieved with each individual action is only a matter of inches, and generally it is done in a continuous manner so that the line maintains a steady progression through the water.

Although this method can be used with all types of line, it is fair to say that it is most commonly used with floaters through to slow-sink line densities.

The 'steady progress' of this retrieve is ideally suited to rainbow trout feeding behaviour and less suitable for wild fish in most scenarios. It is a vital part of buzzer and nymph fishing as no other retrieval method can imitate the natural movement of insect larvae so effectively.

It would be erroneous to imagine that a figure-of-eight retrieve always imparts movement to the line, as the method is often used merely to combat the drift speed of the boat or current. It is also employed prior to the commencement of other forms of retrieve in order to let the flies reach a predetermined depth.

I dare to say that no modern fly fisherman can perform adequately without this technique in his armoury. At varying times, due to external factors such as high drift speed, or cold immobile fingers, I have tried to replicate a figure-of-eight retrieve by slow, steady pulling, but never successfully.

2. INDUCED TAKE

The 'induced take', or the 'lift and hold' as it is often referred to, is only a part of a retrieve system and can be added to any of the listed retrieval systems here described.

Basically, it is employed believing that there is a fish moderately interested in the flies but needing a spur to commit. The mechanics of the induced take is, at the end of the retrieve, to raise the rod from horizontal to near vertical in a steady movement and then to let the flies rest with the top dropper near to, or in, the surface film. The philosophy behind this manoeuvre is to attempt to persuade a following fish to imagine that its target is about to escape, and it can be remarkably successful.

It can be used with all lines from floating to fast sinking. In my wild trout heyday, using floating lines and wet flies, most anglers would lift and skate or bob a top dropper fly to emulate hatching and emerging flies, but with the demise of many freshwater insect species this tactic lost its power. However, an adapted technique at the end of the retrieve allowing the flies to simply 'die in the water' without the 'lift' component largely supplanted the bobbed or skated fly.

In wet fly fishing it is normal to fish bushy, palmered flies on the top dropper when using this tactic because they have the mobile dressings to seduce fish. When using reservoir techniques, I tend to fish a vague imitator in this position, reflecting items in the food chain.

3. STRIP

The simplest, dare I say the original, line retrieval method was hand-lining, pulling or stripping, call it what you will. This involves picking up the line near to the butt-ring and pulling a couple of feet of fly line through the eyes, whilst holding the rod handle in the non-stripping hand.

In the good, old, wild fish days, the rod was generally held above the horizontal which produced a retrieve with an almost continual progress broken into regular periods of slow and quick movement. Nowadays we tend to hold the rod horizontally or almost touching the water, which breaks the retrieve into a stop/start rhythm. The modern approach to line stripping (rod tip in or just above the waterline) has nothing to do with providing a more attractive retrieve style, but everything to do with better hooking practice for rainbow trout. I still prefer the old-style rod position for wild brown trout, but always employ the modern style for rainbow trout, and this has more to do with how each species takes a fly than any other consideration.

There is no set speed for stripping/pulling, which is dictated by trout preference on the day. Nor is there a fixed formula for length of individual pull. It can be long, which equates to a smooth pull, or short, producing a sort of staccato effect. My preferences are the former for wild trout, and the latter for rainbows (and, surprisingly, saltwater sea-trout).

Standard wet flies, mini-lures, large lures, sparklers, blobs and even boobies can be employed with this technique.

4. ROLY-POLY

The roly-poly retrieve is designed to reproduce the actions usually associated with trolling, i.e. fast steady travel without breaks or interruptions, and comes from the Midland reservoirs.

An explanation of this system goes something like this – make a normal cast, tuck the rod under the armpit of the casting arm, and then using both hands in succession, strip the line back from the butt eye towards the stomach. Both the uninterrupted progress of the flies and the speed will attract fish, and pattern is not the major factor, although flashy, bright and highly mobile lures tend to work best.

As regards line choice for the roly-poly, generally speaking sinking lines and intermediates are favoured.

5. MIXED

A mixed retrieve is one in which a variation in pace to any of the both is added to spark interest. I have found this to be more useful for rainbow trout than for wild fish, and why this should be is a mystery.

It could be argued that mixing the retrieve makes it more likely that by adding the element of variation makes it more likely to find the correct element which will be successful on the day. However, my strongest objection to a mixed retrieve is that one must continually think about the variations inserted into the retrieve and this compromises rhythm, which I believe is a major component of any retrieve style. I find that a retrieve style one can slot into almost subconsciously brings the best rewards.

But when fishing slowly, in such techniques as buzzer or nymph fishing, it is possible to add minor variations in pace which will not compromise rhythm. It is more difficult with a fast retrieve.

Having said all that, the best mixes I find are stopping dead during a fast retrieve or adding a short burst of pace to a static one.

A mixed-up retrieve can be used with any line density and all manner of flies.

6. NEGATIVE RETRIEVE

What is a negative retrieve? It is one in which line is recovered but the leader flies do not move. How is this possible? Generally speaking, this is a method by which contact is kept with the flies whilst not allowing slackness to develop in the line. Classic conditions for this are most often found in boat fishing, but can occur in bank fishing, primarily when casting into the wind.

The best way to achieve this is to use the figure-of-eight retrieve, and to watch the line as it responds to line recovery. If the line moves, slow down; if slackness persists, speed up. When buzzer fishing this is an essential technique. If not used appropriately then many takes will be missed.

This season was a prime example of how to use a negative retrieve in a variety of situations. At the start of the buzzer extravaganza, a very small amount of tension was required and trout would swim away with the buzzers and hook themselves. As the fish became savvier, sure enough a figure-of-eight retrieve was required to keep the line straight whilst leaving the flies to settle. Takes were subtle and easily missed. As the big buzzer hatches faded, interest was best achieved by a slightly faster figure-of-eight in which the flies moved gently through the water.

Dry fly fishing also requires a negative retrieve at times. If the wind is slight, then no line recovery is best. I do like some slack line between me and my dries, this allows the fish a chance to turn way with the fly, feeling no restriction, and also allows a modicum of natural drift to the flies. However, in a decent breeze, especially from a boat, some line retrieval will be necessary without involving unwanted movement in the flies. Normally in such a situation I will incorporate short, slow pulls but a figure-of-eight retrieve will also fit in very well.

If small or large amounts of dry fly movement are wanted to imitate what is happening with naturals on the water, then you move out of the negative retrieve and into something from the list above.

IMPORTANT CONSIDERATIONS

A) When we talk about retrieve we tend to think about lateral movement (towards the angler), but it should always be borne in mind that, even with the fastest recovery, there will be some degree of vertical movement (sinking of the flies or line/leader). The path of recovery will, therefore, include more than one vector.

In very slow retrieves – buzzer and nymph presentations – flies will tend to move into and out of the killing zone as a natural process, and thus operating practically and successfully for only a percentage of the retrieve. This can be combatted by using a sacrificial buoyant pattern, such as a booby or FAB, on the point position. This is what we know as the 'washing line'.

B) We, as a whole, tend not to think of the gravity factor that affects retrieved flies. We generally only think of retrieves as a one direction movement i.e. towards the angler, blissfully forgetting that all the time the flies, and some lines, are trying to sink.

This goes a long way to explaining why some retrieves work better on low density lines (floaters, midge tips, and intermediates) and less well with high density lines (sinkers). To put it clearly and simply, the slow retrieves work best with low density lines because the slow rate of sink won't pull the flies out of the fish activity zones too quickly. Faster retrieves with faster sinking lines work best by not allowing the sink rate to compromise the forward motion of the flies.

– 19 –

The Month of May

MY MENTAL VISION of May is a young man, full of piss and vinegar, ready to take on the world, or in this case, the year. Poets ramble on about nodding daffodils, young girls dancing round maypoles (ooo-er, missus!), fleecy clouds, and gambolling lambs, but then bad poetry has always been like too much make-up on a maiden aunt, an assault on the senses and a fragile veneer of fantasy covering up the harsh realities!

May is the foundation of the fishing year and it tells us a lot of what the following months will bring. In contrast to what we hope for, it can be an awful month with more of winter than summer. I've sat out in blizzards, or slipped on an icy boat thwart, and returned chilled to the bone. We in the East of Scotland often experience a deeply unpleasant period of very cold weather we refer to as the 'Gab o' May'. Experts differ as to whether it occurs in the early, middle or end of May. This is because sometimes this month is too much 'Gab' and not enough May.

But the intriguing thing about May is that the weather rarely seems to matter to the fish. You get a cold, bleak spell in July or August and it can set things back weeks and really interfere with natural cycles, such as fly emergence. But in May, things just keep trundling along. I'm often asked when's a good month to visit the far north for a spot of fishing. I generally suggest June because it's relatively safe – the fish are feeding hard and the weather is, more or less, settled. But May can be better for those man enough to face sleet, hail, horizontal rain, and winds capable of lifting you off your feet.

The reason for this is that wild trout are on a strict timetable. When the water temperature and light levels start to pick up in early months the annual cycle of growth and production kicks in and the aquatic food ladder starts to re-assemble itself. The food items which make up the trout's larder are also on a strict timetable of feeding preparatory to reproduction. Fly larvae crustaceans and molluscs take advantage of improving conditions and plentiful food and become increasingly active. This stage in the aquatic year peaks in May, and with plentiful and hyper-active food, trout indulge in some of the hardest feeding of the season. Wild brown trout are binge feeders and will always feed hardest and longest when the living is easy. Although they are prone to take advantage of 'windfalls' when available, such as terrestrial falls or explosions of fish fry in August and September, predictable feeding binges always occur in May and June, with a simple but important caveat that hill/mountain or extremely deep lochs may be a few weeks behind the norm.

It is forgivable for the poorly informed to look upon fish as 'scaly' humans with fins that need three square ones a day. The reality is different, however. One of the common dictums about eating has it that we should eat like a king at breakfast, like a gentleman at lunch and like a beggar at dinner. To realign that 'old saw' to coincide with trout feeding regimes, they binge in spring, have modest diets in high summer, and pick at their food in the autumn. This, of course, tends to apply to trout which plan to spawn in the on-coming winter because, with the onset of sexual maturity late in the year, they basically give up on feeding. Parallels can be drawn with their close relatives, salmon. Trout which are planning a maiden winter (i.e. not to spawn) will, in all likelihood, continue on feeding at a normal rate, relative to food availability, throughout the year.

We like to think of trout as surface feeders, intercepting hatching and hatched insects. Attractive though this picture is, there isn't a lot of truth in it. The greater part of a trout's fare comes from, or is sought out, at depth, although the term depth is relative. Trout are fish which like shallow water except where environmental pressures bring about localised behavioural change. In the deep, inhospitable, and nutritionally-challenged glacial lochs of the Highlands trout can only grow big by hunting the char shoals which haunt the deeps, but in fertile waters trout prefer to hunt in depths of less than 2-3 metres, whilst being able to retreat to deeper water when temperature or oxygen levels dictate. Generally speaking, when trout are in fertile waters of over 3 metres they are not actively feeding unless there is no alternative, shallow-water feeding, available.

In May the largest proportion of a wild loch's trout population will be attracted by shallow water. This is a hangover from earlier months when feeding activity can take place in some very shallow water. As the year progresses and light intensity increases, fish will drop back out of the very shallow water, and in May can usually be found in moderately deep water just on the edge of shallows. In June and July this will continue with fish only entering the shallow water in periods of low light intensity and particularly at night. The Harray Loch in Orkney is a classic trout loch in which all of the above behavioural activity is very pronounced. By May, boat fishing rules the roost with very large numbers of trout accumulating in the deep water on the very edge of skerries. Due to the water clarity, which is now very good after a rapid decline in the late 1980s, these areas are very well defined by colour change – the skerries show up a khaki/brown, the deeps as an almost aquamarine green.

The tactics are to drift the edges and flies are placed on the demarcation line. Nymph or buzzer tactics can be employed on the green side of the line, but not straying far from the shallows. In other waters which lack off-shore shallows it is generally best to concentrate on shoreline drifts. Start the drift by zig-zagging from very shallow to deep, noting where trout are being contacted. It is normal that a precise depth will show most fish and once that depth has been defined then its best to stick to it, avoiding exploratory work away from the area and depth of activity.

Another very good tip for wild fish hunters is to stick to very slim and sparse patterns in May. As the season swings on trout preference will change and bulkier, bushier patterns will become more acceptable, but in the early months there is a marked appetite for slim patterns. I think that this has much to do with what is naturally on offer. Swimming shrimp, midge pupae and larvae (bloodworm) and insect nymphs have very slim and often straight profiles. Artificial flies reflecting these properties and general colouration will generally work best, leaving the brighter colours and bulkier profiled flies to rest up in the box for later in the season.

I like intermediate lines at this time of year when water surface temperatures can be chilly, because even though trout are regularly seen swirling and feeding at or very near the surface, the bulk of the feeding activity will be sub-surface. A good ploy is to vary the distance of casts; a short cast will tend to fish the flies higher in the water than long ones. This is very likely to show the depth at which trout are most inclined to feed, and once ascertained a cast distance can be adopted to increase catch rate.

Line retrieve rates can be critical also. I normally adopt a moderate retrieve because, by and large, most food items are not turbo-charged, and meander along at modest speeds relying on numbers rather than evasive speeds and manoeuvres for safety. However, some of the nymphs, particularly those of the Olive family, can be pretty 'nippy', especially when ascending to hatch and a modified retrieve can pay dividends in such circumstances.

I mentioned earlier that it is quite common to see fish 'on the top' in May, and many of us have a tendency to sharply switch to dries in such circumstances. It's generally best to resist such impulses unless nothing else will work for you. I have spent some pretty fruitless hours trying to get surface-feeding fish to take dry buzzer or olive patterns when it appeared that this was a wise option. Buzzers are very often taken at the point of hatch but that rarely means that trout feeding thereupon will take a dry imitation. The best bet is to target rising fish with some form of buzzer pattern because the surface 'rise' you have just seen has been created by a fish deviating from its normal behaviour which is picking off ascending pupae somewhere between the bed of the loch and the surface. Olive nymphs can also mislead. Very often trout take them in the surface film amongst fully fledged adult duns. The misconception is to assume that the rise you are witnessing is to a dun. Nine times out of ten it is not. The rise is almost always caused by a trout rocketing up from the deep to take a fast ascending nymph. These little buggers don't hang about and, in the sort of depths of water we are talking about here, a nymph can break from the bottom, hit the surface and hatch in the blink of an eye. Trout hunt the nymphs at depth, following them up and generally taking them as they momentarily pause in the surface film. Keep your flies wet as a fail/safe and you won't go far wrong.

So, while the 'piss and vinegar' of May is trickling down your neck and wicking through your breathables, just remember that though there is snow on the hills and a fresh north-easterly is trying blow your hat off, down below the trout are hard at it, packing on the inches which will be the difference between life and death on the spawning gravel. Let the poets ramble on; there are plump succulent trout to be caught!

– 20 –

Hatches –
Love Them or Loathe Them

IT'S A FUNNY thing but I have an intense love/hate relationship with hatches. In your mind they become exceptional opportunities to have a red-letter day. In reality the letter in question is more like one from your bank manager containing the line "with regard to your overdrawn account."

The major problem is that a 'hatch' is not a single event. It tends to be composed of the pre-pre-hatch, the pre-hatch, the hatch itself, and the post-hatch, and all of these minor events require a dedicated approach and precise tactics and techniques.

Last night was a prime example. Early in the evening, a large bank of cloud swept over the loch, dimming the light down to that muted level that anglers adore. Only people with serious skin complaints hate sunshine as much as fly fishermen – a weather forecast in July promising a sun-powered heat-wave will have serious fishermen drop-kicking the cat into the neighbour's garden, whilst his wife corrals the kids in the cellar to sit out the emotional storm and swear words.

As the unrelenting glare of the sun faded from the memory, a couple of fish tentatively 'rose', a big, fat buzzer was seen resting gently on the ripple, and a concentration of large orange shucks starts to accumulate on the downwind side of the boat. A nice fish falls to an optimistic Crippled Midge, and you think "Here we go! A few more of these will go down a treat!" Then a blink of sunlight breaks through the cloud and, like a chap lounging about in his garden and spotting a couple of Jehovah's Witnesses coming down the street, the trout skedaddled at high speed, and you're back to stage one.

Is this the pre-pre-hatch? Well, no it isn't. What it is is a promise. It's a bit like half-watching some boring nonsense about cottage renovations and getting an advert in it stating that Miss Pneumatic 2011 will be starring in a film about beach volleyball dressed in three postage stamps and a short length of dental floss … but you'll just have to wait.

So, what to do whilst waiting? No, not for the film – for the bona fide, full-out hatch, because this is when the problem of the pre-pre-hatch has to be addressed. What is going on down there, pre-hatch, far from the questing eye? Well, it all depends on what species of insect will comprise the hatch, and to a large extent this is enlightened guess work. A lot of insects don't go in for much preamble prior to the hatch. Ephemerid nymphs and caddis pupae tend to go for it in a no-nonsense way, giving trout little opportunity to make an event out of the pre-hatch, but chironomids (buzzers) don't do anything in a rush. The act of hatching causes extreme physiological changes in the bodies of individual pupae and these take time. Like cross-country runners milling about on the start line I imagine buzzers to be making dummy runs just above the sediments and venturing further and further from their muddy homes. I believe, without a whole lot of evidence that, in ascending order of importance, it is a combination of season, temperature and light level which starts the aquatic ballet. The time of the year can be delayed by a week or two by the winter's degree of severity (as happened this year); buzzers will hatch on a cold evening, but rarely; never in bright sunshine, preferring late in the day or cloudy, humid daytime conditions. Of course, I am being specific here. The species I'm discussing is the big, deepwater 'grey boy' buzzer. Others like 'big red' and 'big brown' are not quite so light-phobic, and I do wonder if the very deep habitat of the 'grey boy' is the critical feature, as the others don't seem to necessarily need excessively deep home territories.

Sometimes a lot of feeding goes on during the pre-pre-hatch, but mostly out of sight. Some early hatchers will cause one of those big, bulging rises that gets any angler's juices flowing. The odd head-and-tail rise will take an adult, sitting in the film. These odd events are like the ribbon round a chocolate box – attractive and all that, but not what you are really interested in. During this period, you have two options. Well, three if you happen to have a box of chocolates with you. You can fish wets at a depth where you imagine fish are feeding. This can be very fruitful and enjoyable. Vague representations of midge pupae can work well but knowing what will look right and work well in any given variable of wind, weather and ambient light is a mind teaser. Snatchers, muddlers, suspender buzzers and traditional wet flies can, and often do work well, but not all at the same time. Sometimes one or other will get all the action and deciding on a team of flies is

Hatch fishing – two on at once

a great skill. Selecting a line is a degree easier. I generally start with a Fast Glass, pulled slowly, but, if it is brighter than would appear perfect, a DI-3 can be better.

The other option at this time is to try to pick off one or two of the haphazard risers with a dry fly rig. It is surprising how effective this method can be given that normally there are so few natural 'risers' about. I've used the term 'pick-off', but the best method is to fan cast about in front of the boat, at a moderate range, and only leave the flies on the water for half a minute or so. I call this 'search and destroy'. That way you can cover a lot of water, and fish will come out of the 'blue' to your flies. It is best to ignore a rising fish unless, of course, it is a continual riser. A 'oncer' will normally be heading down to the proscribed feeding level and be unaware of any fly alighting behind its tail. The 'search and destroy' dry fly method is an immensely satisfying technique because (a) it is a very pleasant way to take fish, and (b) quite often fish caught at this time, in this way, can be the biggest of the session. Dry fly has always had a tendency to sort out the big browns, but even better, small fish much prefer a pulled, subsurface fly. Why this should be is a bit of a mystery, but it seems to be a fact on most waters.

But more often than not sod-all happens. It is as if the fish know what is going to happen later and are content to sit out the intervening period. Then it doesn't matter what you do because, like the trout, you are going to have to be patient.

The light fades and that big orange ball sinks behind the western hills. Now is about time for the pre-hatch to start. The pre-hatch is a precise period when the pupae have reached the surface and are struggling to get out of their pupal skin. Depending on the ultimate size of the hatch – from sporadic to blizzard – this can be a brief or extended period. It is the best time to catch fish because so many options are open to the angler. Pulling wets, twiddling neutral-density buzzers or Suspender Buzzers, dries, or even pulling greased-up muddlers or Sedgehogs will take fish as they slash and rise amongst the emerging buzzers.

It can get a bit hectic, this pre-hatch period. The trout seem to know that if they don't get a gut-full now the actual hatch is going to provide lean, and harder to hunt down, pickings. Fish are feeding everywhere, and big, bulgy rise forms can be seen all over the surface in the half-light. Quite often the angler goes a little daft, trying to cover every rising fish. I have come to the conclusion that this can be wasted effort and the best tactic is to lay out the flies anywhere, keep the line tight and wait for the fish to come to you. This requires intense discipline and I wouldn't blame anyone for cracking at this juncture and start whipping the water to a froth, trying to cover every rising fish in range. The takes, regardless of whether you are fishing below the surface, just sub-surface or 'on the top', are savage and positive. If fishing dries or semi-dries I just keep in contact and wait for the line to go tight, but 'soft hands' are an essential or it is possible to get smashed to pieces.

The ambient light is the critical factor. It controls the buzzer behaviour, and the trout's reaction to it. As the dusk gathers, the angler will see a lessening in the frenetic activity, and as the adult buzzers gather above the boat in squadrons it is time to react accordingly, because this is often when the big boys seem to appear. Over the years, I have noticed a peculiar but recurring theme about hatches – the biggest fish always appear late, sometimes when the hatch is, to all intents and purposes, over.

Anyway, we have gone from pre-hatch, through the hatch without even really noticing it, but as the insects leave the water (the actual hatch) trout are left picking off the cripples, aborted hatches and those adults who don't realise the inherent dangers of 'taking five' before getting airborne. My favoured technique during the post-hatch is to have a rod set-up with a brace of suspender buzzers, with very buoyant heads, in claret or black for good silhouette properties. The head buoyancy is critical for reasons that should be apparent – fish are hunting very high in the water and that's where the flies must be. Also, the water disrupting qualities of the foam head will attract attention.

Casting a short line and using a figure-of-eight or slow-pull retrieve will bring home the bacon. Unlike during the hectic period of the pre-hatch, I tend to cast towards the sound or sight of rising fish, there's just not enough fish left 'on the prod' to cast speculatively. My best fish in good buzzer hatches have always come in this tricky period when the 'sussies' have sorted out the wheat from the chaff. You won't get many but what you do get will warm the cockles of your jaded heart.

Getting it right during all the stages of a hatch is well nigh impossible. There are just too many variables, and by that I don't just mean tactics, patterns and techniques although, god knows there are plenty of those to be going on with. A hatch occurring in a flat calm may be fine but generally it will have you tearing your hair out. Wind direction can dictate that you are facing away from the only light left in the sky, peering myopically into jet black nothingness full of rising fish. Sometimes the fly come and the fish ignore them – work that one out – but conversely, on the odd occasion, the fish will be up there when nothing is hatching, probably out of habit. And things are changing all the time. Just when you think you've 'cracked it', something subtle alters and, although the fish seem just as busy, you are catching nothing. Two of the most annoying scenarios are when the flies that worked so well last night simply fail tonight, and the area where all the fish were yesterday is suddenly deserted today.

Hatches can be the best of times or the worst of times. Is it any wonder that I can't quite decide if I love them or loathe them?

Gateway to an angler's paradise – Amhuinnsuidhe Castle

– 21 –

Amhuinnsuide – Simply the Best

IF I HAD been a couple of hundred feet above the loch, I would have been blown off my feet. But at loch level the wind had reached that point where big, silvery fish threw caution straight into it. Fishing wasn't a problem; getting the boat back up the drift without mechanical aid most definitely was.

Jonesy stroked the boat a few feet to the left, and said, in a confident voice, "Any time now!", and the rod slammed down. Is there anyone smugger than a ghillie that gets it just right when the rod keeps up his end of the alliance? We smiled at each other and, in a bizarre moment in a day packed with many such, simultaneously remarked "Carnage!"

There are a few places that should raise the hair on the back of the neck, places that announce boldly, 'this is a portal to fishing excellence'. Here are a few which definitely do it for me – the car park at Loch Leven; the white bridge at the southern end of Loch Arkaig; the OTFA boat site on the Stenness Loch; and the front door of Amhuinnsuidhe Castle. To be warmly welcomed at that door and then shown to your accommodation is to experience how things used to be done in an era when the sporting break was one of the high points of the year.

I had been before and marvelled at the organisational excellence of this island estate, and way back then it provided me with one of the best salmon fishing experiences of my life. Innes Morrison guided Ian Muir and me over the hills to Loch Ulladale, a trip that very nearly killed me but produced a three-salmon day augmented with a splatter of modest sea-trout.

There were about half-a-dozen rods in the castle at the time, but I had had the best day of the week, and only because I am immensely capable of subsuming my ego, listening intently to my guide and sticking to his advice to the letter. In those days, Innes was a guide/ghillie in control of the outer reaches of the estate's fishing. He took unwary guests on 'jomps' which separated the men from the boys. His infectious enthusiasm and unrelieved optimism kept the rods going in even the least hopeful situations.

Nowadays, Innes is the boss. It's his remit to oversee all the sporting assets of the estate and his enthusiasm and optimism have not diminished one whit. He jealously guards the reputation of the estate and is able to spot an irrational complaint and deal with it accordingly. He may well be in control of marvellous fishing – arguably the very finest sea-trout and salmon loch fishing in the UK – but has no say in the provision of wind and water – sometimes too much, often none at all. My attitude to the vagaries of climate and weather is to take it all on the chin and work my guts out to bring fish and fly together. I owe it to myself, to the ghillie and, ultimately, to the estate. My standpoint is never to grump about things out of my control; fishing is more than just catching fish.

But I must say that Amhuinnsuidhe has never let my expectations down. I've had hard days when wind and weather have conspired to make even presenting a fly correctly, and keeping it under control, a major achievement – Harris is a very windy place in the late summer – but hard work and a sketchy understanding of the behavioural characteristics of migratory fish usually means I get my share.

So, I returned in 2013 in late July to chance my arm again on this fabulous collection of lochs and mini-rivers. The happiest coincidence that occurred was that I was re-united with my old mucker, Ian Jones, who is currently ghillieing at Amhuinnsuidhe. Jonesy is a very accomplished angler (he fished with me in an international event on Rutland as part of the Scottish team), top class company in a boat, and probably the most enthusiastic and hard-working ghillie it has been my pleasure to work with. Innes, knowing of our past connections, teamed us up for the two days of my visit, which was great news for me at least (I can't speak for Jonesy!) Having a ghillie of his calibre in the team doubled my sense of anticipation and optimism. Come hell or high water (and we got both), I was supremely confident that we would get fish.

One of the joys of an Amhuinnsuidhe visit is that a short walk will take you to the mouth of the Castle River, where summer salmon mass, waiting for the welcome rain. To see so many fins cutting the freshwater outflow is a delight. It is permissible to fish this area, with strict provisos, but I had never felt tempted. Don't ask me why it fails to get my hunting instincts going – it just doesn't. Many others take full advantage of the situation, but I just like to watch them, happy in the knowledge that I am witnessing a natural phenomenon denied to many others.

It was grand to wake up in my sumptuous bedroom to discover that it had rained overnight. On this type of spate-influenced system with its significant lack of top-soil, water rises come on fast and clear, and overnight rain is a major blessing, bringing fish up, helter-skelter, from the sea bays. Jonesy and I were bound for Scourst, probably my favourite loch on the estate, renowned for its very big sea-trout and a large head of salmon. Scourst isn't a big loch, but takes its runs of fish from the south, whilst its close and more famous, over-the-rise neighbour, Voshimid takes its fish from the north and is approximately twice the size. Scourst is justly famous for its specimen-sized sea-trout (the estate's biggest from 2013 was a Scourst fish of 11¾ lb), and most years produces its top weighing trout.

I must admit my strike record on sea-trout at Amhuinnsuidhe is dismal and I put that down to my fishing style which seems more attractive to salmon than trout. My tactics almost invariably take the form of muddlers on floating lines. Muddlers are lethal on these west coast salmon but not so effective on sea-trout, but having said that, the top sea-trout in 2013 (mentioned above) was taken on a Black and Silver Muddler. Perplexing, though the only other notable sea-trout water where I have seen muddlers work well is Loch Lomond.

Travelling to Scourst provided us with excellent views of the Scourst River running high and clear. Not one of us doubted for a moment that fresh fish were running this stream as we watched. Our excitement was mounting. Dark clouds swept alongside the surrounding hills as we arrived at the boathouse, pushed along by a fresh to strong south-westerly wind, and some white water was visible at the northern end of the loch. It all reeked of fish and preparations were done at a trot.

End gear construction, for me at least, depends an awful lot on wind and wave conditions. A good breeze will keep everything up in the water where salmon, in particular, like it. A muddler on the top is *de rigueur*; a bushy palmer in the middle stops the top fly skating; and another muddler on the point balances everything up. On this day of days, I chose a Stone Goat Muddler for the top, and a Jungle Cock Ballcock for the middle. Often the point fly is sacrificial, as it proved on this day. It acts like a 'holding midfield player' – it won't score but makes everything else 'tick'.

We started our drift in the extreme southern end of the loch, angling towards the west shore. This happily took us down an extended sunken ridge which is usually a banker for a salmon or two if, and it's a very big 'if', they are in very shallow water. Sometimes they are; sometimes they are not. I know it is perceived wisdom that all loch salmon must be sought in the very shallowest of water, but in my experience a strong wind and a lashing wave can force them just off the shallows into water which will be completely deserted in calmer conditions. We managed a lovely bright fish off 'the stones', but that was on the first drift when the wind hadn't peaked. It slashed at the Stone Goat Muddler and produced a very typical, head down, dogged fight almost on to the west shoreline, a distance of approx 60 yards, but when you're on the business end of a Hardy Zenith you fear no evil. We never saw another fish in the shallows. It appeared that the strength of wind and wave had pushed them out into more comfortable water slightly offshore. This may be considered a problem, but it is actually a great opportunity. The movement of fish from their chosen lies may very probably increase the likelihood that they may 'come on the take' as they roam, restlessly looking for some comfort in the storm.

Whilst we were still under the mistaken belief that we would find fish in their normal locations, we worked the west and east shores with no response. Jonesy suggested a drift into the northern burn-mouth and, although I had 'ma doots' whether fish would gather in the maelstrom that represented the north shore, I wasn't about to tell him his job. As we approached the designated spot, we had to negotiate a weed bed just off the burn-mouth. Wham! We were into another fish, another sparkler but a tad smaller than the first. This tourist decided to be a bit more athletic than its predecessor and performed some stunning aerobatics which raised the blood pressure. Knowing I was going to release this, and not wanting him to over-exert himself, I leant into him… and pulled the hook out of his face. Long distance catch-&-release, we in the trade call it. We continued into the burn-mouth, but as I suspected, despite the attractive flow of freshwater, it was devoid of taking fish.

Rather than make the long haul back to the top of the wind, Jonesy positioned the boat above the weed bed in a drift destined to take us down the other side of it. Jings, crivvens and help ma boab, we were fast into another fish. This was the fish that Jonesy had prophesied and had elicited our dual response of "Carnage!"

This salmon was a real flyer and we were well on our way to the burn-mouth without any inclination on behalf of the fish to come to the boat. I suggested that we play out this fish from the shore for a variety of reasons – to give Jonesy's arms a rest, and to ease my battered and weary bum. Keeping the boat and startled fish in the area where a conglomeration of fish had gathered wasn't the best way of guaranteeing continued sport, so Jonesy acquiesced.

Playing salmon from the shore, especially 'the boy racers' of the clan, can often be more exhilarating than fighting them from the boat. They really don't like coming into the shallow water if that's where the restraint is coming from, and the fight can be prolonged and spectacular. I wanted to keep one very fresh fish, so I wasn't concerned about playing this one to exhaustion. Then we had a bit of a disaster. I brought the fish in close to the net, Jonesy made to lift it, the fish recovered dramatically and tried to set off again, and Jonesy only managed to jab it in the posterior. The grilse went absolutely ballistic... and that was the last we saw of it. Jonesy was mortified, but I could only laugh. This was real sport; a day to remember; fabulous entertainment.

We were quickly back in the boat – we got going whilst the going was good. There was no reason to think that the sport was over, and now we knew where the fish were gathered. Buoyed by the excitement of the day, Jonesy chanced his arm. "Just about...!", and a fish roared out of the water with the Jungle Cock Ballcock wedged firmly in his scissors. This was the most savage take of the day and a testament to rod and leader that it was still firmly engaged. We made no mistake with this fella, try as he might to visit destruction upon us. Of the six fish hooked, this was the only one to be attracted to the middle fly rather than the muddler on the boo.

Two more salmon came to the boat that afternoon, and we all had that wonderful feeling one gets from a day when everything (well, almost everything) worked according to plan – a day filled with fish, fun and frivolity. We had witnessed the other fishing parties beating a hasty retreat from Voshimid earlier in the afternoon, the ghillies exhausted by rowing in a gale, but the modicum of shelter supplied by the surrounding hills and Jonesy's desire to keep at it, kept us fishing and catching until the fish, inexplicably, switched off.

When we pulled into the mooring point, Jonesy was played out. He tried to encourage me to have a wade, but my heart wasn't in it. In the storm the fish were probably not reachable from the shore and, well, you can have too much of a good thing. We de-geared and set off back to the warmth, shelter and welcoming arms of the castle. After indulging in a deep, hot bath I joined the rest of the party for a few wee drinkies before dinner. I could have sold a hundredweight of Stone Goat Muddlers that evening, but on reflection I am convinced you could have thrown them a ham sandwich that day and the fish would have happily accepted them. Circumstances had conspired to provide a perfect day – a rise in water, a run of fresh fish, a good wind and wave combination, and the expertise and resilience of a first-class ghillie.

I got the place of honour at the dinner table that evening, and though I humbly stated that it was just good luck and better fortune, and that without Jonesy's input things could have been a lot less spectacular, the 'hot-seat' was mine, and it topped off what was a day to remember for the rest of my life.

Stone Goat Muddler

Hook:	Fulling Mill, Competition Heavyweight, #10 & #8
Thread:	Black
Tail:	Hot yellow golden pheasant crest
Rib:	Silver wire
Body:	Claret seal's fur
Body Hackles:	Claret, dark magenta & black cock*
Collar Hackles:	Blue guinea fowl over black hen (or bottle-green peacock body feather, for more 'kick')
Head:	Black deer hair

* In small sizes, strip one side of each palmering hackle. In large sizes tie them full

− 22 −

Lanlish – Extreme Fishing

THERE IS A time, during the wee sma' hours, when the body reaches its lowest ebb. I think the French have a name for it, but then they have a name for most things that happen between dusk and dawn. It is the time dreaded by long-distance drivers, shift-workers, hard drinkers, inveterate party-goers and serial sea-trout fishermen. It is said that if you are going to be lucky enough to pass away in your own bed – bend the water-receptacle of Life round the defensive wall of Mortality and into the top-corner of Infinity – odds-on it'll be round about four in the morning.

The evening meal was preparation for what we hoped would be a successful night's fishing. As I mopped up my gravy with the last remnants of my bread roll, I knew I was going to need a lot of nutritional help to fish past the dreaded 4 a.m., so I ordered chocolate pudding for dessert. Booze was out, but kip for a couple of hours between ten and midnight was an essential.

Iain Muir, Colin 'Puck' Kirkpatrick and I had gathered at the Cape Wrath Hotel at the start of what came to be known to us as 'The Muckle Troot Hunt'. Our mission was to spend six days on three waters attempting to catch one or more trophy wild brown trout.

What constitutes a 'trophy' trout is for each angler to decide. On some water anything over 12 ounces is a specimen, but you might not necessarily want to hang it on the wall in all its ferocious and majestic beauty. For the sake of argument, we had collectively decided that four-pound was break-off point. Anything under that could well be a very fine fish but it would not qualify as 'trophy'. To get things into perspective, a trophy fish should be the fish of a season, if not a lifetime, and they tend to come along when they decide to, and the angler has very little say in it. We had gone out on a limb at the beginning of the year and worked out a plan in which we would do the dictating, and trophy fish would be the outcome.

Almost everyone said we were mad and doomed to fail. To plan a June trip in January, on waters of which we had only a passing knowledge, with the essential factor of weather being in the lap of the gods. This wasn't just a wild goose chase; this was searching for a needle in a field full of haystacks; hunting the Snark; seeking out the Holy Grail with spots on. Surprisingly, we were pretty optimistic.

Puck is one of the finest, most reliable non-professional 'field' photographers in the world of fishing 'snappers'. As a more than competent fisherman himself, he knows the 'score' and will be there ready, at your shoulder, when and if the fish comes along. Good light, poor light; day or night, Puck will get the shots. This was important as we didn't intend to kill any fish on this trip if we could possibly help it. Iain is a dynamo; he'll happily fish away, through hell and high water, long after others have given up hope and retired defeated. He also has a happy knack of snagging a good 'un when the chips are down, as I had come to appreciate on our many and varied trips together. And then there was me – a self-confessed big trout junkie, with a creditable history of removing big, reluctant trout from water that they'd much rather stay in. This was the team on *Mission Seriously Unlikely*.

I could write reams about big fish. I have studied them and hunted them for as long as I can remember. I've never really been interested in anything else in my whole fishing career but big, wild fish. And big, wild trout are as fascinating a subject for a fisherman as there is. The Cape Wrath Hotel, which controls the loch, has stuffed specimens and photographs of Lanlish fish which make hardened anglers dribble saliva down their shirt-fronts – no joke! I've lost count of the time I've spent looking wistfully at their final remains, hung on the wall. And one thing I've learnt is that there is only one way to catch big trout – find the right place (you can't catch 'em if they ain't there), be there at the right time (preferably when they are awake and feeding), fish in an appropriate manner (give 'em something they'll accept as food), and be prepared to spend a whole lot of time – almost all of it, in fact – not catching anything! That in a nutshell, is how to snag a trophy.

We were in the right place, at the right time. I knew that Lanlish fish had a predilection for big, lure-type flies, so had equipped Iain and myself with plenty of Humungous-es – marabou-tailed, bug-eyed, sparkly monstrosities that, it saddens me to admit, big, wild trout simply love. (My first ever experience of this type of lure and its effect upon big fish was one evening on Loch Clumly in Orkney, when

Sandy Leventon put on what he referred to as a Bloodworm, and I called a Red Dog Nobbler, and damned near emptied the place with it before I lured him away with hints that the bar would be closing soon). I can only assume that it is the action of this style of fly that is so lethally attractive, as pattern doesn't seem to matter much as long as there is weight at the head and a long, mobile, wavy tail at the end.

We have already established that trophy fish hunting is not like standard trout fishing and you have to do strange things to comply with fishy behaviour.

We were due on Lanlish at approx 2.00 a.m. and would fish until the dawning sun's rays touched the water. This is a great part of the day to try for a specimen trout. In the far north-west, June nights are never very dark but, in what passes for darkness, big Lanlish fish will stir themselves and go looking for something to chew on. Also, being as wary as long-tailed cats in a rocking horse factory, regular periods of low human disturbance are their favoured activity times. As the wind howled round the hotel, and heavy rain battered the windows, we left the happy drinkers at the bar and went to try and grab some sleep before the 'off'.

You know it's windy when descending the hill is just as hard as climbing up. The south-easterly gale that met us trying to reach Loch Lanlish at 2.00 a.m. on that June morning was producing weather which, by any assessment, was hardly conducive to perfect fishing conditions. I can safely say that if the party had not been comprised of hairy-arsed Hielan' men, a decision would have been made that it was simply too windy to fish. But Iain, Puck and I were on a mission, and nothing was going to stand in our way. Not lack of sleep, flying golf balls or a wind desperately trying to blow us back up the incline we were determined to climb down. Flying golf balls? Lanlish sits on the south-eastern corner of the Durness Golf Course and is home to some of the finest and biggest wild brown trout to be found in the UK. Mind you, our plan to fish from 2.00 a.m. 'til sun-up probably eliminated the golf ball hazard unless there were others out there as single-minded (or mad) as we were.

The one and, perhaps, only good side to fishing in a gale is that flyfishing effort must be restricted to the down-wind shoreline, cutting down on the search area. Even big trout will find the maelstrom at the tail of a gale more than slightly uncomfortable. I got myself into the water just in front of the golfers' shelter/hut, and, trying hard not to get blown into the water, I lengthened my cast and was suddenly into a decent fish! It really isn't supposed to happen this way. These waters, by definition, are damned hard! Their trout populations are low, and individual fish are fussy, sneaky, wary and wild, not to mention downright difficult to catch. You just don't catch fish in the first spot you try, on the first fly you offer, within minutes of starting. Having said that, it wasn't the monster we were looking for, but it was a nice fish for all that, just over two pounds, with a #10 Gold Muddler wedged in its scissors. It was about this point that a dog otter popped its head up to see what all the commotion was about. The things you see at two o'clock in the morning when respectable people are in their beds!

Puck was swiftly on the scene and the trout was quickly played out, 'snapped', and returned. Give that trout another year in this 'protein soup' and it would most definitely be a trophy fish to gladden someone's heart. We had made a sprint start but the 'night' was young, and the best of it was still to come. Iain had strolled over to see what a Lanlish fish looked like, and vowing to get one bigger, wandered off in an easterly direction to try some fresh water. I stayed exactly where I was, on the assumption that 'where there's one, there's two', and proceeded to pull out a succession of fish, unfortunately each one being smaller that its predecessor.

Meanwhile, Iain had got himself into the south-eastern corner of the loch, and what transpired next I will leave to him:

"Nearing the end of the loch I began wading the short downwind shore to cover the last of the available water. We've all been there, eking out the last bit of water before deciding what to do next, casting way too close to shore and rocks. And then, for some of us whom the gods favour, the old cliché: 'I thought I'd caught in a rock…and then the rock took off'. And so it was. Suddenly there's something in the water able to challenge the wind's hold – if the wind wants to push the water this way and that, this unseen thing is pushing it that way and this.

A natural force stronger than a Force 9 wind? Through the dim light a massive trout throws itself into the air, the wind stripping it of spray. Its monochrome profile confirms this to be the trophy fish we are seeking. The rod, previously only obeying the wind's command, is pulled screaming across wind. Excited shouts bring Puck and camera, slipping and tripping, cursing and gasping, onto the scene. I'm on adrenaline, tenterhooks and unseen slippery rocks. The battle ensues, with line and confidence lost and gained in seemingly equal measure until, in time, a beautifully silver wild trout weighing some 6½ pounds is brought to heel and to net. This is a fish to wonder at, drool over, and quickly fall in love with. It is, by a long way, the best of many memorable fish I've had from the Durness lochs in a decade of fishing there. The fish returned, the fishable water fished out, we make our way back to a rude golfers' shelter and slump, dazed, amazed and exhausted while the sun rises over the horizon as if nothing had happened."

And what can I add to that? Just this. As we sat in the three-sided shelter with the wind still screaming over the loch and throwing the odd handful of sand in our faces, we mulled over our small miracle. We, as a team, had accomplished what so few wild trout anglers had managed in many lifetimes of fishing – a truly wild Scottish brown trout of over 6 lb. Truth to tell, having safely negotiated the 'little death' of 4 a.m., feeling wind-battered and weary, but successful, what was really at the back of our minds was hot tea and fried breakfasts. Well, after all, we still had five more days hunting mythical monsters.

If you are going to release, bring them in quickly

– 23 –

Catch & Release: A Cognitive Approach

SO, WE HAVE come to the end of another season. Now we have time on our hands to consider the past, present and future.

We fishermen are in the business of catching fish, which is why we spend hours and days on the water. At a time when our sport is under scrutiny from those who are, positively or negatively, very interested in our actions, our relationship with our prey needs some serious consideration. We must justify our behaviour to others and ourselves, or our ability to continue to fish may be removed. To do this we must retain respect for our quarry.

A couple of years ago whilst fishing on Rutland I was privy to the disgusting and unedifying sight of a well-known angler, who should have known much better, throwing captured brown trout over his shoulder back into the water. He had reached his limit of browns and wanted to catch rainbows. Such disrespect for another living organism opens us up to criticism and censure from friends and enemies alike.

I fish for a great number of reasons. Because I love the sport, find it fascinating and challenging, and love to feel part of nature as a hunter. A true hunter not only deeply respects his prey but also ensures that that which is killed is utilised. Therefore, because I am a hunter, I believe it is necessary to eat part of my catch and return unharmed that which I have no use for. This confirms my position as part of nature's plan that species should interact and, through reliance on each other within the plan, continue to exist and flourish. I believe that to distance oneself from nature is to jeopardise not only the natural world but also ourselves. If we don't accept that we are an integral part of the workings of the planet, and adopt our part in it, the jigsaw breaks up and the ecological and environmental chains, which keep everything together and working, will fragment. Nature is a dynamic process in which destruction must equal construction, consumption be balanced by production, exploitation be set against sustainability, and we humans must play our part.

So, what has all this got to do with fishing behaviour? Like all human behaviour, fishing has become a thing almost unrecognisable from the activity of our parents and ancestors. It is now almost purely an artificial construct, designed to gratify our least honourable and selfish requirements, controlled by stocking policies and weird self-justification concepts such as 'catch & release'. We deceive ourselves by thinking that to hook, play, capture and return a living creature is honourable. Individual actions of this type may be justifiable, for example in natural waters where stock levels are low, but as a blanket, cover-all policy it is fundamentally flawed. Many people think that mandatory C&R is the way forward and will not only enhance our stocks of fish but also save us from the onslaught of bodies who would like to our sport terminated. I have grave doubts about such beliefs, mainly because C&R has become almost a religion with some people who are fundamentalist in their belief and evangelical in their attitude. There is only one way, and it's their way.

Catch-and-release as a philosophy was largely born in the USA where stocked waters receive extraordinary pressures, and imported into this country where it is, to a greater or lesser extent, less applicable. Blanket application of C&R is more popular in England than it is in the other three countries which make up the UK, and I believe there is a very simple reason for this – English fishing prior to the great stillwater revolution was largely concerned with coarse fish, the majority of which are inedible, or at least, unappetising. The tradition of 'one for the pot' is not as entrenched there as in other countries where fishing was largely for salmonids. If you are brought up returning everything you catch the conditioning is strong and easily transferred to areas in which its application is less appropriate.

The vast majority of rainbow trout in this country exist for only one reason, to be caught by angling practice. They fulfil no other purpose and their place in UK freshwater ecology is questionable. They are produced by humans to provide enjoyment for humans, and if they didn't fulfil this function, they'd likely not exist in this country at all. For rainbow fishery managers to apply rules and restrictions, such as C&R, is understandable. That rainbow trout have now achieved the status of a commodity and that anglers treat them as such should surprise no-one. The angler turns up at the fishery, pays his money and expects to catch his allotment, much as a shopper purchases cans of beans or packets of biscuits. For fishery staff to be able to sell an individual fish to a number of different customers makes excellent business sense, but eventually coarsens the attitude of the angler. That is why the saying "a fish is too valuable to be caught once" reflects attitudes which have nothing to do with respect for fish or our sport. I believe that if I catch a trout and the next chap in the queue steps up to the water and catches it again, the experience is undervalued, grave doubts are cast on our relationship with another living creature, and we are all inevitably demeaned by the whole sordid affair.

However, in most of the UK, without rainbow trout swimming in many of our lochs, lakes and reservoirs there would be no trout at all. But is the artificiality of it all somehow seeping into the soul of the angler and making him/her respond in ways which have nothing to do with our hunter/gatherer past? I'll say it again – modern stillwater fishing has more in comparison with a trip down the supermarket than it does with the pursuit of a wild creature in its natural environment.

So, what are the ramifications for wild trout resources? With each passing year I see more and more wild fishery owners attempting to mimic the management styles of their southern counterparts due to the pressures of a very competitive market and the changing aspirations of fishermen. If the modern fishing market is driven by the need to produce a 'product', the vagaries of an uncertain sport, affected as it is by weather, season, the variability of stock recruitment, environmental changes, etc., undermines the attempt. Wild fishing is all about the unpredictability of outcome and success has more to do with angling skill than gullible fish

And there's the rub. Modern anglers don't just like to catch fish, they damned well insist upon it, regardless of their own ability to fish. They've paid their money, and, by God, there had better be a return on their investment or there will be hell to pay. The commercial fishery attempts to solve this problem by continually refreshing their stock of fish with infusions of gullible, easy-to-catch 'stockies', in a 'never mind the quality, feel the width' sort of fashion, and this goes a long way towards satisfying the less discriminatory angler. Any wild fishery manager who attempts a similar route to commercial success endangers his stock of indigenous fish. And, surprisingly, there are many who, in the face of all evidence to the contrary, believe they can get away with it.

There is an erroneous belief prevalent throughout the country that the problems of each and every fishery can be solved in a hatchery. Witness the steady decline of our beloved Loch Leven in the fairly recent past. Every problem – be it poor water quality, cormorant depredation, falling angling numbers, algal poisoning, competition from other fisheries, changing feeding behaviour of indigenous stock – has been addressed by stocking more and more fish into the loch. At no time has there been the slightest evidence that these stockings have been reflected in better fishing, apart from a brief honeymoon period in the early nineties when alien rainbow trout swelled the catch returns. The simplistic logic that 1 wild trout + 1 stocked trout will eventually = 2 wild trout, fails to factor into the equation the underlying problems which have led to falling catches.

Wild fish in Leven were under extreme pressure. The spawning burns were in a dreadful condition with compacted, silted-up gravels and low (if not non-existent) summer water levels, and this has seriously reduced natural recruitment. Cormorants, no doubt attracted by increased numbers of rainbow trout, were gobbling up vast quantities of those wild parr that did make it down the burns. The moratorium on stocking any sort of trout into Leven has created greater numbers of trout, more than any stocking policy did in the past.

Am I hopeful? Not really, because I don't think it's a numbers game, it's just that the Leven fish are becoming dreadfully difficult to catch because their behaviour has changed. The virtual loss of the vast majority of insect life has the fish looking for sustenance elsewhere. Almost every fish I caught on Leven last year contained midge pupae and bloodworm, incontrovertible proof of bottom feeding for the first part of the season. It needed good hatches of adult fly to bring fish up through the water column. Brown trout are designed by nature to feed above their holding level. The positioning of their eyes and mouth shape gives this away. If such a fish then decides, through necessity, to bottom feed it will have to virtually stand on its head to do so. The chances of it seeing the angler's flies in such a position are remote.

The continued and growing use of hatchery stock to 'enhance' wild populations to satisfy the selfish needs of unskilled anglers is a form of long, drawn-out, suicide. Management dare not stop stocking in case the punter, faced with more challenging fishing, goes elsewhere. But as the hatchery lorries continue to spew out confused, disorientated 'stockies' into the natural environment, catches of indigenous fish drop, necessitating greater and greater stockings of hatchery fish. The loch goes into an out-of-control nosedive spiral of decline. The once self-sustaining loch has become a giant put-and-take fishery, with the few remaining anglers desperate to know where the last stocking took place so that they can get there as fast as possible and 'bag up'.

As far as I can gather, modern day fishery management addresses the need for sustainability by encouraging C&R and sprucing up the hatchery. South of the Border, where trout waters and populations are largely artificial, a future with self-sustaining trout populations is probably an unrealistic dream But where trout naturally exist, self-sustainability must be defined and achieved if we are to continue to enjoy quality fishing.

Is the future brown? It can be, but I very much doubt it, given human nature and the economic factors. I suggest we need a radical rethink of existing attitudes, policies and perspectives. Management must stop trying to solve environmental problems with economical solutions, and anglers must recognise that they can become part of the solution by not adding to the problem.

The Cap'n's surprising salmon!

– 24 –

Loch Naver – Charlie's Ghost

IT KINDA CAME out of the blue. As we approached the burn mouth, in amongst the lifting wavelets and patches of foam, out of the corner of my eye I saw a good fish aggressively launch itself through the air in front of the boat.

Colin grunted and Davie gasped. Colin struck with his dapping rod, and the fight was on.

Another thing that came out of the blue was our day on Loch Naver. I hadn't planned to fish there but Becky at the Altnaharra Hotel added it to my itinerary, and at the end of the day I was mightily glad she had. Even more chuffed was Colin, as events will show.

I had fished for salmon and sea-trout in Loch Naver once before, but as I remember it, the loch hadn't fished well, and the weather was hardly helpful, and I had no fishy response whatsoever. So, I wasn't overly optimistic as we set out, but that never has had much effect on the amount of effort required from me. You are either cut out for it or you're not. Continually chucking flies at the horizon in the vague hope of a special fish is not for the guys who measure quantity over quality. It's a waiting game, and sometimes the wait goes on forever. Some misguided non-fishers think this requires patience. I can readily assure them that even the tiniest measure of patience is not required. What is required though is confidence in your tactics and techniques, your ghillies (should you employ one) and an understanding of the fish you are targeting.

Many people steer clear of ghillies. I suppose that may stem from bad experiences in the past, economic dictates, or perhaps just an anti-social temperament. I always like to use a ghillie, this being a team game after all. My ghillie on Naver was Davie McKay, one of the very best 'men on the oars' I have ever met. There is a character profile attached to Highland gents of a certain age which implies a degree of grumpiness and a surly nature. Whilst this could describe me fairly accurately, nothing could be further from the truth as far as Davie is concerned. A chap who would rather smile than scowl, and full of interesting chat and banter, Davie knows his lochs, and even in bright sunshine and a flat calm his optimism never falters. That is as close to perfection for the job as I can imagine.

Now, we were fishing in mid-September, and the expectation of fresh fish entering the system was not high. To all intents and purposes, the salmon run was over, and whilst a trickle of fresh sea-trout could be expected, the bulk of the run would already have taken up residence in the loch. Davie's plan was to stick to the west end of the loch, an area of relatively shallow water where many spawning burns enter. Fish could be expected in this area awaiting the spate that would lead them to the spawning grounds. I couldn't argue with his decision.

The breeze was quite steady from the north-east, so Davie took us up to the plantation on the north shore and we began a drift towards the outflow of the Mudale River, a classic salmon drift full of good lies.

Migratory fish lies are a conundrum that I have pondered over ever since I took up this game, and I have a theory which may cause some controversy. I believe there are a variety of lies available to fish entering a system – perfect ones, good ones and those that are inhabited 'til something better becomes available, or not, as the case may be. In the latter I suspect that fish are unsettled and they may take occasional forays looking for an improvement. It is just before and after such forays that fish are liable to be caught, and possibly during the saunter as well. These are the fish we see leaping, and head-and-tailing. Immediately before and after a wee jaunt the fish will be active and wide awake, and perhaps somewhat irritated. Perfect targets at which to chuck a fly. I also suspect that fish in a 'perfect lie', and to a lesser extent in 'good' ones, are unlikely to feel the inclination to stray far or often, and will only leave said lie because of disturbance (a boat passing close, for example), or a migratory impulse brought about by a spate. The first fish to enter the system (possibly larger early fish, immune to threat or intimidation), will get first pick of lies and will basically sleep their way through to spawning time. I also believe that the more rest and recuperation a fish gets, the less inclined they are to 'take', because it is during that dormant stage that they quickly become sexually mature and lose any desire to investigate objects that stir old freshwater feeding images and memories. As stock levels fall, the number of fish lying in poor lies

Charlie's ghost is watching on

will decrease and fishing returns will also drop considerably. To sum up, a fish in a perfect lie will be dormant, and dormant fish will be unaware of our flies; fish in poor lies will be more active and more likely to take out any aggression on, or piqued interest in, our offerings.

Our first drift in toward the sandbanks which delineate the mouth of the Mudale saw no response, but we were not too downhearted. The breeze was picking up and a good 'salmon wave' was developing. There is little doubt amongst loch salmon and sea-trout aficionados that a good breeze is an essential component of a good day. In a perfect world we would always leave the best drifts for such conditions because the first time over good water will produce the best results. But knowing when conditions have peaked or will reach optimum is a chuck of the dice too far for all of us, and you have to take your chances.

We continued on along the west shore powered by Davie's steady oar work and started to get some very frustrating inquiries from what we perceived to be sea-trout. What at first appeared to be a solid take with some weight behind it, produced no contact when the rod was lifted. We coined the term 'suckers' for these mystery fish. I was fishing a medium-sink intermediate line and Colin was sticking to a floater, and while the floater seemed to be attracting more fish the results were the same – seemingly good takes leading to nothing. Did I mention that this was very frustrating?

Colin has a pattern he calls the WOIGO Kate Muddler (WOIGO = West of Ireland golden olive dyed deer hair), and he puts maximum faith in it, and it rewards him by featuring at the top of his catch returns. Whist I persevered with my own favourites, Colin was seeing a lot of interest to his. I couldn't work out whether it was the fly or his floating line, but I decided to stick with my patterns and intermediate line.

As we approached the mouth of the Vagastie burn, on the west shore south of the Mudale outflow, Colin was into a nice sea-trout of 2½ – 3 pounds which led him a very fine dance. Sea-trout are spectacular fighters. They almost always jump, and are prone to long, powerful runs. People say that sea-trout are soft-mouthed, but I suspect the main reason so many 'fall off' is because of the vigour and extravagance of their fight. This one stayed on, thankfully, and the Naver account was finally opened. Both Colin and I encountered a few 'suckers' in this region with predictable results, but nothing more was hooked or landed. We then decided to try some very attractive water on off the Clebrig shore. Sea-trout have a defined preference for slightly deeper water than salmon. And this stretch ticked all the boxes. But this was 'sucker' heaven, a number of non-productive takes being experienced in this area along with quite a number of small-ish brownies.

Deciding to have a belated lunch, we returned to the launch site, where Davie noticed that the water level had lifted a few inches. This was good news. It would mean that fish numbers attracted to the burn mouths would increase. However, we noticed that the precipitation creating this rise was very localised as the Vagastie burn was flowing well whilst the Mudale seemed not to have changed at all. This was most likely due to a cloud burst in the catchment area of the former. On our later return to the hotel those fishing Loch Hope had had very strange and mixed

The Cap'n's successful dapping pattern

up weather with thunder storms, flat calms and rain. On Naver we experienced none of this. We were blessed.

Lunch completed we decided to repeat our first drift, running the north shore down to the Mudale outflow, across the sandbanks and once more into the burn mouth of the Vagastie. Although we were aware of a salmon build-up in the river mouth and along the sandbanks, they were reluctant to come out to play. It was about this time that Colin decided to try the dap. I enjoy watching the dapping fly dance across the wave tops but find doing it boring in the extreme and riddled with inconsistencies in practice. Why should a salmon or sea-trout have any desire to attack the equivalent of a dead sparrow? I can always think of a dozen reasons why it shouldn't work and damned few why it should. I am, first and last, a wet fly man. I can't settle or relax when dapping. But Colin is an adroit dapper and loves to do it, so I encouraged him to use his skills and was very keen to see what fishy reaction it would produce.

Approaching the southern extent of the sand bars, a feisty grilse of about four pounds roared out of the water and engulfed Colin's dapping Daddy. A mere twitch of the rod and Colin hooked the beast which, very surprisingly, swam round in a small circle and came obediently to the net. We were all convinced that the grilse had no idea what had occurred and only decided to put up some opposition when safely in the net. And, boy, did it go crazy. The fly fell out of its mouth within seconds of the net's entrapment leading us all to believe that had it put up an aquatic fight it wouldn't have remained hooked for very long. Slightly disappointed by the lack of fight, Colin was ultimately delighted in his very first salmon on the dap. Quite an achievement, and by all accounts, a rare one in this neck of the woods.

Whilst all this was going on I was aware that anyone on the upper floors of the Altnaharra Hotel could have kept a close eye on our successes and travails. It also occurred to me that it was about time that the ghost of one of my great fishing heroes, Charles McLaren – sea-trout fisher extraordinaire, inventor of that classic pattern the Kate McLaren, and onetime owner of the Altnaharra Hotel – came to my aid. I was having a tough day and, apart from the frustrating attention of the previously mentioned 'suckers', was looking to add another blank to my list. Hoping to stir some sympathy from Charlie's spectre, I put a large Kate on the dropper and proceeded to stroke the water with it. As we approached the Vagastie burn mouth Mr McLaren interceded and sent a lovely sea-trout of about 2½ pounds crashing on to the Kate. Unlike Colin's grilse, this trout knew exactly what was going on and gave me a right going-over. In this day and age of sea-trout conservation and category-three waters, it is very important to play your fish hard so they come quickly to the net with plenty of vim and vigour left when released. I have always loved playing fish hard, and this one was out of the net, unhooked and back to the depths, in the flicker of an eye.

Our Loch Naver day had accounted for one grilse, two sea-trout and a couple of finnock. Not at all bad for a day I had been dreading. It has to be said that none of this would have been possible without the advice, knowledge and strong arms of Davie McKay, who was our physical and mental support all day. Job well done, Davie.

I would like to relate that upon our return to the welcoming embrace of the Altnaharra Hotel – one of the best, if not the best, fishing lodges in Scotland – I felt a congratulatory hand on my shoulder, and upon turning round, saw Charles McLaren's wraith fading from view, but that would be taking things a bit far. And after all it was only one modest sea-trout, and I'm sure he had better things to do.

– 25 –

Footprints on the Water

THE FIRST TIME I saw this style of pattern was amongst a mix of reservoir patterns sent me by Jeremy Clarke, and I immediately saw the logic and motivation behind its creation. The concept first came to light of day as 'Bill's Big Red', and a little bit of tinkering (mostly by JC) with the original has spawned a family of patterns which, I think, rule supreme in the world of stillwater dries and I refer to them as Crippled Midges.

The whole concept centres not on what we see from above as an adequate imitation of a surface-trapped insect, but what the trout sees from below, and this has to do with the physics of water. Water is relatively unique as a liquid by having what is referred to as *surface tension*. Surface tension is a force created by the interaction of water molecules at the surface of the liquid. To understand it, consider droplets of water; surface tension is what makes a droplet spherical; it is why water runs down a window pane in rivulets rather than just smearing its way across that surface in a uniform film; why falling from a great height into water is like hitting concrete; and why materials which are heavier than water can float on its surface. And the most surprising fact about surface tension of water is that without it life on this planet, as we know it, wouldn't exist. But more importantly to the subject in hand, it is why insects can safely alight on water but also get trapped in the surface film.

We've all watched insects struggling in the surface film, and some of you will have noticed that the water surface resists tearing and bends, stretches and fluctuates almost like a sheet of latex. This is a surface tension effect. Light passing through an undisturbed surface film is relatively unaltered; light passing through a disturbed, stretched and bent surface film is fractured in such a way as to send highlights and sparks of light almost like a beacon. Trout vision underwater is complicated by this same surface film in that they can only observe the above-water world in the

157

area directly above its eyes, the area being increased or decreased by the depth at which the fish finds itself. Any area outwith this 'window' appears like a mirror, reflecting the underwater world. Any distortion to this 'mirror' is instantly picked up by a trout as the presence of potential food trapped in the surface film. It will home in to the said distortion until the source of the disturbance is in the 'window of view' and then accept or reject the item.

The trick is to accentuate the distortion, thereby increasing the signal sent out. And that is where the parachute hackle comes in. Without the 'para' hackle this pattern would still create a disturbance in the film, but it could be a weak one. The spray of hackle points, each equally capable of bending the surface film, produces a signal like a searchlight in a desert night. The concept is a bit like wrestling, we are using the trout's strengths, in which it is totally confident, to defeat it. This is dedicated and targeted fly-tying in its purest form.

I could go on for pages listing the occasions when this pattern has turned a mediocre day into a red-letter one, but I will restrict myself to just a handful to illustrate my points.

It had been a totally fruitless day on Loch Leven. The loch was just not fishing worth a damn during the day, and a brief period of activity immediately after sunset was the only chance of sport. But I had to be off at 5 p.m., so I searched the water column in the increasingly vain hope of a pull. This was in the bad old days of rainbow trout stocking, and even these 'protein hoovers' seemed immune to my piscatorial blandishments. It really wasn't a fishing day; the water had that steely, hard look that is common in winter and during the summer states categorically "nae fish!" If that was not bad enough there was a brown stain to it which always makes fishing difficult. With about an hour to go I found myself drifting in Queichy Bay. There is some very shallow water at the head of the bay into which fish will often wander in the late evening, and there is a spectacular drop-off out in open water which usually can be relied upon to hold taking fish throughout the season. I drifted it a couple of times, more in anger than in hope, with no change to my luck, and then thought "Testicles (or a word to that effect), if I'm going to catch sod-all fishing with sinking lines, I may as well catch sod-all on a floater!" With time fast disappearing, I put up the floater, a co-polymer leader and a couple of Crippled Midge patterns and chucked them out. It is indicative of my lack of optimism, that I immediately switched my attention from the flies on the water to those still sitting snug and dry in my box in the hope that something other might suggest itself. I just caught the rod as it launched itself from my lap and clattered off the gunnels. "Bloody hell! A fish!" And it was – a firm rainbow of about two pounds. I went back up the drift and took another, turning a hopeless day into the start of a long and profound love affair with the Crippled Midge.

I wouldn't want you to think that this style of pattern is purely for rainbow trout because brownies are real suckers for it as well. I've an English pal who cadges a few off me most years for Ullswater brownies, and the Duck Fly version (see below) salvaged a really poor duck fly trip on Corrib this spring. My most enjoyable evening on Leven last year saw the standard version take three for 8½ pounds – the best basket off the loch on that evening.

While I was writing this piece, I decided to take the dog for a walk and grab a 'breather'. There is a moribund 'stocky' rainbow trout fishery quite close to me which hasn't been stocked in a couple of years and, although it was drained to the dimensions of a big puddle last year, there were unsubstantiated rumours that there was still the odd fish in it. I had my doubts, but it was a perfect evening for a fish to be 'up on the fin' so I popped over for a stroll round. And sure enough there were some rising fish – not many, but enough to make the blood stir. The next evening, I popped back, this time with a rod and a few Crippled Midge patterns. The fish were real spooky and even a heavy footfall had them seeking sanctuary in the relative depths. This hardly matched the fishery of old where the 'bows would come along and nibble holes in your wellies, but I didn't complain, this was more like the thing!

I stood and watched for a while, my dog 'pointing' every rising fish. There was one which seemed to be larger than the others, rising in a very tight pattern a hundred yards along the bank. I slipped into 'red injun' mode and slunk up the bank. Because the fishery had been shut for so long the bank-side vegetation was a damned nuisance and my fly line kept getting tangled up in last year's dead thistles and rushes. Eventually I got within casting distance of the targeted fish and I studied his movement pattern. He was moving in a clockwise direction in a circle with a diameter of about four metres. I dropped the single Olive Crippled Midge (see below) on the edge of his swim path, and he rose up and took it like a carp on a dog biscuit! The slurp of a good trout on a dry must be one of the most sensual and primordially stimulating aspects of flyfishing – I'd probably be censored if I told you its effect on me, let's just say I love it! People talk about a screaming reel – it doesn't even come close.

The fish thundered off to the left, heading for the island, and even some exaggerated side-strain didn't faze it one bit. Just as I was watching my backing-line preparing to get wet, he turned and ricocheted back to his starting position. I got some line on the reel and was thinking "This must be a rainbow of about five pounds! How the hell did he survive the drainage?" when the sod repeated his blistering run back to the island, only this time he thought it would be a wheeze to go around it. However, this time the side-strain changed his mind for him, and he played every trick in the book to put-off the inevitable. Festooned with weed, the leader was beginning to look like a washing-line. This fish was not just wild – it was seriously pissed-off!

After one of the hardest fights I've had for many a long year and making the eight-pound trout of last year feel like a puppy-dog on a lead, a superb three-and-a-half pound wild brownie came to my hand. I've been flyfishing for so long now that my memories have cobwebs hanging off them and I suppose I am entitled to be a bit blasé, but I almost danced for joy that night and had a grin on my face that a crowbar couldn't have removed. We all knew that there had always been a head of wild brownies in the place, but they were rarely seen and hardly ever caught. This was triumph by nature over man, and in a totally atavistic way and in celebration of a real worthy opponent... I knocked it on the head, took it home and ate it the next day! And it tasted sublime.

PATTERNS

The Classic Crippled Midge

Hook:	Fulling Mill All-purpose Medium, #12 and 10
Thread:	Brown 8/0
Tail, post & breathers:	Glo-Brite white fluorescent floss
Rib:	Fine oval gold
Abdomen:	Rich orangey-brown seal's fur (Sherry Spinner)
Hackle:	Light furnace hen
Thorax:	Hare's mask fur with lots of guard hairs

The original and best. Will work everywhere and is, in my mind, not only the best stillwater dry but also the most versatile.

The Crippled Duck Fly

Hook:	Fulling Mill All-purpose Medium, #12
Thread:	Olive
Tail, post & breathers:	Glo-Brite white fluorescent floss
Rib:	Twisted medium red holographic
Abdomen:	Sooty-olive seal's fur
Hackle:	Dark furnace hen
Thorax:	Hot-orange seal's fur

This has saved the bacon for me on a number of times when a long, hard, fruitless day on the buzzer has come good in failing light with the application of this wee beauty.

The Olive Crippled Midge

Hook:	Fulling Mill All-purpose Medium, #12 and 10
Thread:	Brown 8/0
Tail, post & *breathers*:	Glo-Brite white fluorescent floss
Rib:	Fine oval gold
Abdomen:	Olive seal's fur with a dash of hare's fur added
Hackle:	Grizzle, dyed sunburst
Thorax:	As abdomen

I tend to use this pattern when fish get a tad fussy after being fished over hard for a number of days, the sort of conditions one often experiences on the run-up to a major competition.

The Fiery Claret Crippled Midge

Hook:	Fulling Mill All-purpose Medium, #12 and 10
Thread:	Brown 8/0
Tail, post & *breathers*:	Glo-Brite white fluorescent floss
Rib:	Fine oval gold
Abdomen:	A mix of fiery-brown and claret seal's fur
Hackle:	Light furnace hen
Thorax:	Hare's mask fur with lots of guard hairs

I have a collection of strange mixes of seal's furs, but this is my favourite. Adding a dash of claret to fiery-brown gives the mixture a depth which the constituent parts, in isolation, lack. It's a great bright day colour.

TYING NOTES

The furs incorporated in this style of pattern should always be very sparse in the abdomen region – slightly heavier in the thorax – and well teased out. I don't usually use a dubbing scrubber, instead I dub loosely and rely on the ribbing to pull things together and then rub and pull with thumb and forefinger. This produces the same effect without slackening the rib.

A gallows tool is essential for this style of dressing. They are cheap and easy to use, if not always easy to source.

Use a dubbing needle to stop the hackle climbing up the post. Winding in a clockwise direction around the post I come in low and tight on the thorax side and lay the needle at right angles to, and tight down on, the hook shank on the abdomen side and wind the hackle under it. With the post tight and the turns tight, this makes the hackle build-up locate tightly down as low on the post as humanly possible.

I like genetic hen hackles for the Crippled Midge, but Indian hen will work fine.

Perfection. A Carrowmore salmon on a tough day

– 26 –

Carrowmore

IT'S A STRANGE thing but I often think fishing in the UK is a very solitary thing, even when in company. It is as if one is undertaking an activity ignored by the rest of a totally uninterested community. Fishing seems to be considered a weird, unattractive, esoteric business by the vast bulk of society

Perhaps, not surprisingly, I never feel that way when in Ireland. I always seem to have the belief that everyone around is willing me on to success, that everyone I meet is somehow involved. Is it simply because UK fishing is a minority interest whereas across the sea its Irish equivalent is considered a laudable, justifiable endeavour, something well-understood by everyone? Sit in a bar and mention a lough, and someone will appear out of nowhere and provide you with all the information you'll need to locate it, buy a permit, flies to use and where exactly to employ them. Whereas over there this is a regular, reliable occurrence, in the UK you'd be damned lucky not to get blank or pitying stares, the sort normally reserved for those released back into the community. Even in what one might consider 'fishing centres' such as Kinross or Banchory talk of golf would raise more interest than fishing.

I was tired. Very tired. I had been fishing in Ireland for seven days non-stop – two days each on Sheelin, Corrib, Mask, and a day on Conn – and I was running on fumes, mostly Guinness and cognac fumes. The body and mind seem to be able to dredge up energy out of nowhere when you have a passion – a life's mission – in which to indulge. When away from the water I was running on autopilot. And today I was due another long shift on Carrowmore Lake.

My life was falling into a simple routine – eat, drink, sleep, FISH, eat, drink, sleep, FISH. But this rhythm has its upside. One becomes very relaxed and peaceful – even the extraneous fluff that the conscious mind keeps dredging up to confuse the thought process vanishes and you can concentrate on the job in an almost tranquil fashion. Here's a classic example from my past – I was due to attend a club outing on Harray, but I had an almost terminal head-cold. My brain was full of porridge, and I didn't know if it was Shrove Tuesday or Sheffield Wednesday, and I thought "There's no way I'm going fishin' today!" Unfortunately, I didn't factor my boat partner, Norman, into the equation. I *was* going fishin' even if he had to throw me into the boat! I vaguely remember us setting up the first drift from the Brig o' Brodgar to Kirk Bay, getting a fish in the first few casts and, after that... nothing.

When I resurfaced to a state approaching normality, I was stunned to learn that I had won the match at a canter. Norm told me later that I never dropped a fish. Everything that came to me I hooked. Seems I didn't have to be fully conscious to catch fish. Maybe sometimes it helped.

Paul Caslin, Peter Gathercole and I set out from Foxford on the reasonably short journey to the West End Bar in Bangor Erris where proprietor Seamus Henry was going to provide us with the keys to paradise. Ireland seems liberally besprinkled with these havens for fishermen where decades of fishing talk have bestowed a calming atmosphere which truly welcomes brothers of the angle. I love them and their friendly atmosphere. You get a hint of it this side of the Irish Sea when in a fishing hotel, but for the full-on, undiluted essence of the real thing UK citizens have to travel.

As we had motored west I saw a gradual change in landscape. The soft, fertile soils of the archetypal Irish landscape was giving way to moor and mountain, a landscape which states with unequivocal passion sea-trout and salmon. The best migratory habitat is harsh and unforgiving heather and rock. The best of brown trout exist in fertility; moorland drives fish to sea.

Carrowmore has a very strong reputation as a migratory fish water, famous in the past for its sea-trout. But with the universal decline in migratory trout due to the evil that is salmon farming, Carrowmore is now more of a salmon water. Its spring salmon fishing is nationally important, and I had long dreamed of trying my hand on Carrowmore, although this was June not January. Paul was going to do the guiding whilst wielding a rod, and Peter was going to record the catch if, indeed, there was a catch to be recorded.

Every stop was a struggle, a fight against the desire to shut my eyes and drift off to sleep, but when we arrived at the boat dock I got that surge of energy. This

Norman Irvine - In my opinion, one of the best wild trout fishers to have cast a line

was a sight to gladden the heart of any boat angler. Most boat launch sites look like they could be reclaimed by nature in a few man-free months. This one, however, looked like it had been uplifted from a more urban setting – like a health centre or something close. Good tarmacked surface and white lines to demarcate the parking slots. A group of people had worked hard to make the facilities at Carrowmore as good as physically possible. This place was loved, if not actually worshipped. I was impressed. But the midges, and the beckoning water, made it impossible to hang around and enjoy the view.

Carrowmore is a shallow lake with loose bottom sediments, and its waters can become turbid in a strong wind. In such conditions it does not fish. We were lucky in that the breeze was gentle, and I found myself in the peculiar position of not hoping for more wind. Salmon and a good wave are synonymous on all of my other haunts, but not here.

I have two ways of tackling silver tourists from a boat. A two-fly cast with a muddler up top, and a three-fly cast with muddlers top and bottom and a bushy palmer in the middle. The former has a 8′ to 9′ gap between flies, and the latter about 5′ between flies. The former is for light winds and the other for a good wave. There was little doubt in my mind which was going to be most appropriate today as the breeze was a bit 'wimpish' to say the least. Having good cloud cover I went for black and claret flies.

Early in the afternoon, with no fish coming to us, we all noticed a distinct rumble away to the south. Thunder was approaching, which went a long way to explaining why the fish wouldn't bite and the midges wouldn't stop. The breeze, such as it was, fell away to nothing, and the wee biting beggars flocked offshore and attacked us in droves. We had to actually get the outboard started and do a slow 'putter' round the lake to get away from them. Thunder is no good for fishing at the best of times, but for salmon and sea-trout it is total disaster. The dramatic changes in air pressure involved makes fish sulk, so motoring about out in the lake in the flat calm, whilst the thunder storm threatened, was as good a ploy as any other. Nature was disrupted by the nearing storm. Even the herds of donkeys wandering the hinterland around the lake seemed disturbed as choruses of braying broke out.

After an hour or so, in the late afternoon, the massive storm moved away north-westwards and a reasonable breeze picked up from a north-easterly direction and the heavy, oppressive cloud cover started to break up. The midge attacks had stirred me from my torpor, but with the steady breeze and a beautiful long drift along the White Shore, I was getting into that tunnel-vision mode as referenced earlier. I was almost cut-off from outside influences, what concentration I now had left was 100% devoted to the rod in my hand, the flies on the cast, and the water I was casting into. As we commenced drifting the White Shore I made a radical change of top dropper fly, taking off the Stone Goat Muddler and replacing it with the Voltas Muddler. This change was in answer to the increased sunlight. Many salmon and sea-trout loch anglers wouldn't change their flies for this reason, but as a wild trout fisher of many decades I am convinced that light and colour are imperative factors in fly choice, and what works for trout works for their silvery brothers and cousins.

I realised that Paul and Peter were losing hope of turning the day into anything vaguely resembling a success, but I knew it only took an instant doing the right thing in the right place to transform disaster into glowing triumph. It had been a hard day – trying to catch one reluctant fish always is – but it's never over 'til it's over. We were approaching the point at the end of the shoreline, a place where we had decided we would pack-up and head home. I was determined to fish it out to the very last cast, and maybe then steal another one. This bold decision was still rattling in my head when the line stopped dead. When you're running on autopilot you don't miss chances. Experience takes over and everything slots smoothly into place. You don't respond too quickly, too aggressively, too slowly or, worst of all, not respond at all. No, everything is as clockwork. The rod comes up, the pull gets pulled against and the hand is ready to give line in an instant.

Everything was going to plan, when... *HEE-HAW... HEE-HAW*, right in my seriously offended ear. I looked shoreward and there, not more than 20 feet away was a donkey, all ears and teeth, congratulating me on a job well done in the only way it knew. I had never seen the brute as we approached, and I damned near wet myself, or worse. My companions, recovering from the shock, were roaring with laughter, but the sound of line rapidly leaving my reel told me this was no time to be distracted.

Salmon from a boat, pound for pound, are not the best fighters in the flyfisher's world. The struggle is more of a dour 'pull me, pull you' with the odd jump to stir the heart. It is the rarity of chances, and the beauty of the fish, that captures the imagination and brings you back for a fresh encounter. This brief moment in time was no different, and as the fish slipped over the rim off the net the mood of my companions was more relief than celebration. I had never doubted that a chance would come, though I sincerely doubt whether my boat buddies shared my optimism. The late substitution of the Voltas Muddler from the bench had scored again, as it regularly did. I won't say that is an essential pattern for the job, but if the conditions call for it then I will fish it with ultimate confidence.

The job was done, and there was nothing left to do but eat, drink and sleep, no doubt to dream of big silvery fish and laughing donkeys.

Above: The stunning beauty of a Loch Eye trout   Below: A drift onto the south shore of Eye

− 27 −

More Than One in the Eye

THERE IS A preconception of Scotland which paints a picture of towering heather-clad heights, tumbling streams, massive lochs, and grandiose wilderness. This is a reality which applies to less than half the landscape, and much of that is found in the far north and west. Scotland is much more than this.

The east of Scotland is characterised by gently rolling countryside, wooded hills, stately rivers and fertility. Given that the north and west contain the vast majority of the UK's surface water, lochs in the east are not common. You can travel a damned long way in the east without seeing a loch worthy of the name. Caithness, in the far north, has some very good waters, including Watten, St John's and Heilan; East Sutherland has Craggie and Shin; Eastern Inverness-shire has Ruthven; Kinross-shire, further south, has majestic Leven. And, by and large that's about it. There are parishes in the west of Scotland that have more good trout lochs than the whole east coast put together. The east is the Kingdom of Salmon. The Republic of Trout lies to the north and west.

But many years ago, I heard whispers of a very good trout loch in the unlikely area of Easter Ross. I never followed up this rumour which, in light of recent events, was a great pity. In the late '90s I worked for the Conon and District Salmon Fishery Board, and during my forays for this august body I often passed within a mile or two of Loch Eye. All my colleagues knew of my passion for loch trout, but no-one ever mentioned Eye. It was a mystery. It almost seemed to be a fairy loch which could only be found if accompanied by a virgin, riding a unicorn, under a full moon. Maybe not so wide of the mark, given that the whole area is littered with ancient, and inscrutable, Pictish remains.

A very unlikely virgin, in the shape of Roger Dowsett of www.troutquest.co.uk, contacted me early this year and asked if I'd like to fish Loch Eye. I jumped at the chance, and in August this year, Roger and I met up with Chris Gregory on the side of Loch Eye in what I would have to say was pretty damn good fishing conditions. A north-west wind was gently blowing into the launch site, and the odd patch of blue freckled the otherwise grey sky.

Loch Eye is a fairly large water (1¾ x ⅔ of a mile), but the relatively shallow nature of the loch is the critical factor. The greatest depth is about 7′ and the mean depth is about 5′. This is the sort of environment which trout adore; the bottom of the loch will receive life-giving warmth and light at all times, and no matter how deep fish lie the surface is just a short dash away. This basic loch-type is a Mecca for those who like to fish traditional flies on a floater or midge-tip. The one factor which threatens the welfare of the loch is the number of swans and wintering wildfowl. The amount of nutrients gleaned from the surrounding agricultural land being introduced into the environment by wildfowl can tip the balance between fertile and eutrophic. Many such lochs sit on the razor's edge, with a natural and renewable harvest on one side, and death and putrefaction on the other. In the past algal blooms and proliferating weed growth has hampered flyfishing activity and threatened trout health, but I was pleased to see, on my visit, that water clarity and weed growth indicated a healthy balance.

Whilst Chris took landscape shots from the shore, Roger pulled the boat out a hundred yards for a drift into the jetty. In such a situation, on a new water, I either take local advice or stick to my fail-safe cast – a Silver Invicta on the point, a Kate McLaren on the mid-dropper and a Green Peter muddler on the top. Roger talked of black flies and silver-bodied flies, the Alexandra was often mentioned, but I thought the light wasn't just right for such a selection and set about proving myself right.

Now, human pride and smugness notwithstanding, there are generally pointers in fly selection to be had from the water colour and the ambient light conditions. You've got to start somewhere when your experience of the venue is nil. If, as I do, you have a favourite team, a sort of percentages line-up, it helps if it is well thought out. The Silver Invicta is a one-off – it will catch all game fish in stillwater locations from Shetland in the north, to places in the south where a pair of fluffy dice, a girlfriend called Shaza, and watching interminable soap operas is the height of culture. It is not incapable of failure, but somewhere close. The Kate McLaren behaves similarly, and a black fly on a cast for wild trout is pretty much a given.

The Green Peter muddler is as good a top-dropper pattern as you are going to get if the water is clear. Generally speaking, none of the above should be compromised by ambient light conditions. Black is good in strong sunlight and none; silver is slightly better in poor light, but the addition of light dressing materials helps when it is bright; and green is equally good in good and poor light; and all fit in with likely available food items.

That's the theory. The practice can often be something else. Roger and I started the drift and flogged the water to froth and moved nothing. We did, however, see a few good rises, which were obviously the product of good fish, but I could see nothing on the water to justify such vigorous action. I decided to have a go with dries nonetheless. The effort was fruitless, so Roger suggested a move, and we picked up Chris and headed east.

The move was a good one as Roger was swiftly into a fish which had taken his Alexandra. Not being slow to cop on, I stuck a Peter Ross dabbler on the point, and instantly joined the action. We were drifting across the mouth of a shallow bay in the south-east corner of the loch, and onto an extended point, and fish were everywhere. There wasn't much showing but they came to the flies with the sort of gay abandon one normally expects from half-pounders rather than the 1lb – 2lb characters we were catching. It was starting to verge on the surreal; beautiful, colourful, fat, fit and hyper-active fish after fish came to the boat, jumping and sprinting, and never giving up until the net enfolded them. It reminded me of a cross between Leven and Watten – the cracking quality of the former and the large quantities of very surface-active trout of the latter. Loch Eye is a riddle wrapped up in a conundrum. How is it that such a fine trout water isn't universally lauded? Perhaps the reason is that it exists in what is largely salmon fishing country with the Kyle of Sutherland system closely to the north and the Conon, Beauly and Ness to the south.

Roger and I adjusted our fly teams. He put a heavily dressed and ginked Loch Ordie on the top dropper and I slipped a Hielan Laddie muddler into the fray. Bigger fish started to appear through the rank and file, until Roger topped the day off with a cracking fish just shy of the three-pound mark to his Loch Ordie. Silver-bodied flies and a degree of surface disturbance was the medicine on the day, and I doubt if we could have improved on it. We kept looking for that elusive four-pound fish, but it was not to be. Was I disappointed? Not in the least. I had experienced a day's flyfishing redolent of former times when trout seemed numberless and all suicidally devoted to eating artificial flies presented right in the surface layers.

Chris, our photographer, was gob-smacked. He was a tyro fly fisherman and couldn't believe his eyes. Trout, larger than he had ever caught, were coming on a conveyor belt to the boat, being admired, photographed, unhooked and returned in a bewildering number. He simply didn't know which activity to photograph at any given time – the tussle of a freshly hooked fish at one end of the boat, or the unhooking of another picture-perfect fish at the other. Roger could see he was virtually itching to get his hands on a rod, so he contrived a deal – if Chris would agree to row the boat back to the jetty (petrol outboards are banned and electric jobs have only recently been accepted) Roger would give him his rod for a go. After a bit of tuition and a number of aborted tussles, Chris landed his best ever trout, a beauty of about 2¾ pounds. He was ecstatic and, I'm sorry to say, permanently lost to the world of normality and reasoned behaviour – he was now a fully committed fly fisherman! He also learnt a bit about rowing and was enthusiastically encouraged by Roger and me as we relaxed after our exertions.

You may travel a long way to fish for trout – Orkney and Shetland attract thousands every year, and Durness has its devotees who return annually; Ireland is frequently irresistible, as are the islands of the far west. I've been to them all and enjoyed the best they have to offer. But Loch Eye ranks up there with them all. It's a 'Brig o' Doon' sort of place, full of enchantment and magic. And may I suggest if you want the best out of the 'Fairy loch', don't forget to cast some silver into it!

– 28 –

Stay Calm

AS SMOOTH AS polished glass; not a ripple to be seen; the odd decaying sign of a rising fish; the air slightly misty with tiny midges drifting slowly by, going about their inscrutable business; all enough to make the bravest heart quail.

Flat calms are the bane of the fly fisherman's life, and if the pursuit is catching wild trout, a windless day will probably be full of frustration. But you are ever optimistic and determined not to be defeated by conditions that some will describe as hopeless.

The single biggest problem is that during such conditions trout get spooky. The surface of the water has always held deep terror to brown trout – that's where they are most susceptible to attack – and when it is calm, predators from above or below have clear views. This is obviously a learned phobia as it doesn't seem quite so well-defined in small trout. I suppose just as we can look at the surface of the water with apprehension, trout can look at the 'surface' of the air with similar fears – it's a dangerous world when you are not adapted to survive in it.

It is patently obvious that, within well defined parameters, the more the surface of the water is disturbed by wind the more likely that trout can be successfully approached high in the water, and the reverse is also true. Finer tackle, smaller flies and delicate techniques can be employed to offset the lack of surface disturbance, but I am convinced that fish detect the presence of boats (and noises from within them) much more easily in calm weather to the disadvantage of the fisherman. 'Water noise' associated with fly lines and surface disruptive patterns will also betray our presence to spooky fish. Although fish may be feeding avidly during calm conditions, their desire to stay safe and secure will always take precedence over any desire to feed. The odds are stacked against the fly fisherman.

Apart from the difficulty in approaching trout in still weather there is the added problem of lack of boat movement. Whereas rainbow trout, which tend to be constant 'movers' throughout a body of water, can be expected to come to the angler, brown trout are largely sedentary and territorial, and the angler must be continually covering fresh ground to come across new fish to tempt. If a flat calm occurs as a brief interlude amongst windy weather there will be water movement created by previous windy conditions which will cause the boat to gently drift across fresh ground, to a greater or lesser extent. However, if the calm conditions have prevailed for some time water movement will be markedly reduced or non-existent. There are few successful ways of dealing with this apart from continually being on the move yourself (oars and electric outboards are better than petrol-driven outboards to achieve this) or using natural features like burn or river mouths to provide boat movement.

So, what can he/she do to turn disaster into some degree of qualified success? Let's start with the obvious. Noise and disturbance must be kept to an absolute minimum. One thing which never ceases to surprise me in modern anglers is their lack of respect for their prey. They have little understanding of the finely-honed survival instincts of wild trout and make little effort to build any such awareness into their preparation or on-water behaviour. A dropped bailer or a clumsy cast will virtually clear the surrounding area of fish and, if they remain, they will be as wary as a turkey in Bernard Matthews' back garden.

Way back in the early 1980s, while most of my comrades cursed and fulminated at calm weather, I discovered that with an appropriate set of gear I could catch a reasonable number of fish by targeting individual 'risers'. Whereas most around me were fishing unnecessarily heavy lines I was using a #4-weight floater, an 18-foot leader of 0·18 mm nylon and, in calm conditions, only one dropper. I must admit I was lucky back then as I could tie and devise my own flies. Almost everyone else had to buy theirs from the tackle shops, which meant that, unlike me, they couldn't vary the bulkiness of patterns to suit wind and wave conditions.

My erstwhile comrade-in-arms, Norman Irvine and I experimented with patterns and eventually came up with a couple which suited flat-calm purposes. Norman devised a Greenwell's Glory variant which was absolutely superb at convincing bigger than average trout that it was a hatching midge, and I came up with tiny mini-muddlers which were very good as general food imitation when chucked in front of rising fish. There certainly was something about the construction of a mini-muddler which, regardless of colour, appealed to midge-feeding fish and I put it down to the surface-bulging capabilities of the deer-hair head when fished off a floating line. These same patterns and techniques also worked remarkably well on waters farther south, such as Loch Leven, in very similar conditions.

But, of course, calm conditions don't necessarily mean midge hatches or any other sort of hatches, for that matter. There is only one thing more daunting to a wild trout fisherman than flat-calm water without a sign of a rising fish, and that is a mirror-flat calm under a clear sky which seems to increase fish reluctance to come anywhere near the water surface, food availability notwithstanding. Pulling wet flies on a floating line in such conditions is usually a complete failure.

Fly selection for a 'flat' is always a problem when there is no obvious evidence from the presence of natural fly life or fish activity. However, the adoption of rainbow techniques in recent years has helped greatly. In the past many would simply give up when traditional patterns failed to make a mark, but as I noted above, those who could devise patterns to suit conditions had the advantage. The simplest advice for struggling anglers faced with no wind is select flies which are sparse and slim, and again the rainbow tactics filtering up from the south provide a plethora of suitable candidates.

BUZZER TACTICS

There seems to be an unwillingness by wild trout fishermen to adopt buzzer techniques which, given their undoubted effectiveness, strikes me as strange. I wonder whether this distaste stems from lack of experience, the absence of major midge hatches on favoured waters, or, simply, because those firmly wedded to pulling techniques feel that simply allowing flies to drift through the water layers is tantamount to 'doing nothing'.

I have colleagues who, when introduced to buzzer fishing far from home and being intrigued by it, have tried it at home and been stunned by its efficacy. A few years ago, a friend of mine accompanied me to Corrib to experience the duck fly hatch in late March. He was simply stunned by the technique and how effective it could be on wild fish. On his return to the far north-west he tried out his new skills and was pleased to discover that it was an extremely useful method when conditions dictated.

Obviously, buzzer fishing works best when trout are actually feeding on the natural. This can happen at depth or near the surface. There are few things more gratifying or enjoyable than carefully dropping some imitative artificial over the visible rise-form and simply waiting for the line to go tight when trout are visibly feeding on hatching insects or ascending midge pupae,

There are lochs where buzzer fishing will not work, so it isn't a comprehensive panacea. Lochs which fall into this category are those which are very low in productivity, brackish waters or, for some bizarre reason beyond the comprehension of man, those in which trout appear to be totally unimpressed with buzzer techniques.

During the early 1990s, Ian Hutcheon developed buzzer fishing which suited the majority of Orkney lochs. These static fly presentation tactics were adopted by all or nearly all of his colleagues and were tremendously successful when called for. Only two of our lochs failed to co-operate – Stenness and Swannay; Stenness because it was very brackish (very limited midge hatches), and the trout prefer very shallow water in which static fly presentation is virtually impossible; and Swannay, which for no good or obvious reason just wouldn't play ball.

An interesting aside re: Swannay – my old mucker, Norman Irvine, and I developed a minor tactic for evening flat calms. We would fish a short leader with a heavily weighted pattern (in this case a leaded shrimp, although pattern didn't seem to matter) and accurately cast it into the rings of a rising fish. After a count of 2 or 3, the rod point would be lifted, and more often than not the fish would savagely hammer into the fly. The only difference between our 'shredded limp' tactics and pure buzzer fishing was the very audible 'plop' as the fly hit the water, and we were convinced that it was the noise close by that initially attracted the trout, and the sudden lift in the fly which brought about the desired reaction. These fish were feeding on hatching midge, so the failure of bog-standard buzzer methods was even more baffling. Sometimes there are no answers, just more questions.

Another minor aside – when I travelled to Corrib for the duck fly hatch I noticed a marked reduction in the appeal of superglue-style buzzers as years went by. I now wonder if we are seeing a similar phenomenon on Loch Leven, as there seems to be little doubt that catching on buzzer techniques is no easy matter these days. In 2010 the catches on buzzer were phenomenal, not as good in 2011, and deplorable in 2012. Again, no answers, but plenty of theories. none of which you would stake your life on.

NYMPH TACTICS

Perhaps the use of the term 'nymph tactics' is too restrictive. Basically, all I really mean by the term is the use of slim, sparse, semi-imitative wet flies fished slowly. However, the use of fundamental patterns and styles more commonly associated with rainbow trout fishing won't take one far from the mark.

I well remember a specific day on a highland reservoir, Loch Glascarnoch, in Easter Ross, when this minor tactic saved me from frustration and a minor amount of embarrassment. Glascarnoch must be one of the least productive waters in Scotland. The use of the water for hydro-electric generation, and the vagaries of Scottish weather, causes radical fluctuations in water levels which badly affect food production in the shallows. I was working in the area and had rashly promised some browns for a barbecue that evening and thought (wrongly) that the extraction of a dozen ¼ pound fish would be the work of a few minutes.

After a couple of hours of casting a variety of options, wet and dry, to a 'sprackle' of rising fish I was stumped and baffled. Surely these fish wouldn't cast a scornful eye on any decently presented fly. They could, and they did. I had noticed a few duns (claret or, perhaps, sepia duns) drifting in the fragile breeze. I re-hashed my gear and presented the 'troot' with a couple of Diawl Bachs off a very slow intermediate line. A simple fast figure-of-eight retrieve across their bows quickly fulfilled my promise to provide the barbecue fish course.

I've been about a bit and have had some very spectacular and memorable days, but that Glascarnoch day readily comes to mind. It taught me many hard-earned lessons; principal amongst them is that trout living in a virtual aquatic desert can be as picky and discerning as your fattest, well-fed chalk stream inhabitant. That may come as a bit of an unwelcome surprise to many voyageurs heading north to sample some easy, thought-free, wild trout fishing.

The basic principles of 'nymph' fishing for wild browns are to use vaguely imitative, slim, sparsely-dressed patterns in a manner which trout expect to see edible items progress through the water. This is not always easy, as most of the little 'critters' have specialised means of locomotion. Some are deceptively fast (e.g. ephemerid nymphs), some medium-paced (e.g. shrimp and damsel nymphs), and others ponderous (e.g. water lice and snails). With no evidence to help I generally adopt a medium-paced retrieve, either with a figure-of-eight retrieve or simply long, slow pulls.

Colour choice can be important, and I generally go for colours suggested by the clarity of the water and the background colour of the weeds and sediments, plus a few small hot-spots to attract attention. On Leven I prefer olive/green Diawl Bach style nymphs with either chartreuse hot-spots or small jungle cock cheeks. Farther north I go for standard Diawls with fluorescent hot-orange spots.

DRY FLY TACTICS

My general advice for those trapped in bottle-flat calms is to avoid dry fly tactics, regardless of the temptation. Dry fly fishing just creates too much water disturbance when you are slowly moving or not moving at all. The sole result of continually chucking dry flies at the odd rising fish is to push it farther and farther away from you or simply put it down. On prolific waters where the average size can be small, dry fly in a calm can be productive. But to catch quality trout in such conditions it is always better to get sub-surface.

The great and fundamental secret of flat-calm fishing is to disturb the surface film as little as humanly possible. This is done in buzzer fishing by long periods between casts and fishing well below the surface; in nymph fishing by infrequent casts and the use of slow intermediate lines.

Remember that wild browns are very spooky in calms, and paranoid when near the 'top', and will quickly scurry away at the slightest disturbance on the surface. Even the commotion of trying to get the leader to sink will 'put the wind up' them. The odd fish can be caught by alighting a fly right on his nose, but you can't base a whole technique on such slight chances.

The basic rules for flat calm flyfishing are:
- create as little noise as possible
- be prepared to abandon standard techniques
- fish as fine as you can
- reduce number of droppers
- use oars rather than the engine, when possible
- and, don't get frustrated – stay calm.

The Sheelin fish which made the day for me

– 29 –

Sheelin: The Fairies' Lough

THERE IS A saying which goes "You can't cross the same river twice!" This also applies to lakes and lochs.

I have lost count of the number of times that I have returned to a fishing location to find my experience totally different to the mental pictures dredged up from the past. Sometimes even the landscape looks different. So, going back to that old saw about crossing the same river, is it you or the river that has changed, or perhaps both?

I know that when I returned to Sheelin this year for the fourth time in twenty-one years, my expectations were very high. Many phone calls to Kenneth O'Keefe, my good friend and guide for the trip, had, I believed, prepared me for all eventualities. I had mayfly dries that had worked extremely well in 2012; dedicated Welshman's Button patterns for sedge hatches which were more than likely to occur; and a new Campto Midge dry which was aching for a drink of Sheelin water. What could go wrong?

In the run-up to my arrival in Ireland, the news was good. The mayfly was just getting started, the fishing was taking off, and everyone was getting very excited about the prospects. Shane O'Reilly of the Inland Fisheries Ireland was also keeping me informed on the days before my arrival.

I was booked to stay at the Lakeside Manor hotel in Virginia, a warm and welcoming establishment sitting on the banks of Lough Ramor. When I arrived, and after booking in, I just had to take a walk to the lake shore to look over the water. I don't know if I'm unique in this – somehow, I doubt it – but as an angler I find it impossible to resist the appeal of water. When I was a kid, I couldn't pass a puddle without peering into it, hoping that some passing deity had placed therein a fish just for me. There should be a medical name for such a condition. Let's just call it *fisherman's syndrome*.

Standing beside the marina – Ramor is more of a yachting location than a fishing venue these days – with the drizzle clouding my spectacles, the first thing I saw was a mayfly drifting towards the breakwater. I thought this was a good omen, and an even better one when a trout engulfed it. There wasn't a major hatch on, it being early evening, but a few duns floated in off the main lake, and not one made it to shore. I could feel the excitement building. Tomorrow I would, at last, be back on Sheelin after a four-year absence, and Kenneth and Shane would be busting blood vessels putting me over the best possible fishing they could find.

Kilnahard is a place to gladden the heart of any fly fisherman. A launch site to dream of; whenever I arrive there, my legs start to shake with barely controlled excitement. As an old buffer, I am getting a tad jaded so there are only two launch sites that grab me by the unmentionables – the Pier at Loch Leven and Kilnahard on Sheelin. These are places where old, tired dreams are rejuvenated. Where every fish is a picture, and days become indelible memories.

Of course, into every life some rain must fall and, unfortunately, we seemed targeted on that first day. The weather was atrocious with heavy, thundery bouts of rain, but the mayflies kept hatching, and in some sheltered bays the water was alive with freshly hatched duns. However, the biggest *but* was that the fish seemed totally disinterested – not uninterested, because there was the odd rise, and gawd knows what was happening below the surface – it was as if the trout were saying to themselves "Yeah, well, mayflies! So, what's new? Maybe I'll have a few tomorrow. If I can be bothered, that is!" I suppose those with more experience in this field would not be surprised at this, but I was perplexed. How could the trout ignore such a bounteous bonanza? Ever since, my mind has returned to this conundrum and the only explanation I can come up with is that what was to blame was that old perennial problem – 'atmospheric pressure'.

Some people seem unaware or simply don't understand why variabilities in atmospheric/air pressure should affect fish and fishing. After all we, as humans, are only vaguely aware of extreme changes in atmospheric pressure, and even then, most of us don't associate the vague feelings of lethargy or lightness with ambient air pressure. But fish are highly sensitive to changes in air pressure for one major reason – one of the most important organs in most fish is the swim bladder. The swim bladder is a sac stretching the length of the body cavity which is full of gas –

Not exactly typical dry fly conditions

mostly nitrogen with small quantities of oxygen – which gives the fish buoyancy. To all intents and purposes, swim bladders render fish weightless in water. The gas in the swim bladder must be at the same pressure as the water surrounding it to achieve this weightlessness, and the water pressure is in direct proportion to atmospheric pressure. During thundery weather conditions, and particularly during thunder storms, atmosphere/air rises and falls in a chaotic fashion, and that affects the gas pressure in the body cavity of fish. Imagine you had a balloon in your gut and an outside agency kept inflating and deflating it irregularly. Imagine how you would feel?

Thundery weather can be worse than actual thunder storms because with thundery conditions there is no relief whereas after a storm has passed fish can react very positively and come 'on the take' in spectacular fashion. This is, however, not guaranteed, but one can always hope. Kenneth, Shane and I were on the receiving end of the most negative effects of the awful weather and fishing was becoming unrewarding and bloody hard work. I was determined I would get my

Roll-Over Mays to work in the face of all the evidence to the contrary. Kenneth was putting his faith in a Mosely May and getting the odd fish. I stuck to my Roll-Overs and was being 'skunked'. The annoying thing about this state of affairs was that I could spot the Mosely May amongst a batch of naturals but couldn't differentiate the Roll-Over from the duns even at fairly close range. If I could see the difference surely the fish could too? In 2012 the Roll-Over Mays had been irresistible to Sheelin fish, but now they were being treated with disdain. Such is fishing, I suppose.

But one of the best features of Sheelin fishing is that if one tactic fails for you there are other alternatives. The lake has some of the most reliable buzzer fishing available. If the weather is kind and favourable, campto buzzer will hatch most evenings in specific areas. I distinctly remember during my first visit to Sheelin in '95 taking a boat out from Finea one August evening. I hung around Sailor's Garden and witnessed a good rise of big fish continuing on 'til darkness fell. Seeing a good number of sedge hatching I assumed that's what the fish were on. I fished dry Sedgehogs until I was blue in the face, and never moved a fish. I was later informed that my assumption was wide of the mark, the fish were on hatching buzzer. Lesson learnt and stowed away for future use.

After a very frustrating day dodging downpours and fruitlessly chucking dry mays, Shane, Kenneth and I retired to the Crover House Hotel for a bite to eat, mulling over the possibility of a wee venture out at dusk. The vital factor for a successful jaunt of this kind is air temperature. If it falls too much in the evening from the daytime average, the fish won't come on even though a hatch may occur. Basically, if the water temperature exceeds the air temperature, fish will avoid the cooler surface layers. A good way to test if this is the case is to dip your hands in the water. If the water feels warm, then the air temperature is colder than the water. A common misbelief is that the water is so warm that the fish don't like it. The contrary is true. The cold evening air is chilling the surface layers, and it is this that the fish don't like. The water test shows that your hands are being cooled by the air to a temperature cooler than the water. However, if the evening air is even slightly warmer than the water your hatch and associated fish rise is very likely to occur.

After our grub, a wander to the car park showed that the air temperature had not fallen excessively, so we decided to give it a go. Kenneth decided on a trip to

Campto Crippled Midge

Hook:	Fulling Mill All Purpose medium, #12 & #10
Thread:	Very pale yellow
Body:	Mix of natural and golden-olive seal's fur
Tail:	Sparse bunch of white floss, tied short
Rib:	Flexi-Floss, red or claret
Post:	White floss
Hackle:	Light furnace hen
Thorax:	As body
Head:	Post material, tied and trimmed as breathers

Sailor's Garden and, not that I had any say in the matter, I concurred. Time to get things right and set the record straight.

Prior to travelling to Ireland, I had prepared a few patterns just in case we did get a shot at the evening midge hatch. Kenneth had suggested Griffith Gnat type patterns, which I tied up, but I also wanted a dedicated campto midge pattern tied Crippled Midge style. I have found this style of dressing to be very effective during evening sessions on Menteith and Leven due to the footprint size vs pattern size ratio. In other words, for a fly that is relatively small it produces a very large impression in the surface film, drawing as much attention as a strobe light in a deserted field.

When we got down to Sailor's Garden, there was still just enough ripple to start off with a two-fly cast. I stuck my Campto Cripple on the point and a Griffith Gnat variant on the dropper. Multi-dropper dry fly casts are an exercise in hope over expectation. When you've had a lot of experience in chucking dries for trout, especially browns, you'll find that a very high percentage of takes will come to the point fly, somewhere in the 80% – 90% region. If you find that you are getting more offers to the dropper fly than the tail, or any at all in fact, immediately ditch your point fly, replace it with your dropper pattern and select a new dropper replacement... And settle back for some hectic action.

As the evening light diminished, fish began to show. Good, sizeable fish in the 2 lb to 5 lb range. But they were very spooky in the quiet conditions. I was faced with a problem as the ripple diminished and the light faded. I knew I should change from a two-fly combo to a single dry, but which should be sacrificed, the Campto Cripple or the Griffith Gnat, the new boy or the local favourite? I stuck to my guns and 'benched' the Gnat. A good, long, accurate cast could get you in the area of the fish, but in which direction were they cruising? Decisions, decisions. An accurate cast was likely to get attention, whilst an inaccurate cast would be ignored. This was no easy game.

Kenneth and I got a few opportunities with fish which ventured close enough for a try, but I seemed to always get the direction of cruise all wrong, and Ken was faring no better. Then it happened. A fish was showing to my right and seemed a confident feeder, holding to a set direction across my fishing area. I made the cast a few feet ahead of his last rise, and waited, hoping the leader was sunk. Then there was that sound that every dry fly fisher loves to hear – 'slurp'. I lifted slowly and gently and felt a surging resistance. He was on. Boy, was he on. These Sheelin fish are in the prime of condition and don't hang about when they feel the hook, using every ounce of muscle to test your gear to the maximum.

Eventually Ken got the net under him and he was unhooked, admired, photographed and released. The Campto Cripple had scored, and I was well chuffed. It is not often that a new pattern imitating an insect never seen except in photographs will seduce the spookiest trout known to man. As the light dimmed, and the temperature dropped even further, we both had a diminishing number of half-chances, but nothing came of them and we knew the short 'rise' was fast drawing to a close.

As we motored back to Kilnahard I speculated on how that previous visit to an evening rise in Sailor's Garden, twenty-one years ago, would have turned out with the knowledge and experience I now had. The rise then was pretty spectacular with considerably more fish 'on the go', and I didn't remember them being particularly spooky either. But this was the same 'river', and you can't cross it twice.

– 30 –

Myths

BIG FISH – HEAVIER MONOFILAMENT

I believe that in selecting leader strength there are three factors to be taken into consideration. In diminishing order of importance, they are:

- Hook size
- Balance of tackle
- Individual fish weight

One of the biggest strains one can impose on leader monofilament occurs during casting. That period during casting when the flies go from backward movement to forward movement. During this action fly speed can be 700-plus mph. The crack you hear when the fly has gone from your cast is caused by the speed of the end of your monofilament breaking the sound barrier as it turns at the end of the loop. The strain created by these forces can snap monofilament like cotton thread, if the angler is employing heavy hooks on light leader material.

In contrast, using very light hooks on heavy monofilament means that the flies are not presented in a life-like or attractive manner. There has to be a balance between fly weight and the bend or flexibility inherent in leader material.

Most monofilament will have some spring in it, as will most fly lines and all rods. Pre-stretched monofilaments have their ability to stretch reduced, so it is worth bearing this in mind, especially if you are prone to break-offs in fish or are consistently discovering that flies are mysteriously disappearing from the leader. A leading tackle manufacturer supplies some lines in which the core is stretch-free. They are designed to improve the ratio between takes and successful hook-ups. If using lines of this type it is generally necessary for the angler to beef up his monofilament breaking-strain because it is regularly in the moment of 'the take' that most leader breaks occur. In order to convert energy into power, so that a rod can cast a line, rod spring and flexibility are essential. Rod springiness will not only help cast a line but will also absorb shock during fights with fish. Steady pressure will never break leaders, but sudden shocks will, particularly if the rod is horizontal and pointing at the fish. It is impossible for a leader to break in all but the most bizarre circumstances if the rod is vertical or near vertical.

As regards tackle balance, imagine you are on a spring salmon beat with a 15′ double hander and an 11-weight fly line, chucking a cone-head. You wouldn't link all that together with a 0·18mm leader. That would be ridiculous, I'm sure you'd agree. It is all to do with rod strength. Every rod has a test curve, which is the strength/weight needed to bend the rod a prescribed amount. This requires an appropriate leader strength. A leader which can't perform this action with reserves will break at the slightest shock. Balanced gear is vitally important.

So, if you are fishing a water where big fish can be expected, get your rod right and match it with appropriate monofilament – any break will be due to angler mistake.

IT'S A PERFECT DAY – LETS GO FISHING

Our understanding of the activity and feeding patterns of fish is so weak that we really don't have a clue when fish will be active and when not. To simply look outside or at a weather forecast before going fishing can lead to bitter disappointment. Feeding fish, particularly in fertile waters, will feed when the opportunity presents itself, and that means when there are plenty of food items such as in a hatch or bloom. And blooms or hatches can be triggered by factors beyond our comprehension, there being so many factors involved.

It is often thought that mild south-westerly winds and high cloud cover will always provide good fishing. It is also thought that bright weather plus cold northerly or easterly winds provide hopeless fishing conditions. Neither prophesies can be relied upon. I remember some years back when I was closely monitoring what made good and bad fishing conditions on a particular loch that mild westerly weather was proving hopeless and sudden easterly cold snaps saw better than average catches being returned.

For example, I was out on Loch Leven one evening in June with my club. It was bright, very cold and windy – virtually hopeless conditions, with no hope of a hatch. I thought 'top of the wind' to take any advantage of reduced wind chill and shelter which was available. After a couple of fishless hours, we decide to head a bit further down the wind in the region of Castle Island, which had been providing some sport in better conditions. Shortly after getting into position, I saw a fish rise... then another. Gulls had arrived from nowhere and were obviously feeding. I switched to dries and managed three good fish in what turned out to be a frenetic but short-lived buzzer hatch. From an objective perspective, if it hadn't been a club outing I would have been tucked up at home in front of a blazing hearth thinking I was missing nothing in such hellish conditions.

Anyway, you pays your money and takes your chances.

TROUT ARE JUST LIKE US

The clumsy word – anthropomorphism – should be tattooed on an extremity of every fly fisherman. It means crediting animals or other non-cognitive creatures with human behaviour, emotions or thoughts, and is one of the major stumbling blocks that bedevil fly fishermen. Where this wrong thinking affects us most is in trying to understand trout feeding regimes and basic behaviour.

In the early months of the season many fishermen expect to find fish in deep water. Whilst large numbers of fish may well inhabit deep water in the spring, they will not be feeding and be, to a great extent, uncatchable. Feeding fish will be in shallow water where weak spring sunshine can penetrate the water, reach the loch bottom, trigger algal growth upon which will feed shrimp, caddis larvae, and snails. Sunlight is the catalyst without which the food chain will struggle to exist.

Another omnipresent myth that clouds our thinking concerns trout breeding. A large proportion of wild trout anglers believe that the overwhelming majority of trout – if not all – spawn every winter. This belief couldn't be further from the truth. In any wild population of trout only a percentage of fish will spawn in the late autumn/winter. This means that in the spring the greater bulk of fish caught will be non-spawners (maidens), whilst the spawners will be virtually comatose in deep water waiting for the late spring food bonanza before becoming active.

While we're on the subject of fish being comatose, trout, being cold-blooded creatures, have the ability to render themselves inactive for long periods of times during the year. This generally happens in the spring (see above) and after the binge feeding which happens in the late spring/early summer. How often have you heard of folks out searching the waters with fish-finders coming across large populations of fish in open water, which prove impossible to catch?

One of the interesting aspects of this behaviour is that many of the trout caught when general prey activity is low have empty stomachs. I am almost wholly convinced that these fish have only recently become active after a comatose spell and are more opportunistic than fish which are more tuned into the natural cycles.

Another aspect of this behaviour generates that other great myth – "They've got to get hungry sometime!" Well, no they don't. Trout have no need to feed on a daily basis because, again, they are cold blooded. In the very fertile, productive bodies of water trout get very hatch-centric and they binge feed when the going is good. And fishing outside hatch periods can be very unproductive and frustrating. Hunger is an alien concept when applied to fish behaviour.

C&R IS ALWAYS A GOOD THING

There is a growing trend amongst fishermen to return every fish they catch, particularly wild brown trout. This is perhaps understandable where they are rare and endangered, for example in the southern part of the UK which is verging on being climatically unsuited to Salmo trutta. But in Scotland, and the bulk of Ireland, I venture to suggest this is an eccentric view.

Don't get me wrong. I return the vast majority of my trout, and only keep those that are destined for the table. But I have a natural horror and deep distrust of mandatory catch and release. It can be, I believe, inherently damaging to wild stock, and is riddled with anthropomorphism (yes, that word again).

The moral justifications for releasing or killing individual trout is beyond the scope of this piece, but the sustainability and welfare of wild trout environments is not. What concerns me most about blanket C&R policies is that it doesn't take into consideration any environmental or ecological factors pertaining to individual waters and their stock dynamics.

Let us take two totally different trout environments. The first is a low-nutrient, low pH water with good spawning facilities, and high stock levels. The second, a highly productive environment with reduced spawning availability, and low stock density. To impose an identical, catch-all (if you'll excuse the pun) C&R policy to those locations would benefit neither, or, at best, only one.

The typical Highland loch environment (the former) will produce high quantities of small fish in any given year, and to identify young from old fish is inherently difficult. I believe that in such locations bigger than average fish display a positive reaction to the water ecology and should be preserved at all costs. A general, positive harvesting campaign will not affect stock levels, and will provide improved feeding throughout the population. This should be of prime importance in any C&R policy.

In the latter, every fish in the low population will be capable of good growth, achieving trophy fish proportions. Small fish are tomorrows 'lunkers' and should be preserved at all costs. A high quantity of sexually-mature big fish competing for sparse spawning space at the end of the year will lead to redd overcutting and potential population diminishment. In such scenarios the removal of the odd adult fish, which has already passed on its genes in previous years, does no harm, as long as some degree of restraint is observed.

I've said it before, but it bears repeating – C&R is a valuable tool if used like a scalpel; used as a bludgeon it is worse than useless.

BIG TROUT WON'T TAKE DRY FLY

I have heard that there is a growing myth that big trout won't take dry fly. This puzzles me greatly because I have always believed the exact opposite.

In Orkney some years back, when I was experimenting with dry fly as a replacement for standard wet fly tactics for wild browns. I caught all my heaviest fish from all the major lochs – bar Stenness, which is brackish – on dry fly.

Why should dry fly be attractive to bigger trout? My theory, such as it is, is that nutritional economics lies at the heart of this mystery. Small trout can race about attacking anything and everything in sight and get a decent nutritional return on their effort from eating small, fast, active food items. For a big fish to do this would be suicide. Big fish burn up a lot of energy moving about and to get a positive return from a food item it either has to be big or, at least, require a minimum expenditure of energy to hunt down and eat. In a nutshell, big trout like a sure thing, and nothing's surer than slow or static food items. (Is this why so many big trout are caught on buzzer patterns?) I believe that fish instinctively know this.

What can be more effortlessly eaten than a fly trapped in the surface film? What can be more frustrating and nutritionally void than chasing a fast nymph to the surface, only to have it snapped up in front of you by a quarter pounder? To slip up a calm lane, sipping down hatching fly, is a very good deal for a big fish, leaving their smaller brethren to attack the ascending pre-hatch nymphs.

Trout like a dry fly. Well, big brown trout do, and that's a fact.

PATTERN IS ALL THAT MATTERS

Here's the situation: You and your buddy are fishing from a boat. He is catching, you are not. He's fishing a midge tip, and you've got your favourite full floater on. You reckon the fish must be a bit deeper – at a level he is reaching but you are not – so you add a few feet of mono to let your flies sink a bit deeper. Nothing changes. You still don't catch, and he's into his zillionth fish. He is becoming so smug you want to hit him with an oar.

Where is everything going wrong? Well, assuming that it's a level playing field and your flies are theoretically acceptable, one can only assume that your presentation is 'off'.

Presentation is a factor of flyfishing that most ignore. An old friend once tried to convince me that presentation is more important than pattern. I couldn't accept that then; I can accept it now. And what has led me to change my mind? The proliferation in modern line choice and nymph tactics for rainbow trout, that's what. Every line option, every change in retrieve style, will present your flies differently to the fish.

I now believe that it is better to present the wrong fly well than the right fly badly. Good presentation convinces trout; bad presentation puts them right off.

My classic example of this fact happened on Loch Leven and shook my long-held beliefs to the core. I was fishing with my fellow club mate, Bill. He had had a lot of success fishing a DI-6 and sparklers so I copied his end gear to the letter. Out we went, and Bill took a trout within minutes. Then another ... and another ...

and another. Meanwhile I hadn't had a touch. I was doing something wrong, but for the life of me I couldn't work out what.

I reeled in and thought about the variables on option. No obvious answer presented itself, so I thought I'd just watch Bill in action. Realisation struck me like a thunderbolt. Whilst I was holding my rod-tip below horizontal on the retrieve, Bill held his at an angle of 20°–30° to the horizon. My presentation was stop – start, whilst Bill's was smoother, the developing curve of line hanging from his rod tip maintaining a slight but regular 'pull' on the flies. That was all that was needed to convince the trout to take. Adopting Bill's retrieve technique, I quickly got back in the game and ended up with a very respectable basket.

One day Jimmy and I were having a miserable time. We tried all the lines and patterns and couldn't get a pull. Conditions were good, we were in the right place, but a blank was staring us in the face. In frustration I reeled in very fast to make another, probably futile, fly change ... and, wallop, I was into a fish. The secret was to retrieve as fast as was physically possible. Pattern didn't matter a jot, but speed through the water was everything.

Not in the best of condition but the fish is alright

– 31 –

Loch Lomond and the Anadromous Trout

THERE IS A name which we must get used to – anadromous. The term 'sea-trout' is now defunct. Trout (*Salmo trutta*) which migrate to sea and return to freshwater to breed are anadromous trout. The old term is too confusing to carry on in popular use.

All trout are, to a greater or lesser degree, migratory. If they drop down a river or burn, if they enter a loch, or if they even take up home in an estuary, that is a true migration. In its most extreme form, migrating trout go to the sea and fatten there to return as sexually mature fish. We all know that loch trout, if they can, will run up spawning burns to spawn. What the 'sea' trout and 'brown' trout do when sexually mature is exactly the same process.

To use the term 'sea-trout' implies that their home is the sea. Not true. Their home is the one that they fight back to in order to create the next generation. And that brood will spend years in freshwater before setting off to pastures new to achieve enough growth to produce another generation.

I love big lochs and they don't get much bigger than Loch Lomond. I know that a lot of people are very much daunted by big waters and I can understand this. Where do you start? Where are the fish? Where are the hazards? How deep is the water beneath me? All these unknowns can put you in a negative frame of mind.

I was lucky. I was going out with the two Colins – McCrory and Riach – and their combined knowledge of Lomond is truly comprehensive. Colin McCrory has his own boat on the loch and a better equipped vessel I've rarely seen. Haven't found the jacuzzi yet but it is in there somewhere. The single most important feature is the 'fish-finder' which is, of course, not required for finding fish, but for ascertaining depth, which is critical.

I could write books about the mysteries of sea/anadromous trout. Why is it that they inhabit very shallow water in the sea and relatively deep water in the lochs?

In Lomond somewhere in the region of 10′ is prime holding water, as it is in many other sea-trout waters. Salmon and brown trout in the same loch would prefer much shallower water. That is why the fish-finder is so useful.

As we prepared to set off the day did not look promising at all. Sunshine and a flat calm are of no use to those searching for sea-trout in stillwater. But the forecasts all said that conditions would improve with a freshening westerly breeze due about late morning, and high cloud to make an appearance round about the same time. So, when all were aboard and more or less ready to rock, we slowly putt-putted our way out of the Balmaha moorings.

As we headed through the channel between the land and Inchcailloch, a bird dropped out of the sky onto the calm surface of the loch. It was a "What the ……?" moment. We were staring at the presumably dead bird, when a peregrine falcon swooped down out of nowhere, picked up the apparent corpse and flew off with it. Fishing is a lot more than just fishing on the wild lochs of Scotland.

An acquaintance of mine always reckons that seeing a raptor on the way to fishing is the best of omens. I didn't mention this to the other chaps, but it was very much in my mind as we turned the corner and spotted a definite wind ripple amongst the islands.

Lomond migratory trout are pretty unique in many ways. They tend to have more colour in their 'jackets' than the typical specimen, with yellow gill covers being, more or less, standard. There are a few opinions why this should be. I tend to favour a DNA/genetic variation, others reckon that it may be due to environmental factors in marine habitat. Of course, some maintain that many of the supposed 'sea-trout' are, in fact, brown trout or, at least, have a tendency to wander from fresh to salt in a chaotic fashion, perhaps missing a sea season from time to time. I have fished anadromous trout all over Scotland and expect to see colour variation. Shetland fish aren't similar to Orkney fish – The Shelties looking like the archetypal, steel-grey fish whilst their neighbours can be strikingly like loch fish especially in breeding colours. I have caught sexually mature migratory trout on the Scottish West Coast that very much resemble Baltic fish, being a strange reddish-brown in colouration. There is no set pattern even though we think there should be.

Another aspect of Lomond sea-trout fishing which gives me pause is that whilst the floating line is invariably the 'go-to' throughout Scotland, this is not the case on

Preparing the plan of attack

Lomond, where an intermediate or a slow-sink line is favoured. Colin Riach went out with a slow sinker on while I set up a midge-tip, and it was only after Colin had three fish to the boat and I had only managed to raise a solitary individual that I changed to a Snowbee 'Kelly Blue'.

But we are maybe getting ahead of ourselves here. The favourite area to hunt these fish in Lomond is around the islands that lie between Aldochlay and Balmaha. It is an area of shallows and troughs, perfect freshwater habitat and there is always a chance here for a salmon or two, and that's where we were heading.

As the breeze picked up we set up to do a drift along the southern edge of Inchmoan, taking advantage of the weak southerly element of the westerly breeze. Colin McCrory guided the boat with one eye on the sounder, holding to the correct depth. Cap'n Fishy (aka Colin Riach) was into a good fish damn smartly off the Short Point, a trout that led him a merry dance before coming to the net. A very typical Lomond fish of about 3 lbs which had all the colouration previously mentioned. Strike one for the slow sinking line.

Very shortly after moving to the Inchlonaig shoreline, Cap'n Fishy hooked into another cracker at the Clay Holes, only slightly shorter than his first. I was doing very little only having moved one good fish which had obviously given up interest when some distance below the fly. Doubts about my approach were gathering in my mind. Colin McCrory mentioned that one of the regulars, a master of the dap, had said that dapping was pretty much a waste of time during the last month of the season. If this was, in fact, so – and I never argue with regulars – then the Lomond October fish seemed to be disinterested in patterns high in the water.

Drifting on the northern side of Inchlonaig was proving problematical as the slight element of south in the breeze was making ripple unreliable and, just as we approached the best of it, we lost the breeze entirely. Time for lunch.

After a convivial repast on the island, we discussed the afternoon's tactics. The wind was still light, so we decided to attack the shores that the wind favoured most. I was in a quandary about line selection. Would going down a few inches improve my chances? It was overcast and mild and I stubbornly refused to believe that fish wouldn't come to a surface-presented fly

We set up to drift the Geggles onto the Crin shore on western Inchcruin in about ten feet of water. Goddamit, Riach was into a fish straight away on his Cortland Blue. A smaller fish of just over a pound, but a fish nevertheless. Damn and bollocks, I was getting this all wrong. I stripped off the midge tip and replaced it with a Snowbee 'Kelly Blue', and got ready for some action. A word on pattern choice – Colin's fish had come to three different patterns, so colour and dressing didn't seem to be crucial. Depth was the factor.

Apart from the Inchlonaig drift, all the other drifts were short, concentrating on specific features such as offshore shallows and promontories and, as in all fishing for migratories in lochs, redoing drifts, or covering water just fished over by others, was a no-no. This necessitated a move.

There is a very productive drift between Inchcruin and Inchfad where exists a relatively shallow stretch of water ranging between 6 and 10 feet. If location details are required, slap-bang in the middle of the channel is a big red navigation buoy. We were drifting on the north side of this buoy, onto Ladies Point when I received a shoulder-wrenching take. A big, shovel-shaped tail waved at us from an impressive hole in the water.

Fare thee well, pretty lady

When one gets a take like that you are either 'in' or not – the moment has come and gone, making a strike unnecessary. I was 'in', no doubt about it, and this big fish pulled the rod down into an extravagant bend. We all knew this was the 'fish of the day', and it only remained to get it into the net. Easier said than done. There was power and there was weight, but none of the usual aerobatics. When it finally arrived in the boat we discovered it had the length of an 8/9 pounder, but the girth of a lesser fish. It weighed 6 lb and was on my most successful fly for the season – the Clan Goat. More questions. Was it an early spawner? Was it a poorly fed fish? Or had it finally reached the end of its days and was, what we call in the trade, a fish 'going back'. Without an autopsy it was impossible to tell, and I wasn't about to knock it on the head.

I had a friend heading home from the North Esk to stay for the night and, although it was only late afternoon, I was ready to go. The Colins debated whether to just drop me at the moorings and return to the fray or call it a day. Finally, they decided it had been a very successful and enjoyable day and one can over-egg the pudding.

A day's fishing is a series of problems that must be resolved. In retrospect, we did very well, but without Mr McCrory's guiding and sage advice it would probably have been a disaster. Cap'n Fishy had caught three fish, which for Lomond in the 21st century, is no mean feat, and I had my personal best anadromous trout which, in other circumstances, could have been the fish of a lifetime. Three very satisfied chaps disembarked at Balmaha.

Sorry! I missed that. What did you say? Oh, you are going to call them sea-trout, regardless? Funny that. So am I!

– 32 –

Lessons from the Corrib Classroom

I ROLLED INTO Headford after picking up Peter, the photographer, from Knock airport. I use the term 'rolled' advisedly because there is something about the layout of western Irish towns that reminds me of John Wayne or the *Gunfight at the OK Corral*. The sense of space is amazing. I was a tiny wee bit disappointed not to enter the Angler's Rest Hotel through swing doors, but meeting Joe Dollan, barman extraordinaire, in the bar made up for that. His wit and humour was a great solace in the evenings after hard hours spent out on the water. The beer and drams also helped.

We've all had tough fishing. It goes with the territory. We've all heard it. "You should have been here last week/next week/yesterday/tomorrow!" It doesn't help but leaves an avenue of excuse for poor performance.

The big problem is that we tend to make fishing plans weeks, months in advance with no inkling whatsoever of how the weather is going to play out. I must admit that my 'trip' luck has been pretty good, possibly because I always bear in mind that early summer in the British Isles and Ireland is plagued by dry easterly winds and cool temperatures, and book trips accordingly. Unfortunately, this is also a period when trout are feeding hardest and benign weather, no matter how rare, can see superb fishing. It is also a period of potential hatch intensity – mayfly, buzzer and sedge – which can provide a diverse flyfishing experience.

I was scheduled to fish Corrib in late May and I knew it was going to be tough. The winds were coming over from the Continent, and the air was as dry as James Bond's martini (or perhaps even drier). There is an inherent problem in this. Late May is mayfly hatch time, but insects are very reluctant to hatch when the air is very dry. It has to do with managing their body fluids. Insects (and other invertebrates) have an outward covering of chitin, a shell-like material which protects internal organs. It also helps restrict water loss, but only up to a point. So, perfect living conditions for non-feeding invertebrates call for a damp atmosphere. Bugs that can and do feed and drink are not so badly affected, but adult mayfly lack that ability and dry conditions in the atmosphere will not see hatches reach their potential. Aquatic insects, understandably, are particularly affected by dry weather during a hatch period.

There has been much speculation as to the causes of hatch demise in recent years. Climactic change, which sees major fly hatches coinciding with a recently regular period of intensely dry weather, may be a factor worth consideration.

Any road up, here we were – Peter, Declan Gibbons, Kevin Crowley and I – all itching to get out on the Corrib and tangle with her world-famous specimen trout. Declan and Kevin are employees of Inland Fisheries Ireland, with the former acting as our guide, and the latter as our … well, I'm not quite sure really. Let's just say entertainments officer.

In bright, hot, calm conditions we headed out for Inchnagoill, with Declan using his phone to try and find out where the action was hottest. Not much news was coming in, the weather conditions putting a halt to what had been in previous days a reasonable hatch of mayfly. On the east side of the island there were a few hatching mays and the occasional fish taking advantage, but they were unapproachable in the calm conditions. Leaving Declan the unenviable task of trying to lure a 'daft yin' to dries, I plumped for buzzers which seemed a more likely tactic under the circumstances. But our efforts were fruitless.

I learnt a lot about buzzer fishing on this trip. It would appear that my previous experience of buzzer fishing had led me to some erroneous beliefs, especially when it came to wild trout fishing. Rainbow trout, being the protein 'hoovers' that they are, will rarely turn down the opportunity of a buzzer correctly selected and fished. Loch Leven trout are pretty much almost always 'on them' in the late spring and early summer, and my experiences of trout lochs in the wild, in retrospect, showed that I had only used them as a back-up to traditional wet fly when conditions very much suited buzzers – calm weather with only midge 'on the go'.

Lessons learnt were that like almost all tactics there is a time and a place, and that buzzer fishing is no cure-all panacea. The Corrib fish definitely switched on to buzzers at specific times and outside these times buzzers were as hopeless as anything else. Also, location was everything. There was no point fishing the

A Corrib trout in all its majesty

artificials where no self-respecting buzzer would exist. Colour and pattern size didn't seem to matter much, within realistic boundaries, but timing, location and appropriate retrieve were essential. I am going to use a term now that will be repeated in almost all my reports from Ireland, and that is 'hatch lakes'. My belief is that trout waters can be divided into two types – 'hatch lakes' and the more common 'typical lakes'. In 'hatch lakes' trout are conditioned to, and expect, periods of intense food availability interspersed with periods of relative famine. During the hatches, very good fishing can be expected, all other conditions being equal. Outwith the hatches fishing can be very tough indeed. Trout, being cold-blooded creatures, fare well by glutting on the plenty and basically switching off when the plenty disappears. Unlike humans, they have the ability to slow down their metabolic rate to a crawl and one really good feed can keep them happy for weeks at a time.

'Typical lakes', or lochs, which lack massive hatches because of climactic or fertility conditions, encourage trout to be more opportunistic in their feeding regimes, and sport tends to be more averaged out throughout the season. The marrow spoon (an almost redundant tool in this age of 'compulsory' C&R) shows this off best. 'Typical lake' trout tend to have a varied selection of food items in their guts whereas trout from 'hatch lakes' will tend to have one type of food item showing. An interesting observation is that regularly on 'typical' waters the fishing is at its best when no feeding activity is noticeable, and fishing on 'hatch' waters can be hellish hard when no feeding activity is obvious.

We roamed around the bays and skerries hoping to stumble on some localised hatches, but we were fast coming to the realisation that the weather conditions had temporarily halted the mayfly hatch, and as the day wore on it was obvious nothing was going to change quickly. Declan suggested a trip into Balynalty Bay.

When I first viewed Balynalty Bay I quickly realised that this was trout heaven. I needed no words from Declan to recognise all the features that made this stretch of water a magnet to fishermen like myself who are inexorably drawn to big-fish water. The surrounding land is low and level, covered in fertile growth, all the hallmarks of prime wild trout water with a rich larder of food. I knew it would not give up its residents easily, but the challenge was undeniable. Probing with my rod it seemed to have an even depth of about seven feet, and the bottom was soft and silty. Prime territory for buzzer in all forms. But what would be the best approach? Dry fly or wet buzzer? A few rises across the bay showed that indeed the residents were large and, more importantly, feeding. The afternoon was fast drawing to a close, so I reckoned that wet buzzer on a floating line would have a limited time left to prove effective. Straight-lining buzzers is a depth-searching method and, as the day progresses, becomes less effective as fish rise in the water column. Chucking buzzers to rising fish can be very effective still, but that requires fish feeding on ascending buzzer and enough fish activity to make the effort worthwhile. On balance dry fly is a better option unless in a flat calm. With fish searching the upper layers there is a high possibility that a take can come 'out of the blue'. So, I thought, I'll give the pupae an hour and then move onto dries if buzzer start hatching.

At first nothing was forthcoming, and still the odd fish was 'boiling' the water with massive rise forms. I was beginning to think I had chosen the wrong option when I got an abortive pull on the buzzers, quickly followed by another one to Kevin's rod employing identical tactics. We were half-way there, only needing to convert abortive takes into solid hook-ups. We didn't have to wait long, a matter of fifteen minutes or so when my line lifted in the water to a solid take. The weight on the end of the line brought the realisation that this was the best fish of the day so far, and the fight was relentless, powerful and heart-stopping. Upon netting the fish I was slightly disappointed to find that my estimate was way over the top, the fish being somewhere between 2½ and 3 lbs when I was expecting something over four. Then I remembered I was using my Snowbee Prestige 6-wt, not my usual 7-wt, so that may explain my over-estimation. It was, however, a beautiful fish, with the classic Irish trout markings which are, to my eyes, unique.

Another drift parallel to the first one elicited no response to buzzers, so I changed to dries. Peter, who was using the second rod in the second boat and also on dry buzzers, brought two fish up, one of which looked like the grandfather of mine, but neither fish fully committed. And then it went deathly quiet.

Declan suggested that we head in Greenfields direction prospecting for a buzzer hatch, whilst Kevin and Peter decided on some wet fly pulling amongst the rocks and shallows between Balynalty Bay and Inismicatreer, where they incongruously took three decent trout on wet mays, long after any mayfly had stopped hatching. There's nowt as queer as trout, but it further underlines the need to be adaptable when fishing Irish lakes. You set off from home dreaming of massive mayfly hatches and teams of dries dancing in the ripple, then spend your day twitching back buzzers through the depths. But that's fishing for you – expect the unexpected.

We staggered back, awfully sunburnt and desiccated, to the welcoming arms of the Angler's Rest where we got a warm welcome from Joe. Alcohol and rest were much needed, and most definitely in that order. Joe provided the first, sheer exhaustion the second. Being the consummate bar-keep, Joe enquired how the day had gone, so we told him a story to make a statue weep copious tears. He, of course, came back with "You should have been here yesterday!"

Nowhere is 'Suggestion' more prevalent than in Irish mayfly patterns

– 33 –

Suggestion and Attraction

IN YOUR HAND is a small creation of feather, fur, plastic and steel. You are going to try to convince a sentient living creature to eat it. Should be impossible, don't you think? In fact, we do this very successfully on a regular basis. Have you ever wondered why?

We use totally inedible flies to catch fish by fooling them into believing they are food. Fish use a variety of senses to decide whether something is edible or not. Coarse-, and many sea-fish, use smell and/or taste to do this, and that is why a large part of our armoury for them is bait i.e. natural food that is habitually eaten. Trout, salmon and sea-trout largely use sight to identify food items, and the critical feature of this identification is movement. In other words, as far as game fish are concerned, if it moves it must be alive, and if alive then edible to a greater or lesser extent. This makes the fly fisherman's job relatively easy in that we can catch multiple fish on one fly, a task impossible with bait. And we can adapt specific fly patterns to make them successful for specific conditions.

So, if flies are visibly identified as food by trout, what are the features of a fly that makes it more successful than another? Modern scientific thinking suggests that trout eyes work very similarly to our own. Therefore, colour, size and integral movement are vital factors. By integral movement I mean utilising materials in the construction of the fly which are highly mobile, such as marabou, hackle fibres, and fine dubbing.

Wet flies (and by *wet* I mean any fly fished below the surface) can be divided into two main groups – imitators and attractors.

Attractors are patterns which bear little or no resemblance to anything natural such as boobies, blobs, FABs, flashy wet flies, and very large lures such as the Tadpole, Humungous, Snake, etc.

IMITATORS

Imitators vaguely represent in shape, colour and size natural food items that the trout can be expected to eat such as buzzers, nymphs, and vaguely imitative wet flies (traditional patterns) such as Bibio, Invictas, Mallard & Claret, mini-muddlers, Irish mayfly patterns, etc.

At first sight, many suggestive imitators may look nothing like the item they are trying to represent, but the fish are the final arbiters. There is a basic formula to the imitative quality of trout flies – the faster a fly moves the less an imitative pattern has to look like the natural. Buzzers are fished very slowly so buzzer patterns are tied to closely imitate the natural. Medium paced insects like corixa, for example, are replicated with patterns that give basic shape and stand-out features like 'paddles'. Very fast nymphs, bugs and fry – damsel fly larvae, beetle patterns, etc. – need only basic colour, shape and size in their replicas to do a good job.

Traditional loch-style flyfishing is the ultimate manifestation of imitators and attractors. It has always puzzled anglers why many wet flies have 'wings', but they come from an age when fishermen cared less for imitation. Many modern tyers care little for such affectations as wings and concentrate more on mobility of tying material. As the decades have passed we tend to fish our flies slower and mobility of materials is vital, especially amongst rainbow trout flies. Rainbow trout are much more discerning when it comes to imitation, and flies for them seem to need to be closer copies of food items. Brown trout, generally speaking, prefer flies fished a degree faster so close copy patterns are not so important, nor effective.

Colour of pattern can be misleading. Very often matching colour leads to failure, because what stimulates the trout to attack may not be what we imagine to be the critical factor. Humans use colour as a recognition point more than fish, at times. In my opinion, presentation of imitative patterns is crucial. The 'right' fly presented badly is much less successful that the 'wrong' fly presented correctly. A buzzer of the wrong size, shape and colour, presented properly will out-fish a close copy one presented badly.

ATTRACTORS

Broadly speaking, attractor patterns are colourful, bright and can be verging on the garish. They are designed to appeal to the predatory, aggressive nature of trout. As such they do not need to imitate anything naturally preyed upon by them. Size, colour or shape are not necessarily important and, generally, they can be fished at a faster pace than natural food items would normally move. Erratic retrieves can also be a factor which make them work.

Many modern attractor patterns, such as boobies, blobs and FABs have been designed to be used for rainbow trout and are largely much less effective for brown trout. Many of the larger lures such as tadpoles, humungous, etc. with long, highly mobile tails can be highly attractive to both species, and the same can be said of sparklers and flashy traditional patterns.

Presentation of attractors is equally as important for attractors as imitator patterns. It is fair to say that most of the time attractors are fished on sinking or intermediate lines. This is not because they work better when sunk, but because:

1. Trout, not actively feeding, can be induced to take by appealing to their aggressive nature, and such fish may often be found lying deeper than is normal for a feeding fish, and/or:
2. The normal speed of retrieve for attractors being above average, a sinking line will hold the flies at the correct depth for a longer duration. Finding the correct depth will be dealt with elsewhere.

It is not essential that attractor patterns be fished fast. Many of the modern ones – FABs, blobs and boobies – can be most effective when fished very slowly or static. This is puzzling because there is nothing living in, on, or underneath the water which resembles them in any way whatsoever, but as I always say, you can't argue with the fish.

Sometimes flies perceived to be attractors, principally amongst traditional patterns, may, in fact, be imitators. Many fly fishers believe that any fly pattern with a tinsel body must be an attractor, but this is not necessarily true. The Peter Ross and the Teal-Winged Butcher are amongst my favourite early-season midge pupae imitators, and my least favourite fry imitators. Strange but true.

MIXING THEM UP

It is common and good practice, whether fishing on lochs or reservoirs, for browns or 'bows, to mix imitators and attractors on the same cast. It is a mistake, I believe, to put all your eggs in one basket.

Just as its good practice to mix up pattern colours on a multi-fly cast, so it is with imitators and attractor patterns. One of the most successful tactics for rainbow trout is the 'washing line' which incorporates a floating attractor such as a FAB or a booby on the point fly position and nymphs and/or buzzers on the droppers. Even when fishing lures for brown trout I will generally add a vague imitator on one of the droppers, usually the top dropper – the attractor pulling the fish into the cast environment where the imitative pattern is often selected in preference. This is one of the great lessons of flyfishing, use the basic instincts of fish against them.

MATCHING THE HATCH?

There are many factors which can and will affect the types of flies best put on the cast. If fish are actively feeding it makes sense to use imitative patterns if the prey item can be identified and, most importantly, if the prey's attracting behaviour can be imitated. Very often trout can be fixated upon food items which are exceedingly difficult to imitate whether because of their size, or because it is their movement which attracts the fish and that can be difficult to replicate. It may not be just the shape, size and colour which must be imitated, but behaviour as well.

It can happen that luring the fish away from their favoured food by using an attractor can be successful. Sometimes during a caenis (an insect notorious for being difficult to replicate) hatch, a small booby or lure pulled across the path of feeding fish can bear fruit.

Another common and perplexing problem which can occur is when imitating a natural fails utterly. I well remember a period when there were masses of daddy-long-legs falling on the water, and the trout were having a field day. I had some proven daddy patterns, but the trout just ignored them. It took me a while, but I discovered that the trout would only take the natural when it was drifting across the water, pushed by the breeze. Any static flies (including my artificials) were perfectly safe from trout attack.

And last but not least, before you go all out imitating an obvious food item on or in the water, be sure you've identified the correct culprit. If you are not killing fish, then spooning is not an option, and observation may best supply the solution. It is very easy to assume that the most obvious solution is the right one, when it may in fact be miles from the truth. A prime example is in an olive hatch. It is always tempting to think the rises are coming from trout taking the adults, when in fact, more often than not, fish are targeting the ascending nymphs, pre-hatch.

The upside of a hatch. Two rods; two fish

– 34 –

One Out of Three Will Do

IT ONLY BECOMES apparent that phases of a fly fisherman's life exist when you get to a certain age.

The first phase, at an early age, is going fishing to catch a fish. More than one is a bonus. A memorable event in my very early teens saw me catch a wild brownie out of the river Eden in the centre of Cupar in Fife. It weighed about twelve ounces, was caught on a tiny little Iron Blue Dun dry fly, and I was so excited I ran all the way to Grannie's house with it in my hand, only to realise a short time later that I had left my rod on the footpath beside the river.

The second phase is to catch lots of trout, and that saw me haunt the Harray Loch like an evil spirit. My great friend, Norman Irvine, and I spent every spare minute we could drifting the skerries catching dozens of fish with an upper limit of about 1¾ pounds, and more was never enough.

In this slaughter of the innocents we would occasionally come across a 'monster' which led me seamlessly into phase 3 – go out and get the biggest fish ever. Funnily enough, Norman was not dragged down that path to the same degree, but for me it was an irresistible urge.

Many people never leave this stage. In fact, all of these phases can see the end of the road for many anglers. However, I have evolved into a phase 4 angler and that involves setting out with a distinct objective in mind, avoiding all distractions to prove or disprove a theory, or achieve something brand new. This involves leaving the well-trodden path and venturing into unknown (well, for me at least) territory. One of my first ventures into the phase 4 zone saw me on Loch Borralaidh in Sutherland on a bright, calm day. Instead of beating my head against a trout brick wall I decided to try something which had been lurking deep in my mind for years – attempt to catch char from the Borralaidh abyss on epoxy buzzers. I stuck on an Airflo Fast-Glass line and a team of buzzers, positioned myself so that I would very slowly drift inside the eastern edge of the abyss and – glory be – had a char on my first cast, went on to have a double hook-up, and then the cloud arrived and I went back to trout. Job done.

Other projects have included catching ferox on fly, luring sea-trout to static wet flies and trying to get loch salmon to accept a dry fly, and in that order they were very successful, occasionally successful and bloody difficult.

However, my initial experiences with char in Borralaidh had lit an unquenchable fire in me that has never gone out. Char are a fascinating fish, largely unknown by UK fly fisherman. Many think they are a rare and endangered species, but this is a misunderstanding of their true status. Where they exist, mainly in the large deep, glacially-formed lochs of the far north-west of Scotland they can abound in very large numbers, and just because we can't see them doesn't mean they are not there. The char (*Salvelinus alpinus*) is a remnant of the last ice age, a fish which entered our freshwater systems as soon as said systems became ice-free about 12,000 years ago. Back then they were migratory/anadromous (as they still are in the Arctic Circle) and came and went freely. As the climate improved and the land masses rebounded from under the weight of millions of tons of ice, relict populations became trapped in specific lochs and lakes, lost their migratory impulses and learned to thrive in waters in which most other fish species couldn't survive.

Generally speaking typical char habitats are very deep, large-volume lochs in which temperature variation from summer to winter is minimal. There exist some sub-species which are fish-eaters, but primarily char feed on zooplankton such as daphnia, and slightly larger life forms such as chironimid larvae and pupae. Char preferring, as they do, deep water, anglers rarely come across them by accident, but they can be sought out and are not difficult to catch if you know what you are doing.

Calder, in west Caithness, is a classic char loch and has been on my bucket list for a very long time, and though I've fished the Caithness lochs and rivers on numerous occasions I first visited Calder in mid-July 2016. I had a plan. Well, three plans actually. Firstly, I wanted to see a good Calder brown. Should be no problem there, I hoped. Secondly, I planned to try and catch a Calder char, and if that worked out, push on for an unlikely ferox. Big trout have been taken there occasionally, but very rarely by design. I suspect their numbers are low in Calder which might be a reflection on char population density. However, as I was to find out, small trout in the 6″ to 8″ range are prolific and are a very good substitute for char on a ferox menu.

But plans fall apart due to factors outwith control. Hugo Ross, Mr Caithness Fishing – who through his affiliations with the Dounreay Flyfishing Association got us a boat – accompanied 'Puck' Kirkpatrick and myself on our expedition and we all set out with high hopes. But a lack of breeze put the trout component of the plan on the back burner. So, the char hunt moved up the 'to do' list. I was convinced that fishing epoxy buzzers at the correct depth, if we could find or reach it, would be the best method for char capture. I was fairly sure that, it being the middle of the year, any char would be lying fairly deep. They will come into shallow water or rise to the surface over deep water, but generally in the spring or autumn, and when the light levels are low. One of the features of fishing which sets it apart from every other field sport is that we have to gain the cooperation of our prey. Attempting to search the whole loch was beyond our reach, so we agreed that to fish over the deepest water and its approaches was as much as we could manage in the time allocated.

Using the historic bathymetric maps of Calder it was very easy to identify Calder's deepest water which lies off the east shore, about three-quarters of the way up the loch in the northern quadrant. It is interesting to note that Calder's greatest depth is universally quoted as being 85 feet, as provided by the Bathymetrical Survey of the Fresh-water Lochs of Scotland, 1897–1909 (http://maps.nls.uk/bathymetric/chart/2156). Since then, a dam has been built to increase its utility as a water supply for Caithness which has increased its depth. One of the best trout areas in the loch, New Bay, in the south-western quadrant didn't exist until the dam was built. The current greatest depth is now quoted as being 120 feet although many sources still use the old figure.

That we were in wild country was soon brought to our attention as we were motoring into position. Puck had rigged for browns and had a Sedgehog on the top dropper. Laying his rod along the gunnel the Sedgehog dropped down near the underside of the fibreglass and a sodding great spider sprang out, grabbed the 'fly' and proceeded to drag it back into its dingy lair. No matter how long you spend in this game, there's always something new to consider. Eat or be eaten seemed to be the rule on Calder.

If you can fool a spider, trout shouldn't be a problem

The char hunt began. I rigged up an Airflo DI-7 with a three-dropper cast of epoxy buzzers, primarily black, and fished them in front of the boat in standard practice using a very slow, figure-of-eight retrieve. I started getting takes almost immediately, but all the hooked fish were small browns. 'Guesstimating' that any char were liable to lie below trout levels, I decided to cheat. To reach even greater depths I chucked the flies behind the slow drifting boat and fed out a good few metres of line and let the whole drop into the depths.

With the line dropping almost vertically into the abyss things went a bit quiet for a while. Then a take. "Must be a char!" I thought. But no, another 8″ brownie. With a near vertical line drop and somewhere in the region of 40 yards of line out I reckoned the flies must have been at least 80 feet – if not more – down in a hole which was measured at plus or minus 120 feet. This was both encouraging and discouraging. It showed that there were feeding fish at an incredible depth. Wee brownies feeding at 80+ feet! Hard to get your head round that. But where were the char? I decided not to attempt to fish deeper as Hugo reckoned we must be approaching the southern extent of the 'deeps' and the depth would diminish as we drifted ever further south.

The venture failed. We never did catch an elusive char. There could be a hundred reasons why not, but I suspect that mid-July, even in northern Scotland, is hardly the optimum time to go searching for an arctic species. But as we contemplated the deeps, there were an increasing number of mayfly drifting the ripple in front of us. There was a good hatch on and it was time to forget about char and ferox and concentrate on the more amenable brown trout.

New Bay is a stretch of recently drowned land in the south western corner of the loch, created by the damming of Calder. It is obviously more fertile than the rest of the water and the average trout size is considerably enhanced as we could see by the water displacement created by fish taking mayfly duns. So, after a day of mind over matter and relative inactivity, we were a virtual frenzy of feeding fish, and some damned fine trout amongst them. Having been through the mind-numbing boredom of trolling the depths with a fast sinking line it was sheer joy to put up the floater with a couple of dry flies. During my travels I had picked up a garish mayfly dry pattern of bright green seal's fur and peach cdc. I suspect it was garnered on Lough Erne from the Dromore boys, but I can't be certain. Anyway, it never did a thing for me in the Emerald Isle, but it knocks the stuffing out of Scottish browns and rainbows, saving many a tough day on Menteith. It came to the fore here on Calder and the good browns slurped it down with relish.

We had spent most of the day in a fruitless challenge, and now it was time to indulge our appetites, and we were more than ready. Hugo ghillied while Puck and I had a wee competitive spell seeing who could snag the most and biggest fish. I have to admit it was pretty much a draw as Hugo took us from fish to fish. After a tough day this was an exhilarating and surprisingly relaxing end. But I will return one day to take up where I left off, to add another loch char to my list. I've had char from Borralaidh, Trealaval, Brora and Oscaig. Calder won't defeat me and must be added to the list.

A brief break from action can help refine tactics

– 35 –

Unfathomable

SOME YEARS BACK I went through a bad spell of not catching. It happens to us all and is as unfathomable as quantum physics or the ways of women.

Fishing success, like success in all forms of sport, is in the head. Darts players who can't let go of the 'arrow', clay pigeon shooters who can't squeeze the trigger, professional footballers who continually 'balloon' the ball over the bar, and normally proficient anglers who suddenly can't raise a smile. It's a psychological problem normally referred to in the trade as 'head up arse syndrome', but is, in actuality, lack of confidence. And nothing locates head up fundament more securely than fishing your loved waters, with favourite flies, in preferred method and being 'skunked'. Not just once, but day after day after day. And, to add deadly insult to mortal injury, your pal, day after day, is 'horsing' them into the boat to a band playing. And the more he catches the more you consider golf or interior decorating as replacement hobbies.

Norm and I had fished together for years. Until I left Orkney, we pretty much fished together all the time. Norm is probably the best wild loch trout fisherman I've ever known. Some of the things he did were near miraculous, and he could be nauseatingly successful in even the most hopeless conditions. A lot of people thought I had taken an easy route by forming a fishing relationship with Stormin' Norman. They seemed to think that because I was sitting alongside a fishing machine that, by some inexplicable osmosis, his talents would naturally migrate towards me. Nothing could be farther from the truth. To even stay in his slipstream, I had to fish my socks off pretty much all the time. I couldn't relax for a moment or I'd wake up to see his diminishing form disappearing over the horizon. Natural fish-catchers will break your heart.

Norm is a classic 'natural'. He is a top-class fish-catcher, who never tried particularly hard to understand the why and wherefore of his ability. His talent isn't the kind you can quantify. Talent of this kind fades when you study it too hard. Have you ever driven a stretch of familiar road and realised, at the end of it, that you couldn't remember the individual miles? That's a bit like this type of ability. Modern sports psychologists say that a learned ability becomes anchored in the brain and if the sportsman lets his subconscious rule and figuratively 'takes his hands off the wheel', perfect shots, strokes, whatever, are the result. I've seen videos of blindfolded clay pigeon shooters performing miracles of this kind.

I, on the other hand, never had the confidence to 'take my hands off the wheel'. I was a 'cause and effect' man. There had to be a hard core of logic in my decisions and actions. I didn't like miracles. I wanted to understand my successes and failures. Because I wasn't a 'natural' I had to be in control. I'd put on such and such a fly, on such and such a line, in an area which I had selected for good reason, and when I caught fish, everything came together in a most satisfying manner. In this way I caught my share plus a bit more, and it was all down to understanding, experience and logic. Norm would do his 'thing' in all the wrong places with a ridiculous choice of fly pattern and come in with a boat-full.

A classic example: We were out on Boardhouse, taking part in a club match. It was a foul night – low cloud, lower temperatures, and a harsh, biting wind from the north-west. Reasonable expectation was a brace or two of trout, hard-earned. Due to the conditions I was convinced that fish were unlikely to 'come to the top', so I decided that a slow sinking line and a team of mini-lures was the percentages bet. Norm stuck to his floater and bushy wets, with a ginked-up Hedgehog on the top dropper. I slowly started to get a bit of interest and winkled out a couple of fish in a 'head down, grind it out' fashion. Norm couldn't get a 'nod from a donkey'! I heard him mutter "Bugger it!" as he delved into his box, coming out with a DI-7 fast-sinking line. Norm never was a guy for half-measures. He simply stripped his leader from the floater, attached it to the sinker and chucked it out. Almost immediately he was into a fish ... then another ... and another... "Sod this!" I moaned, "What are you getting them on?" "The Hedgehog!" "On a DI-7? Do you mean you haven't changed your flies?" "Yeah. They're taking it just as it sinks below the surface." And that was exactly what was happening. The Hedgehog, on delivery, would sit up on the surface, and as gravity and line weight exerted their effect, the Hedgehog would slowly sink beneath the surface ... and a trout would snaffle it!

This was totally illogical. Temperature and wind effect indicated that feeding levels would be a few feet down, not on the surface. Hedgehogs catch fish when they are on or just *emerging from* the surface film, not when submerging into it. Everything was wrong, but it worked. I could have sat out there for days and never adopted such an irrational tactic.

So, it wasn't unlikely that at some stage I would become swamped with Norm's bizarre success and lack of logic and enter a phase of bewilderment and lack of confidence. His solutions to problems couldn't help me directly because there was no cause and effect, and I quickly learnt that to try and emulate his tactics was a sure-fire route to disaster. This came to a head during a period of no-catch for me. We'd been fishing Swannay a lot, and as my catch rate slumped, Norm's started to go through the roof. Like a fool I started to closely copy Norm's tactics and techniques – giving up my customary route to success with logic and understanding and replacing it with a sort of random approach to fly selection and retrieval technique. If a fly seemed logical, I'd ignore it, and when conditions called for specific techniques I'd head off in the other direction. All this came to a head one day while we drifted up through the maze of skerries just off Louderhill. Norm as catching; I was not. And the more acute this became the more I watched him to discover what he was doing that I wasn't. In a blinding flash of inspiration, I realised I wasn't really fishing at all. Sure, I was chucking out flies in front of the boat and pulling them back, but I wasn't 'down there with them'. I was watching Norm like a hawk and copying every nuance down to the grunts, snorts and farts, and was only going through the motions of flyfishing. It suddenly became apparent to me that my flies were operating like dead things being dragged through the water. Confidence in my own ability had gone, and nothing catches more fish than confidence.

I promptly turned my back on him as much as I could, blocked him from my thoughts and did my own thing. I tried to 'swim with my flies' and invest them with life, but most importantly, I relaxed. Slowly my rhythm returned; the rod became an extension of my arm and I was 'with' my flies. Fish started to come, and with them came a feeling of 'rightness', an understanding that a fly in water is just a dead thing without the rhythm and confidence that comes from a oneness that an angler feels when he doesn't try to analyse and control every second. The brain/

subconscious knows what to do; overriding this rhythm leads to a mechanical beat which is an affront to a natural creature like a trout.

I have never been caught out like this again. I have watched other, successful, anglers to get an insight into tactic and technique, but always ensure that what I learn is *added* to my repertoire, *never* replacing items on it.

– 36 –

Three Men in a Boat

I SAT AND thought about it. Giving a short pull to the oars to get us bang-on the contour line, the thought that we should be seeing fish nagged at me like an unreachable itch. The conditions were as close to perfect as possible – moderate westerly breeze, high cloud cover and shirt-sleeve temperatures.

We were into our second, maybe third, drift and we hadn't seen a fin. But Swannay could be like that. Approaching the loch from the Swannay Farm end, on first seeing the loch it was common for Norman or I to say "It looks perfect. Let's go home!"

But this was no ordinary trip out. We had Peter Gathercole with us and he needed some fish photographs to augment an article I had planned.

Norm and I would operate a boat system whenever we were taking a friend or acquaintance out for a day's fishing. And it went something like this:

Just prior to setting out we would all flip a coin. The loser would be on the oars for half-an-hour. Coin flip again for the remaining pair, and this also-ran would be fishing for half an hour. The overall winner would be fishing for 1 hour.

When the half hour is over, the guy with the half hour's fishing takes the oars, and the guy coming off the oars has an hour's fishing, and the remaining chap has a half hour before taking the oars,

A minor modification often used centred round the catching of fish. A rod who has one fish is declared 'pregnant', and should he take another during the same fishing period, he relinquishes his fishing position to the chap on the oars.

Pregnancy was not a great concern on that day, and as I adjusted drift somewhat, it occurred to me that a radical change of some sort was needed to stir up some action. I was a great fan of a long shank Worm Fly in those past days, and had recently constructed some traditional tandem Worm Flies on a whim. They had never tasted water as I couldn't use them in club competitions; tandems were banned for some reason. But as I flipped through my mental fly box, searching for a pattern that would break the blank, those tandem Worm Flies kept popping up.

My 'oar time' was coming to an end, and a decision had been reached – a size 12 tandem Worm Fly on the bob. Being relieved on the oars by Peter I picked up my rod and made the necessary adjustments and started chucking my new fly arrangement down the wind. After a few casts a slight disturbance in the water appeared where I judged the Worm Fly to be. No monster, I reckoned, but beggars can't be choosers. I flicked the flies back over where the fish had showed and lifted the Worm Fly up 'on the bob' and trickled the fly back in what I hoped was an enticing manner. Well you can smack my bum and call me Moira if one of the biggest trout I've ever seen first-hand didn't roar out of the water, engulfing the said fly. In those far off days we used 4 weight rods and 4 lb breaking strain leaders, which were fine for day to day wild brownies but not much use for a bullying big 'un. A cool, calm, reflective mind would have advised letting the trout hook himself on a tight line using the rod as a buffer to absorb the shock. That was what the reflective and objective angler would have done. I, on the other hand, with my chin on my chest and my eyes popping out of my skull, struck like a good 'un. There was a crack like a pistol shot as the leader fractured, and away swam the trout taking my dreams with him.

Silence reigned supreme in the boat. Nobody said a word. Peter and Norm looked at me cautiously, expecting me to burst into tears. I finally broke the stalemate with peals of laughter, a habit of mine when I lose a particularly big fish. This surprises people but I try to explain it like this – man, is a fairly sophisticated, cognisant animal, has just been comprehensively stitched up by another animal with the IQ of a ham sandwich (and if that isn't cause for laughter, I don't know what is); and secondly, because you're in a boat with company you have a witness to your experience who can vouch for you when you tell others of losing the fish of a lifetime.

And that gets to the very heart of the matter. Boat fishing offers you something which no other branch of flyfishing can – close companionship. It has always struck me as being a strange aspect of fisherman's nature that, on the river, anyone encroaching within 100 metres produces strong psychopathic tendencies, whilst we will sit within touching distance of a fellow angler in a boat and develop friendship so strong that it will make your significant other jealous.

I think that's why boat fishing is my favourite branch of flyfishing. I simply love the companionship, the craic, and the sharing of information, experience and opinion. You learn an awful lot about someone you regularly share a boat with, and friendships created in a dinghy regularly last for life.

But putting aside the aesthetics for a moment there are practical benefits to be gained from having one or two others in your boat. For a start an equal distribution of weight in the boat helps with the drift. Those going afloat on their own can get round this by deploying a drogue. Many modern anglers use a drogue as if it is an essential but we old school guys look upon it as a necessary evil to be used only as a last resort. If you are fishing in moderately shallow water and have had a successful drift you may wish to fish it again. If you have just dragged a bloody great big parachute through it you might find subsequent drifts surprisingly unproductive.

As I previously mentioned, the sharing of ideas and the possible solutions to fishing problems makes finding solutions a whole lot more likely with two or more minds tuned in. Many years ago, I was fishing an inter-county match on Loch Spiggie in Shetland. This annual event was held between two six-man teams from Orkney and Shetland and was a home game every other year. It was keenly contested back in those days and competing anglers fought to the very death. One of the interesting aspects of this match was that the local angler would bring along a pal to act as ghillie. That day on Spiggie Stephen and I had local Shetland angler Colin as our ghillie, and, of course, he was giving Stephen as much advice and encouragement as he could without appearing too partisan.

It is safe to say we were struggling. The conditions were excellent, if a tad bright, and Stephen and I knew we should be doing better than we were. There wasn't much chatter. We were too busy searching our minds for a key to unlock the mystery of the missing killing pattern. Colin poured a continual, unending stream of whispered advice to Stephen, to a point where I could tell poor Stephen was heartsick of hearing it. Amongst Colin's never-ending, interminable, ignored whispered instruction, one phrase rang like a clarion in my mind – "Have you tried a Dunkeld Muddler yet?"

Trying hard not to appear to be reacting to Colin's prophetic words, I casually selected the appropriate fly box, withdrew a Dunkeld Muddler, slipped it on the cast... and I was away. Fish after fish slammed into the fly until it started to get a tad embarrassing. Stephen persevered in his search with added frenzy now knowing that there was indeed a killing pattern. That his boat partner had stumbled on it only added desperation to the mix. Little did he know that he had heard the correct advice and rejected it.

Colin offered to net my fish for me, but I was too long in the tooth to fall for that one. He was more interested in getting a look at the killer than in the safe netting of my fish. That evening the weigh-in showed that not only had I given poor Stephen a damned good thrashing, but that I had the best bag of the day. Seeing Colin and Stephen's faces when I announced to all and sundry that I had been floundering in hopelessness until Colin had inadvertently put me on the right track … well, let me just say it's a moment I'll treasure 'til the end of days. Three heads are better than one.

I don't know if many of you remember Bob Carnill, but back at the end of the last century he was a very famous fly-tyer and contributor to the angling press. I had the privilege and pleasure of his company when he made a visit to Orkney. While he was up, I suggested to Norm that we do a 'three in a boat' with Bob. Bob, in his private life, was an ambulance driver and a great raconteur. That 'three men' day we did with Bob will live in my memory for ever. We all laughed until we cried, as we competed to tell the most comedic and lurid reminiscences. Bob was a clear winner. His experiences as an ambulance driver, and all that that entails, gave him a fund of memories that seemed endless.

While we drifted and fished there came a time when Bob was 'on the oars' and he decided to renew his leader. As he did so he continued to tell us an excruciatingly funny tale. I watched him and laughed along with the story, when suddenly I realised that being wrapped up in the midst of his memory train, he had lost the plot as regards leader construction, and had attached one end of the leader to the other, making the length of nylon a complete hoop. As his time on the oars drew to a close, he began running the 'leader' through his hands, searching for an end to attach to his fly line. I watched in fascination as he searched for the non-existent end. After a few minutes I could stand it no longer and let Bob into the secret of his futile quest. Norm and I roared with laughter at poor Bob's expense but, give him his due, he joined in the hilarity, and laughed as loud and as long as anyone. Anybody else out on the loch that day must have thought we were three raving lunatics escaped from an asylum.

Flyfishing is a great delight, but fishing in close proximity to other anglers raises it to an even higher level. I enjoy it so much nowadays that I never venture out on my own and have been known to search the car park for some poor unfortunate who is similarly afflicted with no boat partner. If I was to be cursed with no boat partners 'til the end of my days I firmly believe I would hang up my rods and never venture forth ever again. The chance to share together every success, failure, happy and sad moments, insights and experiences is a delight denied to almost every other fly fisherman, so I thank the fishing gods for my addiction to boat fishing.

Some people have one big fly box

– 37 –

Snatchers

SOME PEOPLE HAVE one big fly box. Because I fish a wide range of waters I tend to carry dedicated boxes – a lot of them – so that I can match fly selection to specific types of waters and circumstances

However, I do have one fairly large box which I refer to as my 'go anywhere, do anything' box. About 25% of this box is made up of Snatchers, a style of fly which can be used to tackle game fish species of wide variation. Snatchers are truly versatile.

For those of you who have no idea what a Snatcher is, let me enlighten you. Snatchers are a very simple concept. They are basically palmered flies on a grub/ midge style hook. The interesting factor relating to this fly style, to me at least, is that in some respects it shows evolution in fly pattern development.

Palmers have always been important in flyfishing circles. In fact, one of the very earliest flies was a palmer, and arguably a Soldier Palmer as we know it today. But the difference between classic palmers and snatchers (apart from hook shape) is that classic palmers tend to be quite bulky whereas snatchers are best tied as slim as possible. I think this reflects the change in trout food items over the centuries.

The name 'palmer' derives from medieval times when crusaders and pilgrims returned from the Levant. They, the story goes, often carried palm leaves for some reason, and so developed the nickname 'palmers'. They were also classified as wanderers in a time when few people travelled more that a mile or two from home. The nickname later passed to 'woolly bear' caterpillars because they are often seen to wander about, seemingly aimlessly. And so palmered flies can either have been named so because ancient anglers thought they were imitations of caterpillars or simply because the fly resembled the insect. I prefer the former theory. After all, it was not so long ago that fishermen thought salmon ate butterflies and hence the garish patterns of salmon flies created in the late 19th and early 20th centuries.

The general belief in my early days was that palmers represented adult insects, particularly sedges of which there were great numbers of species and hatching individuals way back then. Not so any longer, I'm afraid. The range of insect species important to trout is rapidly diminishing. This is having a profound effect upon fishing styles, tactics and techniques, the most noticeable being that today's stillwater flyfishing almost completely revolves around chironimids and, to a lesser extent, daphnia.

Across the Irish Sea, where water quality is less of an issue, the up-wing insect hatches still remain and are very important features of their season. Over here we are not so lucky. And whereas close copy imitations are not necessary, or even functional, there are parameters which we are ill-advised to go beyond in the construction of flies. Overall configuration – size and general shape – is to a degree essential, and thus identifying predominant food items helps us create working patterns.

I believe that for most of the season trout now expect the greater bulk of their food to be made up of various stages in chironomid (buzzer) development and, as all such stages are slim, we now have moved away from bulky flies and tie or buy much slimmer patterns. The Snatcher clan is a good case in point. They are palmers but much slimmer and sparser than the palmers of old. In the good old days, I often tied palmers with three hackles. Today, when tying snatchers, I often strip one side of the one hackle I am using to make the finished fly look even more sparse and ephemeral.

I mentioned above that snatchers are very versatile and are a family of flies that can make that great leap from stillwater to running water, which is no mean feat. But in a loch/reservoir environment there are no bounds to their use. My preferred use is as back up flies behind sedgehogs or muddlers on a multi-fly cast high in the water, but in the early days of the season mid-depth lines can suit them very well also, particularly in an early midge hatch.

There is a prevalent and growing belief amongst fishermen that snatchers are specifically hatching midge pupae representations, and that has led to mandatory inclusion of cheeks, whether jungle cock or biots, to represent wing buds. To the best of my knowledge the original snatchers didn't have cheeks, but it is very rare to see cheek-less specimens nowadays. I prefer jungle cock splits, although I think there is a modern-day over-reliance on this stuff. If you use jungle cock whole feathers, select the small ones.

Given that they are so useful for brown trout and one of the very few wet flies frequently used for rainbow trout, their inclusion in the armoury of all UK and Ireland fly fishers is strongly advised.

When it comes to patterns many of the most commonly used ones come from existing but adapted patterns of yore, such as Kate McLaren Snatcher, Silver Invicta Snatcher, Doobry Snatcher and Bibio Snatcher. There are no restrictions, only the depth and breadth of your imagination.

PATTERNS

Claret & Hare's Ear Snatcher

Hook:	Tiemco 2487
Thread:	Black, 8/0
Butt:	Two turns flat red holographic, medium
Rib:	Same red holographic, twisted
Body:	Hare's ear dubbing
Hackle:	Claret cock or hen
Cheeks:	Yellow jungle cock splits

A pattern devised by my friend Jimmy Hunter. A very functional top-of-the-water pattern for early- to mid-season work. Essential for Loch Leven.

Doobry Snatcher

Hook:	Tiemco 2487
Thread:	Black, 8/0
Butt:	Two turns GloBrite no 4 or 5 fluorescent floss
Rib:	Fine gold wire
Body:	Flat, brassy gold tinsel
Body hackle:	Hot-orange cock or hen
Head hackle:	One or two turns of black hen
Cheeks:	Jungle cock splits

An excellent mid-season pattern when the hatches have slackened off.

Kate McLaren Snatcher

Hook:	Tiemco 2487
Thread:	Black, 8/0
Rib:	Fine silver wire
Body:	Black seal's fur
Body hackle:	Black cock or hen
Head hackle:	One or two turns of dark ginger hen
Cheeks:	Jungle cock splits

One of the very best general-purpose snatchers. I am never without a few.

Silver Invicta Snatcher

Hook:	Tiemco 2487
Thread:	Brown, 8/0
Tail:	Golden pheasant crest, tied sparse and short
Rib:	Fine silver wire
Body:	Flat silver tinsel
Body hackle:	Ginger cock
Collar hackle:	Blue jay
Cheeks:	Yellow jungle cock splits

If you like a Silver Invicta this is the apex modern alternative. Very effective.

Bibio Snatcher

Hook:	Tiemco 2487
Thread:	Black, 8/0
Butt:	Two turns red holographic
Rib:	Fine oval silver
Body:	Black seal's fur with a fluorescent scarlet thorax
Body hackle:	Black cock or hen
Cheeks:	Jungle cock splits

A very obvious adaptation. A season-long necessity.

The Red Lady beguiles another

– 38 –

Hope Springs Eternal

A WHOLE GENERATION of fly fishermen have grown up never having seen a sea-trout, never mind caught one. If you are one such fisherman and wish to address the problem, read on.

The sea-trout is a mysterious creature and, as such, has captured the imagination of a select group of anglers who show a dedication and devotion like few others.

Let's get what few facts there are about sea-trout straight in our minds. All brown trout are, to a lesser or greater degree, migratory. The movement from the birth-site downstream, no matter should it be yards or miles, can be considered migration. The source of the migratory instinct is either nutritional or sexual. Generally speaking, from one hatching of trout eggs there will be varying degree of movement/migration. Many trout will run down streams to rivers, some from rivers to lochs, and a proportion from lochs to the sea. They are all trout (*Salmo trutta*).

Of course, many variations in the habitat can affect the migratory run. Some streams may be so incapable of sustaining year-round healthy habitat that their trout production must mature in the sea. Other environments can produce so much nutrition that the migratory instinct is over-ridden, and very little or no sea-bound movement is undertaken. In the final analysis it is all about the productivity of environment. Low fertility systems produce lots of sea-trout, and rich habitats produce few, if any.

There is also a sexual dimension to the move from freshwater to salt. Female trout have an onerous responsibility to produce a large mass of eggs which produces a need for large quantities of nutrition – to produce thousands of eggs and their yolk sacks needs regular and copious amounts of food. Male fish on the other hand produce milt (sperm) to fertilise said eggs, and due to the massive difference between the size and protein composition of a sperm and an egg, male trout can achieve sexual maturity in some pretty poorly productive environments. A couple of studies carried out in separate important sea-trout systems – one in Wales, another in Scotland – showed that migratory fish returning to freshwater were 75% female. The resident 'brown trout' were found to be 75% male. That just about says it all.

Colin Riach and I were on a trip round the west and north coasts of Scotland, trying, in a very unscientific manner, to monitor the health of sea-trout stocks in historically famous fisheries. We had been unable to gain access to Lochs Maree and Eilt, both fabulous sea-trout fisheries of the past, for a variety of logistical reasons. I couldn't help but feel that the lack of enthusiasm by those involved tended to indicate that there was little positive to report. I hope I'm wrong.

But we had fished Loch Naver and been greatly encouraged by what we had found, and the next day we were on the famous Loch Hope. Some leaked reports from fellow anglers who regularly fished Hope indicated that the loch bucked the Scottish trend in diminishing stocks of sea-trout. I had fished it in the late 90s, one day on the extreme southern end and another in the extreme north. We had seen a goodly number of fish in the north but the south had been disappointing. But that was then, and this was now. I felt that my numerous experiences on sea-trout and salmon lochs between then and now better equipped me to perform at a good level. I was about to find out if this was true.

Davie MacKay was our ghillie again and, after his showing on Naver the previous day, I was totally confident that he would put us over fish from start to finish. A good northerly breeze was pushing down the loch when we got there, and although not totally overcast the skies contained enough cloud to be going on with. From a fishing perspective, Loch Hope is divided into three sections – South End, Middle Bay and North End. The Altnaharra Hotel has access to the South End and Middle Bay. South End, which has the major spawning water, the Strathmore River, is so productive of fish that it is divided in three parts – Beats 1, 2 and 3. We were on Beat 1 which stretches down the road shore to the right-hand side of the river mouth, about 400 yards long and marginally less than that wide. The water is very shallow all over the beat, so the rods can virtually fish anywhere, which is unusual in a migratory loch where shoreline drifting is the norm. It should be obvious that regardless of wind direction every inch of water is fishable, which is a fantastic attribute.

Flat calm, but Hope springs eternal

We started in a light breeze from the north drifting from the boundary line between Beats 1 and 3, and the number of fish, both salmon and sea-trout, showing, was mind boggling. It is very rare to be in such a situation where you are expecting a fish with every cast. And also, to know that if you aren't stimulating some interest to your fly selection it would be a damned good idea to change the patterns. In a normal salmon and sea-trout loch situation one goes for broke, selects a few flies and hope against hope that one's got it right. Typically offers are few and far between and not getting a response in the short term is rarely a reflection on fly pattern choice.

Colin rigged up with a WOIGO Kate Muddler on the top and a Claret Dabbler on the point. He opened the batting with a double hook-up. Did I mention that the loch was 'hoching' with fish? He didn't initially realise he had two on, and it wasn't until the pound fish on the bob was in the net that he suddenly discovered an estimated 3 pounder on the point. We all do crazy things in moments of crisis and, ignoring pleas that we try and get both in the net, Colin tried to haul the fish in over the side of the boat by hauling on the leader. I don't think I need relate the rest of the sorry tale, you can surely work it out for yourself.

Without finishing our drift to the south shore, we lost the breeze entirely and were forced to watch fish leaping and jumping with little chance of a take to our wet flies. Colin took the dry fly route and after a wait to see if the breeze would recover, I set out to try an idea which had been festering in my brain for years, namely epoxy buzzers. Trout are trout, and if you go along with the concept that non-feeding fish in freshwater are simply responding to memories of feeding in such environments in their pre-marine life cycle, then midge pupae imitations should work almost as well as pulled wet flies. Some may consider this heresy, but I believe that most, if not all, non-migratory trout tactics should work for sea-trout and, perhaps to a lesser extent, salmon. We stick to wet fly tactics not because they are the only ones that work but because we are encouraged to do so, and it is a form of bet-hedging.

As it turned out Colin managed to take a finnock on dries. The water was too weedy and shallow for a decent trial with the buzzers and, thankfully, the breeze picked up from the south and we were back on the percentages game with wets. I reverted to an old tactic of mine – a muddler on point and tail with a bushy palmer in the middle, only this time I greased up the palmer, in this instance a #8 Stone Goat, and it was savagely attacked almost immediately by a fit wee sea-trout of about 1½lbs. The motivation behind the muddler, palmer, muddler technique is to fish the flies as high as possible in the water. Normally reserved for a big wave, here it was working surprisingly well in a very modest ripple.

Then things went a bit quiet. We were still moving fish, but they were refusing to go that extra yard and fully commit. I noticed that the skies were clearing a bit and the light level had increased, so although it had taken me a good fish, I substituted the Stone Goat for a Red Lady, a pattern that has scored for me in bright-ish conditions before. Seemed a likely move, and this was to be a monumental decision as later events proved.

The southerly breeze which had picked up and taken us to the northern extent of the beat apologized for its temporary departure earlier on by suddenly swinging

A brief encounter with a crackin' Hope sea-trout

back to the north, laying out the whole of the beat before us. But just in case this was a temporary blip, Colin, Davie and I headed for the shore to have our long-overdue lunch. Midges can be a real problem on the shorelines of Hope, but the spot we had chosen for lunch was open to the breeze and we weren't expecting any insect attack. What we hadn't factored into our decision on lunch place was the chance of sitting on or close to a wasp's nest. In no time at all the air was full of the striped horrors. Wasps can be pretty aggressive in the autumn, so our period of rest was cut short and it was back out on the water.

As the fish were so high in the water I suggested to Colin that he should give the dap a go. It had worked on the previous day on Loch Naver and there seemed no reason to think it wouldn't on Hope. I don't dap. I can't give you a valid reason why not. I like to watch others dap and find it quite exciting to do so, but give me the wets anytime. Colin is a very accomplished 'dapper' and if anyone could make it work he was the man. As I said, I substituted the Stone Goat in the middle with a Red Lady, and it was attacked almost immediately. The unfortunate factor was that I could find only one of them in my 'big fish' box so I was one toothy fish away from disaster. And, of course, that concern materialised after a couple of sea-trout had their evil way with the Red Lady and chewed up the tinsel body until it lay in tatters. There is nothing more aggravating than finding a 'killer' fly and having it destroyed or ripped off the cast before the day is out. I was in a quandary. The conditions and the trout were crying out for a pattern that I couldn't exactly replace on the cast, but I did have a muddler-headed variant. As I was fishing the already referred to tactic of 'muddler – palmer – muddler' I couldn't stick another muddler in the middle position. This technique really does need a standard bushy palmer in the middle, and the point-position muddler is largely sacrificial in that its primary job is to present the middle and bob flies in the way I want them presented in relation to the surface layer. Would the Red Lady Muddler on the point adequately replace the non-muddler headed version in the middle? Only one way to find out, I reasoned.

It wasn't long until my concerns were addressed by a substantial sea-trout in the 4 lb+ class. Sea-trout of this size provide the ultimate thrilling fight. They are immensely strong and agile and are as likely to spend as much time in the air as in the water. It's a bit like being hooked into a kangaroo x cheetah hybrid, and I never at any point felt I was in charge. Three times I tried to bully this 'un-bully-able' fish to the net, the leader singing under the strain ... and then it departed without as much as a kiss goodbye. In the past I might have made the air blue with some well-chosen spicy language, but these days I tend to be a bit more philosophical. Dammit, you are going to release it anyway, and at least this way you know it is going to have plenty of vigour left to recover from its exertions. With a chuckle and a sigh, I bade it a fond farewell.

Colin was getting very frustrated with the total lack of interest shown to dapped flies. The dap should have been bringing fish up if only for a cursory examination, but not a single fish had shown the slightest interest. He quickly switched back to wets and was rewarded by another finnock to the WOIGO Kate. And then something bizarre happened. We were discussing the day – and there was a whole lot to chat about, theories, counter-theories and assumptions filled the air – when

I casually looked down where my bob-fly was slicing through the ripple. There, in the gin clear water, was a brute of a fish homing in on the Red Lady Muddler. I had to keep the flies in the water although normally this would be the point in the retrieve when a new cast beckoned. Leaning back as far as I could – Davie was convinced I was going to topple out the back of the boat – and raising the rod to the perpendicular, I managed to more feel than see the fish take. I was never convinced that the fish was well-hooked, but it rushed off towards open water where I was hoping I could use its own weight and momentum to ram home the hook point.

This turned out to be a false hope. Before I could tighten the line, the fish turned through 180° and shot across the front of the boat, almost knocking the oar out of Davie's hand and spraying Colin with loch water. This was a big sea-trout with a defined social conscience – it wanted to get everybody involved. However, its social conscience did not extend to staying 'on' and letting us get a good look at it. Another long-range release, I'm afraid, but a very thrilling one.

A great day's fishing is always hallmarked, for me at least, by a deep and profound silence at the end of the day. My mind and memory are so overloaded with images and recollections that I can barely put them into words. I had never seen so many fish, or so much action, on a sea-trout loch in my lifetime. As I previously mentioned, sea-trout are a fish of mystery. Are they, against all the odds making a comeback, or is it only in this particular place that hope springs eternal?

Red Lady (variant)

Hook:	Fulling Mill, Competition Heavy-weight, #10 & #8
Thread:	Black
Tail:	Golden pheasant tippet fibres, dyed orange
Rib:	Medium oval gold or wire
Body:	Brassy gold, flat
Body hackles:	Hot-orange and black cock
Head hackles:	Orange dyed golden pheasant rump under natural golden pheasant rump

Originally devised by John Murdo MacRitchie of Lewis, I have added a scarlet dyed golden pheasant rump feather under the natural golden pheasant rump feather to add more 'kick' and colour.

Red Lady Muddler

Hook:	Fulling Mill, Competition Heavy-weight, #10 & #8
Thread:	Black
Tail:	Golden pheasant tippet fibres, dyed orange
Rib:	Medium oval gold or wire
Body:	Brassy gold, flat
Body hackles:	Hot-orange and black cock
Head hackles:	Orange dyed golden pheasant rump under natural golden pheasant rump.
Head:	West of Ireland golden olive dyed deer hair

– 39 –

Nowt As Queer As Trout

ANTHROPOMORPHISM ISN'T A commonly used word. But it is a very common feature of human behaviour. Anthropomorphism is the act of endowing (non-human) animals with the emotional baggage and responses of humans. Walt Disney made a fortune out of this bizarre human trait – grieving fawns, celebrating sparrows, maliciously evil wolves and gullible piglets are products of the human imagination which do not occur in nature.

We humans find it easy to empathise with individual creatures, and almost impossible to repeat these feelings for whole species. The stranded whale or seal pup, the injured bird or rabbit, the dead fox or badger is capable of motivating whole groups of individuals to anthropomorphic outrage and distress, when, in reality and the cold light of day it matters not a jot to the whole species. One dead or dying animal, in the larger scheme of things, is an irrelevance. If the human race could take the concern for one stranded whale and extrapolate that through the whole species certain oriental and Scandinavian countries would become vegetarian tree-huggers overnight. It's a confusing world and human knee-jerk reaction isn't helping!

It's generally acknowledged that in order to understand the behaviour of social insects such as bees and ants the scientist/layman must accept that each individual acts as an intrinsic part of the whole. This may be hard to envisage but the much-admired footage we regularly see of the co-ordinated sky dances of starling flocks, and bait-fish shoal manoeuvrings when under attack, help give an insight into this phenomenon. This is an important lesson to be learnt for fly fishermen. We must, to better understand our prey, think of them as a vast organic entity and not as a series of individuals because that is how, by and large, they respond to external stimuli.

Now, we are talking wild trout here, not those disturbed, genetically modified, confused, inbred mutants, which we lovingly refer to as 'stockies'. So, how often have we been flabbergasted to realise that the majority of fish taken on any given day by a disparate group of anglers have fallen to a specific pattern and technique? It is easy to say that is because the fly resembled a specific food item, that the retrieve imitated the locomotion style of the food item. That would, alas, be interpreting the evidence from a human perspective. An individual trout is a very basic organism and that which affects one tends to affect the population as a whole. I believe that this is a behavioural specification designed to protect and enhance the entire population. Basically, the qualities of the whole are greater than the sum of the individual parts – one stick is easy to break, a bundle of sticks is virtually impossible.

I first became fully aware of this feature of trout behaviour some years ago after a club match on Loch of Stenness. Stenness is a very difficult and temperamental water – the trout fishing equivalent of climbing the North Face of the Eiger. After this match – which I think ran from 12.00 midday to 6 pm – it turned out that only five fish had been caught between, say, thirty anglers. I had been lucky enough to get two – one at 2.05 pm and the other at 2.18. On checking with the other lucky anglers, it turned out that each and every one of the caught fish were taken between 2.00 pm and 2.20 pm. Now this could be easily explained if a) Stenness was a wee pond with an area of a few square yards, but it is a big loch of approximately 2,000 acres, or b) all the boats were fishing one tight corner, but they were spread to the four winds, and I hardly saw a boat all day.

So, what does that insular event tell us? Firstly, it tells me that the fish switched on at, or about, 2.00 pm and were back in 'their kip' by 2.30 pm. Secondly, whatever it was that caused the brief flurry of activity was recognisable to trout but passed unnoticed by us anglers. Thirdly, this scenario also casts light upon the weird feeding behaviour of trout. Stenness is basically a bowl of protein soup; the range of food items is vast as are the numbers of individuals in the prey species. For example, the production of stickleback fry is mind-blowing and under every submerged stone are enough freshwater shrimp to make a decent sandwich. Plenty of available grub only compounds the problem of course because, just like jaded gourmands surrounded by the tastiest and tempting morsels, trout need only nibble a bit here and there to keep body and soul together.

Some of us probably think that each and every trout gets up early in the morning have a slight snack, nibbles at something pre-packed at lunch time, and then rush home to the wife and kids for a slap-up feed around about sunset. Okay, none of us really believe that, but the truth is just as bizarre. Apart from a period extending from April to June when food supply is at its maximum and binge feeding common, the bulk of a wild trout population is comatose, inactive and totally oblivious to the world round them. This can go on for months, especially if the springtime binge-feed has been particularly rich. We are all aware of this without necessarily knowing why. Serious wild trout anglers know that the best fishing occurs in May and June and accept the fact that July and August will see less organised feeding binges by trout and an associated lack of action.

Individual waters with peculiar food production regimes can buck this trend. It is no secret that Loch Leven, as a fishery, has fascinated me for decades. It is and has been, by and large, a wild trout fishery for most of its history, but it didn't historically follow the above template for wild trout feeding calendars. Historically, peak production time by way of caught fish and fish food was from June to September. This was largely because the staple diet of Leven trout were 'bloom' creatures, amongst which can be included daphnia, midge larvae and pupae, cyclops, and caenis nymphs. Some of these species (daphnia and cyclops) are dependant on algal blooms and so tend to swarm in warm water, the others simply prefer to hatch in the mid-summer months. All fish tend to be most active when food is plentiful, so Leven fish were most productive in the months identified. The corollary between what happens in this type of environment and rainy seasons on the Serengeti is hard to dispute; the rains arrive, the grass grows, the herds gather, and the predators get fat. On Leven the stimulus arrived to promote phytoplankton bloom, the swarms of copepods developed to graze upon them, and the trout got fat. During the famine times Nature holds its breath and the predators wait it out. The parallels are obvious, simple, neat and beautiful. Nowadays things have altered somewhat on Leven. The big midge hatches are unreliable, and midge pupae and larvae make up the bulk of the fishing from May through to July.

So, in retrospect, trout populations are geared to respond in feeding regime to the precise food item populations of their ecosystem. Trout living in waters where food items are, so to speak, traditional – large invertebrates and fish fry – tend to have late spring feeding peaks. These waters tend to have water chemistries with plenty of dissolved salts and a high pH. Trout in waters where 'swarm' foods make up the highest proportion of forage, swim in water full of dissolved nutrients. It's generally quite easy to differentiate low level nutrient water from 'rich' trout waters by examining the agricultural practices in the watershed. If farming tends towards livestock production and/or grazing, lochs surrounded by the same are likely to be 'traditional', and lochs in rich, crop-producing ground are most likely to be nutritionally high, the productivity of the water reflecting the richness of the land.

One of the features of trout behaviour which has puzzled me for decades has been the sudden presence of lots of trout. Where were these trout on the period leading up to sudden activity? At first I was unaware that at any given time only a portion of the whole population would be active, the rest being relatively comatose. Sub-aqua divers have told me of seeing large quantities of immobile fish hanging at depth in deep areas of lochs. Equally surprising is that these fish can be approached and handled without responding. Why would they do this? Apart from the 'security from predators' question, it does make sense for cold-blooded creatures, when not feeding, to conserve energy and body mass by going totally inactive. This will allow very large numbers of fish to inhabit a water without losing condition or reducing the environment to a watery desert. If we assume that there is some sort of relay process by which trout rotate their dormitory and active phases, this goes part of the way to explaining why given the right conditions a loch can suddenly become alive with fish, the presence of which had been unsuspected in previous conditions.

It's not only the sudden availability of food that can cause such a flurry of activity. I'm pretty much convinced that the erratic nature of air pressure during thunder storms can activate previously dormant fish. Some of the most impressive 'rises' of trout I have ever witnessed have been after an intense thunder storm.

I use my marrow spoon a lot when wild trout fishing. It is often surprising how many caught fish have completely empty stomachs. I have recently come to the conclusion that, when there isn't an obvious hatch going on and nothing apparently available to stimulate a feeding surge by trout, the fish we are opportunistically catching are recent recruits from the dormitories. This begs the question "If the opportunistic trout is a recent 'wake-up', are other active trout largely un-catchable until the hatch starts?" The answer I suspect is, yes!

This line of reasoning also provides an answer to the age-old question 'Why are big fish so hard to catch?' Simply, big fish with large biomass and relatively slow growth rate, feed hard for short periods when they are active and sleep longer. Small fish, with small biomass and rapid growth rate have to feed more regularly and may not indulge in dormitory behaviour at all, dependant upon relative size.

Another dawn of realisation which hit me some time ago was that amongst wild populations of healthy fish in productive waters, in the very earliest months of the season, poorly conditioned trout were much more of a rarity than one could reasonably expect. In fact, on Loch Harray, some of the finest conditioned trout caught came from March fishing, and poorly conditioned trout which almost looked fresh from the spawning beds were more likely to be present in the catch from May until July. I assume from this that maiden fish (non-spawners in the previous winter) had enough stored nutrition to cope with the hard times and lean pickings of early-season, whilst the spawners stored what condition they retained after the winter months and retired to the dormitories until the 'feast' months of May and June came around.

Flyfishing revolves around trout feeding behaviour. The more we know about the whys and wherefores of it, the more we should catch. The less we use 'They've got to get hungry soon!' type anthropomorphic balderdash, the better off we'll be!

Loch Arienas. A salmon/sea-trout loch partially destroyed by the salmon aquaculture industry

– 40 –

Loch Arienas – Sea-trout Problems

IT WAS LATE in the day, and I was cream-crackered. We had searched Arienas up, down and sideways for a quality sea-trout and had found many finnock (the sea-trout equivalent of grilse). I had been up since bloody-hell o'clock, travelled somewhere close to 300 miles by car, and fished hard all day. I turned to Mark and said "That'll do for me. All I care about now is food and sleep. But you carry on while I take down my gear."

Gear stowed, I leaned back and took a long draw on a cigarette. I was contemplating the futility of hunting increasingly rare sea-trout when I heard a muffled grunt from the stern of the boat and ... there, a mere cast length from the boat, a very large fish hung in the air. It screamed off to the left and straight into a weed bed, and was gone. It was enough to make a grown man weep, but not Mark. He cast out again ... and was 'in' again. I stared at my carefully packed-away gear and cursed my luck.

Hunting sea-trout in the lochs of the West Coast of Scotland is as hard a job as any fly fisherman can face. Of course, the dwindling number of migratory trout in this area, due to many factors, is the prime concern. But there are others.

Many sea-trout lochs have been consigned to history; some come and go, with false dawns and depressing failures; and others maintain runs of reduced quantity which, whilst not being totally satisfactory, maintain the illusion that hope exists.

Loch Arienas (pronounced *Airy-anus* – Yes, yes, yes, now settle down, class, it is your own time you're wasting...) was at one time one of the finest sea-trout lochs in Scotland. Very large numbers of trout, with some very big ones, used to run this system but, as with so many lochs in the far west of Scotland, it went into a spiralling decline with the advent of commercial salmon farming. In those far off days, like many other anglers and those concerned by the decline of migratory fish, I was heartened by the concept of salmon farming. I naively thought that farming of salmon would take great pressures from the wild stock which would ultimately thrive as the need for harvested wild fish declined. How wrong I was. Commercial greed has turned paradise into a festering wasteland. The inability of business ventures to respect the flora and fauna of natural environments, and a total unwillingness to even consider the impact of their actions upon fragile ecosystems, has led to the virtual eradication of migratory salmonids in many areas of Scotland. Of all the species which have suffered in this scenario, sea-trout have taken the brunt of the pressure.

One of the interesting results of this environmental shake-up is that on some systems increased salmon numbers have filled the vacuum left by sea-trout decline, and on others the descendants of migratory trout simply stay at home. There can be little doubt that genetic inheritance of growth features in migratory trout remain in the 'brown trout' stay-at-homes when the migratory runs decline. These genetic tendencies can produce some very fast-growing trout, especially in lochs which have seen their historical low-nutrient characteristics completely altered by the presence of smolt farming activities which, because of waste food pellets and fish waste product, have seen basic background fertility boosted. This is a common occurrence up the west coast of Scotland and the isles. Lochs such as Sheil, Damph and the Loch of Cliff in Shetland are classic examples. So is Arienas. Due to man's heavy hand these lochs have exchanged their large sea-trout for artificially large 'brown trout'. From a fish's (biological) point of view, there is little difference – trout are simply exchanging one source of food for another; from an aesthetic, fisherman's point of view the change is fundamental. Somehow the capture of a large fish which has spent many a mysterious month hunting the kelp beds and has briefly returned to our mundane world is eminently more exciting than a similarly sized fish which has been grubbing about under a smolt cage.

There are plans afoot to bring all smolt rearing on-shore. Should this come about it will have a profound effect upon the lochs in which at the moment contain cages. The available nutrition which is provided via waste food and fish excreta will disappear and the background fertility of the water will decline quite dramatically. What are the likely effects of such changes? Well, the first likely change we'll see is the decline of large stay-at-home trout. This is likely to take some time but is an inevitability. The second, and most welcome, change likely is that the number of migratory trout in these lochs will increase over the years. There seems to be a balance between a loch's background fertility and the quantity of fish which migrate downstream to the sea. If the fertility is high trout can manage to reach acceptable size and sexual maturity without accessing the high fertility of marine waters; conversely, very low river or loch fertility almost guarantees that the majority of fish will migrate, leaving only a minority of fish remaining as a sort of hedge against a natural disaster. So, the removal of fish cages from freshwater lochs could potentially see a return to the heady days of massive sea-trout runs. One caveat is that this all could hinge on aquaculture practice at sea. If things remain as they are, with inshore waters being polluted with sea-lice emanating from sea loch cages, then immature fish entering the sea may have a very tough time ahead of them. This year I have seen a very large percentage of finnock bearing unmistakable fin damage from sea-lice attack. There are reports from all over the western seaboard that downstream migrating sea-trout smolts are interrupting their marine stay by returning to freshwater in order to avoid the large numbers of sea-lice eagerly awaiting them in the salt. This scenario could ultimately mean that sea-trout will continue to decline as a viable species on the west coast of Scotland and in the isles. Somewhat surprisingly, fin damage on Arienas finnock was not highly significant. Mark commented that he believed that salmon farming in the coastal area had lessened in recent times, and this could account for the healthier than expected small sea-trout.

Arienas is possibly one of the prettiest lochs in the region. It is large without being daunting (2 miles x ¾ mile); the countryside is breath-taking; and it is remote without being inaccessible. It is also a very regular loch with potential fish holding areas easily identifiable. There is a deep hole in the centre of the loch with a depth somewhat in excess of 110 feet (33 metres-plus). The most productive area when we were there was close in, on the northern shoreline, although we did encounter fish on the south side, by drifting a good distance off the shore.

There is a road right down to the shore on the south side and Mark hauled his boat in and launched beside the jetty. The conditions couldn't have been better; a brisk west-by-nor'west breeze, heavy cloud cover with a few breaks. The loch has a west/east axis, so we could get the best of the shore-line drifts, and we initially pushed right to the head of the wind to the mouth of the main tributary from Loch

Doire nam Mart in the far western extremity of the loch. But it wasn't 'til we got out into the main body of the loch that we came across some fish. It quickly became apparent that the recent rains had brought in a very large quantity of finnock, and these small, chubby, beautiful fish were more than happy to attack our flies with relish. What finnock lack in size they more than make up for in dash and energy, fighting twice their weight, and more than happy to spend more than half the fight airborne. But it was their bigger brothers we were hunting for, if they indeed existed at all. Most believe that very few big sea-trout are left to run Arienas, but the inexhaustible supplies of finnock led us to believe that at least some multi-winter sea-trout must exist. And the search went on.

Mark fished his usual Wet Cel intermediate and I stuck to a Hardy midge-tip, and the rewards seemed didn't vary much between the two methods. It quickly became obvious that the northern shore was holding the largest quantity of fish, whilst the southern drifts produced only the occasional finnock. It is notable, at least to me, that sea-trout generally prefer one side of a loch, and in this case the north shore held most of the attraction. My experiences teach me that salmon and sea-trout in the same loch quite often don't share the same preferences for location. There is no fool-proof equation that can be applied to this, but more often than not sea-trout will prefer to have deep water under them or close by, whilst salmon often inhabit water the shallowness of which would scare the heebie-jeebies out of a stickleback. Arienas has never been a particularly prolific salmon water so, in these days of diminished runs, we never gave them a second thought.

After about six hours of continual fishing we had failed to contact any big fish, but we had contacted a few true sea-trout up to about 2 lb, and very welcome they were. Ross, the photographer, and I were ravenously hungry and, after a horrifically early start and a long drive, were running out of stamina, and thinking longingly of the comforts supplied by the Strontian Hotel. As it approached seven o'clock, I bowed to the inevitable and packed away my gear, whilst Mark continued fishing the last of the drift. Within five minutes of me de-tackling, Mark hooked the very good fish which I mentioned at the start of this piece. We never got a good sight of this beast, but as it quickly found a snag and detached itself from Mark's fly, we could not even venture a guess as to its species. Incredibly, his very next cast locked into another fish which immediately launched itself skyward. We both gawped at it as it hung in the air. Here was the very fish we had looked for all day, a superb sea-trout of an amazing 8 lb. Mark had a helluva battle with this fish which tested his gear to break-point, but finally we managed it into the net, weighed it in the weigh-net, and sent it on its way rejoicing.

Sometimes the search for the impossible has a happy ending. Next year I'll go looking for unicorns, the Loch Ness Monster and an honest politician.

'Head and Tail' rise form

– 41 –

The Hunter's Eye

EVER WONDERED WHY some people continually get it right; do illogical things that turn out spot-on; and can 'magic' fish out of unproductive water? You are thinking of someone who has what I call the 'hunter's eye'.

Many thousands of years ago such people kept whole communities supplied with food. They knew the flight lines of birds, where the animals travelled, and the most fish could be caught, and could look at the sky and know whether to go out hunting or stay at home. They had built-in natural understanding hard-wired into every fibre of their being.

In those far off days individuals like that were revered and cherished; nowadays, they are looked upon as rather weird, strange, lonely people who don't quite fit in to the modern world. Mind you, there are not so many of these natural hunters as there were; their talents and abilities are simply not required in this technological world, and many who do exist have sublimated their hunting instincts into something a little less honourable, and a bit more appropriate to 21st century schizoid living – merchant bankers, tycoons, stock market analysts, used-car salesmen and dodgy journalists. Hunting instinct hasn't gone away, it just manifests itself differently.

When I was a kid I literally couldn't walk past a puddle. Seriously, it's true. I had to know what was hidden below the scummy surface. When I wasn't sounding out puddles, I was hell-and-gone up the hill, hunting rabbits, searching for bird's nests, fishing for sticklebacks in the burn, and culling the ever-growing population of stray cats that lived in the car graveyard on the outskirts of the village. Yeah, I admit it – I was a strange little object, now with a certain amount of 21st century shame for some of the things I got up to. Some of the staid members of the community prophesied all sorts of unpleasant ends for my short and miserable life. What they didn't understand was that I was a throwback. Five thousand years ago I would have fitted right in, now I'm an anachronism, only really happy when I'm out huntin', shootin' and fishin' – particularly fishin'!

To many, fishing is a pastime, something to while away the hours. They can spend a whole day fishing and return home without a clue what was going on all around them. You see, what happens on the water surface can heavily influence what's happening beneath and can also be a great indicator of aquatic goings-on. Being aware of the environment, as a whole, can up your success rate.

Everyone is born with the hunter's eye, but it becomes moribund with lack of use, so here are a few exercises and practices to get you operating at a higher level.

One of the things I regularly do, and many of my colleagues omit from their preparations, is to have a look round, before I go out, for evidence of fly hatch. If there is a hut or general buildings about, I always take a look at windows or sheltered walls for signs of insects, especially living ones (it is generally impossible to tell from corpses whether they are recent or days old). Cobwebs are also worth a look at, but most often only contain deceased items. When I've done this, I then turn my attention to any bushes in the neighbourhood. A whole lot of aquatic insects head for bushes in order to pass from mid-life stages to mature adulthood – mayfly are a prime example – and there may be terrestrials which can be blown onto the water. If I am launching from the downwind side of the water in question, the very edge of the water may contain dead or living adult insects, and nymph shucks. All these areas can hold vast quantities of evidence relating to sub-surface insect activity.

When out on the water I keep an eagle-eye on the surface for more evidence. The biggest problem is that good fishing days tend to be a bit breezy and it is often not possible to see much, especially the smaller stuff. However, watching bird life over the water can help indicate whether there are food items 'on the go'. It amazes me sometimes how often small birds, such as swallows, swifts and martins, can be seen hunting over wind-lashed water. What this indicates is that, contrary to what many believe, small insects are continually hatching. This is often backed-up by stomach content analysis which will almost certainly contain the odd small midge pupae at any given time. To show how difficult it can be to spot insects amongst the surface turmoil of windswept water, I was once out on Harray in a good blow and there were big, bulgy rises amongst the waves. It took me a while to work out that I was sitting amongst a very big olive hatch. Only a dun actually blowing into my mouth gave the game away.

Another indication of insect activity is, of course, as I've mentioned already, bird activity. Open water attracts insectivorous birds such as swallows and swifts, and also some of the smaller partially-insectivorous gulls such as common and black-headed gulls and terns. It would be folly not to at least investigate activity by any or all such when seeking trout activity. Some years back I was sitting at the pier on Loch Leven watching common gulls just off the harbour swimming around in tight formation pecking at the water surface. I asked Willie Wilson, fishery manager, whether there was a hatch going on, and he replied that he was sure they were feeding on ascending corixa along the sides of weed beds. Brilliant and simple – Willie has the hunter's eye. I have also noted that when birds are inactive fish are also like-minded. When swans and ducks either have their heads under their wings or are swimming in an aimless, desultory fashion, and when the skies are empty of birds, don't expect a whole lot of action.

The obvious answer isn't always the right one. On numerous occasions rising fish have perplexed me by feeding on non-insect species. It's so easy to see rising fish and immediately, and wrongly, assume insect hatch. The most common species to be involved are freshwater snails, closely followed by sticklebacks. Trout feeding on fry generally give themselves away with slashing rises and associated sprays of tiny fish leaving the water, but sticklebacks in adult form most often live a lonely life and their habit of hanging, motionless in the surface film is often irresistible to trout.

This leads us neatly and conveniently to interpreting rise forms. The ability to read a rise can supply the angler with copious amounts of information, but unfortunately there are mitigating factors which can compromise the art of rise-reading with a degree of difficulty. Rises in a big wave are often impossible to read because water turbulence can mask the finer detail of the rise form. But when the surface is relatively calm all the nitty-gritty is there to be read.

It would take a whole article to clearly define the hidden truths behind individual rise forms, but broadly speaking they can be defined as the broken water rise, boils, head and tail, flattening ripple and the 'suck down'.

'Broken' water rise form

BROKEN WATER RISES

The broken water rise could also be called the engulfing rise and is an aggressive movement, but without the same degree of confidence of other rise forms. I often wonder if there is a degree of surprise in it, as if the fish has just caught sight of a fast-disappearing food item or the hunted item has, in some way, just turned confidence into desperation.

Generally speaking, these are created by fast moving fish and, as such, indicate that the prey is also fast moving and intercepted in, or just under, the surface film.

Broken water rises are often failures caused by the speed of prey, failure of the fish to truly identify where the prey object is in the water column, or because a surface insect has flown off just as the fish was about to take it.

Ephemerid nymphs, emerging insects can be responsible for such rise forms. But, just as commonly, trout lying deep and coming to static, on the surface items, can also produce them.

Always cover a broken water rise form if possible as there is likely to be a confused and 'angry' fish in the vicinity looking for a target.

BOILS

This rise form is most often caused by fish, high in the water, taking steadily and confidently just below the surface. The most common insect associated with a 'boil' is the pre-emerging buzzer, but corixa commonly elicit such a reaction as well.

To produce a good and premeditated catch when fishing amongst trout showing these characteristic signs requires a lot of skill. Flies must be presented high in the water, and closely resembling the natural prey in colour, action and conformity. Remember, these are confidently feeding fish in that they are feeding specifically on one identified item, are sure of a successful strike, and that there are plenty of these items on the go. That, of course, doesn't mean a careless approach or poor presentation will score – fish feeding high in the water are notoriously spooky.

HEAD AND TAIL RISES

The head and tail rise form is the equivalent of the boil but to on-the-surface insects or items and done with the same confidence and deliberation by fish swimming high in the water, but perhaps not just as high as the 'boilers'.

A generation ago this type of rise was common, but for some, perhaps, unidentified reason they are not so common nowadays. In most people's minds the head and tail is closely associated with the taking of adult insects. One of my opinions as to why they are increasingly rare is because they are most often associated with large insects, of which we seem less well supplied than in the past.

I have seen h&t rises to mayfly, daddies, big sedges, and sometimes to even smaller insects, but the one thing which remains steadfast is that it is a rise almost always produced by a big fish.

In the past I was always confident when covering an h&t rise. Don't seem to get many opportunities these days.

FLATTENING RIPPLE

The flattening ripple rise is not a rise at all in the strictest sense of the word, but it shows trout feeding activity. I reckon it is caused by fish moving in a horizontal

Typical 'suck-down' rise forms

manner within a couple of feet of the surface. As such, it is much more common in rainbow trout than in browns, but it does feature in the world of wild trout.

Funnily enough, I tend to associate this indicator with big fish in relatively shallow water, but this may be because it's a physical manifestation caused by a large body moving in a restricted depth/area.

It is closely associated with fish hunting fairly mobile prey and I have seen it when shrimp, olive nymphs and stickleback are on the menu, in other words generally non-surface orientated species.

Trout feeding in this manner can be very specific regarding what they will or won't accept, are operating within strict levels/depths, and thus can be the least co-operative with the angler.

THE 'SUCK DOWN'

This form is almost always associated with deep water and still conditions, although it is such a quiet rise form that it may well be missed in turbulent water.

Closely linked with emerging insects or small items trapped in the surface film, it is the quiet water equivalent of the 'boil'.

The 'suck down' is performed by confidently feeding fish swimming high in the water making almost no visible surface disturbance. It is the easiest rise form to miss, and it frequently betrays itself by its signature sound which is like the noise made by a kiss.

Many wrongly assume that so little commotion must come from a small fish. This is frequently an erroneous conclusion as the biggest fish can often make the quietest rise.

In my experience the 'suck down' is most often come across when fish are feeding on dead or relatively immobile items such as snails, caenis, spent gnat, and emerging or adult midge. After a big caenis hatch, when the water is littered with 'spents' in the late evening, the noise associated with this rise form can be almost deafening.

Because the 'suck down' is the province of very high swimming fish in virtually flat calm conditions, it can be the most frustrating and unproductive sign of feeding fish. A mouse walking through a cat sanctuary doesn't even come close in the spooky league.

Many fishermen can't spot a fish rising. Rising fish are feeding fish, and feeding fish are eminently catchable. Try to train yourself to use peripheral vision to spot movement. This is the quintessential 'hunter's eye'. No hunter actively 'looks' for anything, he simply opens his eyes and allows the evidence to flood in, and movement is best picked up by peripheral vision. I wonder if this was a bonus supplied by nature to help us avoid predators sneaking up. Prey species tend to have eyes on the side of their heads to provide almost 360° vision. Predators, on the other hand, tend to have eyes positioned in the front of their heads, limiting their visual range to less than 180°. Humans have a foot in either camp, having brilliant forward vision and excellent movement-spotting peripheral vision. It's a gift, use it!

And, to close, just a few related pointers:
- always watch or listen to detailed weather forecasts before venturing out;
- watch the skies
- and, of course, watch other boats.

Modern day living blunts the senses, but they are rarely totally lost. Become a better fisherman – train your 'hunter's eye'.

Arguments still rage on about the genetic nature of this fish

– 42 –

Loch Sheil

MARK SAID "A fish just head and tailed to your left, Colin! About 11 o'clock!"

"See it, Mark. Dammit, too far. That was half past ten!"

"Go again, Colin, he's still there" I added.

"That's over him… and he's on!" exclaimed Colin, and a bonny, bright, silvery fish exploded out of the water to muted shouts of encouragement from the excited on-lookers.

There's so much to say about Loch Sheil that I hardly know where to start. There's a historical perspective, a present day one, a geological viewpoint and a trout overview. And, of course, there's a wee tale of how Mark, Colin and I fared on our recent jaunt on this massive water.

Sheil is one of the largest bodies of water in Scotland, only being eclipsed by a few other more famous lochs. It is a ribbon-loch, a glaciated valley some 17½ miles long. In almost all of its length, out from the shoreline, it is extraordinarily deep; but in the lower end it is incredibly shallow in places, boat-run-aground shallow as far from the shore as it is possible to get. The surface of the loch is only just over 3 metres above sea level, and the River Sheil which runs from the loch to the sea is only 2 miles long and quite a placid stream.

One of the strangest facts about Sheil is, that unlike almost every other glaciated, deep loch (over 400 feet in places), it contains no ferox or char. I can only assume that this is because it is more than likely that Sheil was, historically, a sea loch. When the last ice age came to an end it did so in almost cataclysmic style. The sea levels rocketed up and valleys emerged from under the ice only to be flooded by saltwater. The ancestors of ferox and char did not take up residence in saltwater but pushed on to freshwater lochs. Then, as the sea levels dropped as the polar ice sheets formed and the land rebounded from the massive weight of ice sheet, these primordial fish adapted to a total freshwater environment. Lochs which only slowly disengaged themselves from tidal water over hundreds, if not thousands, of years missed being settled by the ancestral ferox and char and lost their chance. The bed of lower Loch Sheil seems to me remarkably like sea bed. To drift over shallow water at the Acharacle (pronounced *Ach-aracle*) end of Sheil is like crossing a tidal sand/mud flat, and one almost expects to see cockle shells and sea weed. Remember that Sheil's height above sea level is less than twelve feet, and the post ice age saltwater inundation would have been inevitable and long lasting. The loch that many generations of our ancestors would have known would certainly have been a body of saltwater.

So, no typical glaciated, deep water freshwater loch species. But there are trout in plenty – sea-trout and brown trout, plus salmon. In the latter part of the last century (and before) Sheil was justly famous for its sea-trout and, to a lesser extent, its salmon runs. Of course, during the 'universal' decline of sea-trout populations in the West of Scotland in the 80s and 90s, Sheil was badly hit. Aqua-cultural activities both in the loch and surrounding sea lochs exacerbated this decline, but in recent years salmon farming has been (to a small extent) closer controlled and sea-trout numbers in Sheil have improved. There are not the massive runs of fish equal to those of the past, nor the massive specimens of the yesterday, but they are making a fragile comeback.

With reports coming through the grapevine of large numbers of finnock and sea-trout waiting for rain in the river Sheil and estuary, Colin Riach and I made plans to join Mark Hirst for a jaunt out as soon as the weather broke, which it duly did at the end of July. More encouraging reports came south of the river emptying its sea-trout load into the loch as the rains fell, and Colin and I packed the car and set off.

We had booked accommodation at the Ardshealach (pronounced *Ard-chelach*) Lodge for an overnight stay, and what a hidden gem that proved to be. I have rarely seen such a comfortable and well-appointed guesthouse in the Highlands as the Arshealach Lodge. Run exclusively by Jill Gosney, the cuisine and wine lists are sublime, and the bedrooms and sitting rooms are fabulously comfortable. But such sybaritic pleasures were low on our priority list – I was heartbroken to miss Jill's wide selection of dinner delights due to coming off the loch late in the evening.

I'd fished Sheil before, launching at the Glenfinnan end. Mark and I had ventured as far west as the Black Rocks and Polloch, but Sheil is dauntingly long

(17½ miles) so we never did get to see the Acharacle end of the loch. Colin was coming 'home'. In the 70s he had spent his summers in Acharacle working in the hotel trade as a ghillie-cum-odd-job-man. He had family links in the area and spent as much time as he could fishing in the broad expanses of lower Loch Sheil. In those days boat power was provided by more than forty Seagull outboards, and long forays up the loch were brave if somewhat inadvisable adventures. So, he had become somewhat of an expert on the lower loch. His reminiscences of days gone by, days of the great sea-trout runs of yore, were fascinating and helped get the recent sea-trout revival into context.

We launched at Dalelia, overjoyed to be away from the loch-side midges and struck up the loch in search of some silver tourist hotspots. All the hillside burns were raging after the recent rains, so burn-mouths with their sweet water were our target. Our first port of call was the burn mouth at the back of Heron Island (*Eilean Druim nam Laogh* on the map). The push of water from the burn was visible from quite away off, and Mark was convinced there would be fresh fish attracted by it. We contacted a few small browns and finnock on the drift in, and suddenly I was into something much bigger. The rod simply laid over and surging pulses shot up through it. The fish was lively, but we knew it unlikely to be a sea-trout as it hadn't leapt throughout the fight, as sea-trout almost invariably do. I did see a flash of red as I forced it to the surface, and I immediately thought 'potted' salmon. But I was totally wrong. It looked like a large brown trout with the most startling colour scheme, and a few big black spots sparsely sprinkled across its hide, but on reflection I am almost convinced that it was, in fact, a stale sea-trout. As I dug the Assassin's Toe out of its scissors, I marvelled at the confirmation of this fish – its superb depth, girth and extraordinary colouration. It was a very fine fish but not at all what we expected, given the earliness of the season. Was this a fish that had run early in the spring and hung about waiting for the autumn rain and the spawning beds? But doubts still lingered. Mark was convinced it was a Sheil brown, as he had seen quite a number of fish of this type on previous forays.

All this brings us to the conundrum of past sea-trout lochs and their present brown trout populations. Almost every west coast sea-trout loch has seen a marked decline in migratory trout numbers whilst its brown trout population has grown in numbers and size. Why this should be has puzzled riparian owners and fishermen for decades. There are facts and there are theories. Amongst the facts we must take on board are:

1. The relative decline of sea-trout and the rise of brown trout numbers go hand in hand. I wouldn't be at all surprised to find out that the biomass of trout within each system hasn't altered materially, and that the drop in sea-trout number and weight is paralleled by the increase in numbers and weight of brown trout.

2. The genes for growth now present in brown trout, and totally absent in historical brown trout populations, must have come from somewhere. The logical answer is that this genetic component must have come from sea-trout.

3. Past sea-trout lochs which now have aqua-cultural enterprise within their catchment have seen the most marked changes in brown/sea-trout population dynamics. One must assume that the aforementioned smolt-rearing processes have markedly altered the aquatic environment to such an extent that individual lochs are now eminently capable of sustaining and growing populations of 'brown' trout of large numbers and individual size. Loch Sheil, for example, now throws out browns of double figures, and large numbers of these fish are met in close contact with the smolt-rearing cages.

4. Scale readings from trout from such environments have shown marked increases of growth which tend to infer artificial nutrient harvesting, probably within and around the altered environments of the smolt cages. There also seems to be a tendency for trout with such a background to take occasional trips to sea. A 20lb-plus fish captured in the River Sheil in recent times was at first accepted as a sea-trout, but results received of scale readings showed a marked and disproportionate growth rate in earlier life years. This suggests that the migratory instincts of these 'brown' trout are not brown trout typical and can be spurred into action by factors we do not as yet understand.

We discussed these matters as we pushed on to explore similar hot-spots. We crossed the loch and popped into Polloch, a renowned sea-trout spot, but the high sides of the channel blocked out any breeze whatsoever, and we quickly moved on. Next stop was Glenaladale which sported a major burn system carrying a good flow after the recent rain. Mark and I had been in this area a couple of years before and come across some fine sea-trout, so we were hopeful. Upon laying on just off the burn outflow, Mark tied into a sea-trout of just over the 2 lb mark on

The majestic scenery of Loch Sheil

his Stone Goat, and it led him a merry jig, roaring out of the water like a miniature Exocet missile. I also met up with a finnock and a small brown, but no further action was forthcoming, so we crossed the loch to have chuck in the burn mouth of Scamodale, a highly rated salmon holding spot but failed to interest a fish. Even Mark's protestations that, at that time of year, there were always salmon at Scamodale, and the enthusiasm that engendered, failed to alter the outcome. Generally speaking, loch salmon at the mouth of a burn in spate will have a go. The only conclusions we could come to were that there were no fish in situ, that not enough time had passed since the rains arrived to settle the fish into a taking mood, or that elevated water temperatures were hampering our efforts.

We tried here, and we tried there, but with similar results I'm afraid, and as the day was starting to wane we started the long journey westwards to the launch site. We had to pass Heron Island on the return home and all thought that a drift to the burn mouth could not be passed over, even though it almost certainly meant missing Jill's best endeavours on the culinary front chez Ardshealach. There is a distinct pecking order and distribution of fish inhabiting a burn mouth; salmon will roam around the out-rushing water and are generally most co-operative when they've got their noses right in the heart of the flow; sea-trout, on the other-hand, tend to sit back off the strongest flow and can be expected in deeper water.

As we drifted in we saw a couple of good fish, almost certainly sea-trout, disporting themselves to either side of the burn mouth, and as we closed with the outer fringe of the burn outflow a fish showed on Colin's side of the boat and, as described in the opening paragraphs, provided him with a bonny fish of about the same size as Mark's, if not slightly larger, and everybody was well chuffed with our day. As Sheil sea-trout and salmon are on the improve, anglers are encouraged to return all their catch, so we returned to the jetty with no tangible signs of success, but we all felt that it had been a damned good day, if tough and demanding. We had failed to get a collective 'Macfisheries' (a fishing equivalent of a MacNab) – a brown, a sea-trout and a salmon – but I'd always rather catch sea-trout than salmon.

Loch Sheil is a wonderful place. It has infinite variety of scenery and fishing locations. I wish it well for the future, but with the cancer of smolt-rearing still eating into its heart, it will be very interesting to see if its recovery will be significant or not. Perhaps if onshore farming operations become a legal requirement Sheil will return to being one of the finest sea-trout lochs in Scotland. Here's hoping.

– 43 –

The Law of Sod

WHILST I SOMETIMES believe that the whole world comes under the sway of Sod's Law, I have no doubts at all that that the world of fishing is governed by it.

For example, why is it that the first time I visit a new fishery, regardless of the conditions, the fishing is wonderful, and never again reaches those dizzy heights of satisfaction and success, no matter how often you return? And it also goes without saying that a trip planned in January for May, will land precisely on the worst spell of weather experienced since the Ice Age. And, of course, that hatch that you plan to enjoy, and which has never been early or late since Noah sailed toy boats on the Sea of Galilee, has been indefinitely postponed.

Such are the joys! You grit your teeth and get on with it because it's part of the rich panoply of fishing life, and you've come to accept that fishing never works out just as you expect it to. And if it did we'd never learn anything.

Quaffing a pint of Guinness in Eddies (sic) Bar, I watched the jackdaws flying backwards over the rooftops of Clonbur. We – Phil, the Buddha, Stan the Elder and I – had meticulously planned our Corrib trip for a late duckfly/early olive sortie. We had visions of light breezes, muted sunlight, chaffinches arguing from the blackthorn blossom, armadas of pert-winged olives, swirling masses of hovering duckfly and, of course, having to beat off monster trout with a stick!

The Law of Sod kicked in with arctic temperatures, winds screaming like banshees, one – yes, count it, *one* – duckfly, and a trickle of frostbitten olives. The dickie-birds, coughing and sneezing from the leafless bushes, provided a backdrop for some of the hardest fishing I've ever experienced on Corrib. We were launching from Tom Sullivan's moorings on the Duras Peninsula, and on our first morning the boatmen – John Somerville junior and Dennis – shared a demeanour similar to that of Casanova arriving in the land of a thousand virgins only to discover that his *cojones* had been re-routed to Bangkok. Fishing is rarely, if ever hopeless. As long as there is water with fish in it and you can spend your time fishing rather than drowning, there is always hope. Well, that's my religion, for what its worth.

John jnr and Dennis had a war-council and decided that pulling wets was probably the best bet and although the easterly/north-easterly winds didn't offer the best drifts, they reckoned we could pull a fish or two. I listened to this advice with a falling heart; I wanted to fish buzzers, for a variety of reasons. Whilst I can pull wets with the best of them, over the years it had become apparent that big fish on Corrib were more likely to fall for buzzers or nymphs than pulled wets; and pulling wets in a 'howler' was likely to bring on a recurrence of my tennis and golfer's elbow from which I had just recovered. Buddha, my fishing partner for the day, concurred.

On the other hand, could we figure-of-eight fast enough to cope with wind speed and boat drift? I was prepared to give it a try, and I was fairly sure that John jnr could find us enough shelter somewhere. That was the first time I heard about Heartache Bay, or Oaklands as it's referred to on the maps. This area is a shallowish enclosure, surrounded by the peninsula on three sides and, from the main lough, by a cordon of islands; a lough within a lough, with a fairly weedy bottom, and about ½ to ¾ the size of a football pitch, as I remember it.

I'd seen places like this before – Stoneyhill on Harray is almost identical – and they always seem to contain better quality fish that are a bugger to get out. Hence, Heartache Bay. John jnr told us that, generally speaking, it was only fished in the evenings when the spotted inhabitants had a tendency to put their paranoia on hold, but he assured us that even then it wasn't easy.

To conform with airline company restrictions, I had come equipped with my Greys G-Tec Travel 10-foot for a #7, and a floater, midge tip and an intermediate, with only a box of buzzers and a few hatching-olive patterns. I felt naked. It generally took a squad of navvies to get my kit in and out of a boat, but needs must when Ryanair dictates.

A fifteen-foot leader with two droppers, graced with a #12 olive quill buzzer on the top, a similarly sized Basil's Buzzer middle, and a plain black #10 buzzer on the point seemed to cover all eventualities when we 'laid on' at the top of the drift. It was, indeed, relatively sheltered in Heartache, especially at the top of the drift, but by the time we had reached about halfway, my fingers were a blur trying to maintain contact with the buzzers. The idea in this style of fishing is to present static flies, settling in the water column, whilst keeping the line relatively taut between rod tip and leader. In calm or light wind conditions this is child's play; in a wind approaching gale force, virtually impossible. Having gone through this before I expected to miss more fish than I hooked. What happens is that the angler feels a sharp knock, then nothing – the fish has picked up the fly on a slack line and the angler becomes aware of it just as the fish rejects it as inedible. A very frustrating business, but the odd one runs out of luck. And this was a better scenario than being unable to lift a pint of Guinness to my parched lips in the evening because my tendons are twanging like banjo strings after a day's pulling in a near-gale.

As in most of these micro-environments, disturbance is the enemy. An outboard motor, running no matter how gently in such shallow confined areas, must send reverberating echoes throughout the length and breadth of the domain. It has always been my experience that, all other things being equal, the first drift is the best. Trout are not necessarily spooked by outboard motors, but the associated noise and vibration certainly reduce activity and put the trout on alert status. So, it proved to be; we saw a fish take an olive dun on the shoreward side half way down the drift, and a heavy fish jump towards the tail-end, so our hopes were high of a positive response to our efforts.

As we approached the downwind end of the drift, I got a sharp 'dig' to the buzzers. I thought I'd missed him but, on lifting the rod, I saw the leader 'slice' off to the left, and the rod slammed down into a pleasing hoop. John jnr jumped onto the oars to keep us well clear of the reeds and I was aware of the Buddha winding in to clear the water for me. Without a word being spoken everyone was aware that this was a good fish, and given the reeds, shallow water and strong winds, the odds were on its side. But we had three very experienced guys working as a team to shorten said odds.

The first sign of the fish was a wave from a big, brown tail. The fish was on the olive quill buzzer on the top dropper which didn't please me; two trailing flies just looking for somewhere to live isn't the best in snag-filled water. Bullying was in order, and the Hardy G-Tec is just the rod for such a job. It has a very responsive tip which is fine for sending signals to the hand (and deriving fun from small fish), but the butt-end is packed with loads of reserve power which springs into action when push comes to shove. This rod reminds me of my old Sage RPL Graphite 3, which I long considered the best fly rod ever made. The G-Tec may have it beat.

I won't bore you with the details of the fight – which was long, dour and heavy – but we were deep into the reeds before Chico got the net under it. It was no monster by Corrib standards. At the time I reckoned it at 6 lb – it was built like a proverbial outside lavatory; deep and chunky, with shoulders like Mike Tyson. In retrospect, given that it measured 23″ to the fork of the tail (and a 24″ trout of standard condition weighs 6 lb) I have re-estimated, conservatively, to 5½. If anyone wants to argue, that's fine, but it was still my heaviest fly-caught wild brownie at that time, and it's still in Corrib somewhere, trying to rationalise its alien abduction experience.

We worked Heartache hard after that, but the wind was building, and maintaining contact with the buzzers with figure-of-eight retrieves was becoming impossible. Slow pulling to imitate a figure-of-eight retrieve never really works satisfactorily because no matter how hard you try it is inevitable that the flies will be 'drawn' more often than not. I missed another good take, but that's the breaks, and although I hoped and continued to hope, I expected no more. The Buddha managed a wee perch which, strangely, seemed to please him greatly. But continually motoring up to the head of the drift was having a detrimental effect upon the willingness of the fish to co-operate and, apart from a monster pike (in excess of 20lb) which swam, fins out of the water, in front of the boat in a lovelorn manner, we saw no more action. We had to move, if only to rest the drifts and it looked like it would have to be a wet fly session out amongst the islands if we were going to continue the day profitably.

I rigged up some hatching-olive patterns which George Barron had sent me, and we ventured out into the maelstrom which was the main lough. I quickly came to the conclusion that the #12 olive patterns weren't man enough for the wave height, so I dug out John jnr's fly boxes and selected a team of big Dabblers in varying colours. Dodging about the skerries and offshore shoals I managed to bang out another couple of fine fish – 1½ and 2 pounds respectively – on a bright green Dabbler, and the Buddha 'fractured his mallard' with a fit pounder, whilst the boat leapt from wave-top to wave-top, like a show jumper at an equestrian event. Everywhere John jnr took us there were fish. I have never before encountered a ghillie so young with that unquantifiable ability to 'stop' on top of fish with unfailing regularity. It's like a sixth sense that can neither be learnt nor borrowed; if its not there at birth, learn to do without. There's no doubt in my mind we'd have been doomed to a fishless day without the bold John Somerville junior!

Later, as we attempted to do justice to the perfectly cooked and immense T-bone steaks in the restaurant of the Fairhill House Hotel, our thoughts were full of Corrib, big fish and the quality of the Irish experience. They do it well over there, with a certain style we lack over here. I put it down to the fact that flyfishing is revered in the West of Ireland; a noble occupation which is honourable work. Over here we tend to look upon fishing as a hobby that should be placed way down the priority list of life. Being an accomplished flyfisher earns no accolades this side of the Irish Sea. How different it is over there.

It also occurred to me that if I'd been a local I probably wouldn't have ventured out that day. It had been a day of foul weather when expectations of good fishing were illogical. But we had ventured forth, and I had amassed a basket of three for somewhere in the region of 9lb. That's good fishing by any standards. That is, also, the upside of Sod's Law.

A Harray trout hooked in the 'Paddling Pool

– 44 –

Orkney – The Changing Face of Harray

AS THE NORTHLINK ferry, MV *Hamnavoe,* ploughed its way across the Pentland Firth I nursed a cup of tea and let idle thoughts run through my mind. I was heading back to fish the lochs where I had served my apprenticeship as a trout fisherman. I planned to fish Swannay, Stenness and Harray in a three-day trip before heading back on the ferry

If you sat down to design the perfect trout loch, you'd end up with something remarkably like the Harray loch.

Surprisingly, Harray hasn't been one of my favourite Orkney lochs for quite some time, because in my day it tended to lack the odd 'monster' which would get your heart racing on Swannay or Stenness. Harray, for much of its history, has been about quantity rather than quality (from a size perspective, anyway). Recently, with the addition of sea-trout running through from Stenness in late summer, things have changed somewhat, a change I welcomed.

The second day of our late spring, Orcadian adventure saw 'Puck' Kirkpatrick, and 'Stormin' Norman launch from the Harray site under the Ring of Brodgar. A better day than the previous one which we spent on Swannay and Hundland, we were greeted with moderate winds and comfortable temperatures. We were going to experience another weather change in the afternoon, but more of that later.

Harray is a long loch. If you are standing on the Brodgar Bridge in the south end, you can only just see the roof of the Merkister Hotel in the north, because the curvature of the Earth intervenes. Harray's axis lies north-west/south-east, with a fairly large chunk of it running off to the west (Esslemont's Bay). Just short of a thousand hectares, she isn't a small loch by any means, but the most remarkable feature is the overall shallowness of her water. Fourteen feet is the deepest you'll find in the summer months, but only if you want to because there are large areas comprised of skerries and shallows, ranging from about 8 feet to sod-all.

Shallow water is a vitally important feature in a wild trout water. Brown trout are, generally, not well adapted to deep water. Some races of trout can adapt to it, particularly in the great glacial lochs of the Highlands of Scotland but, by and large, water less than 8 feet is perfect. This is mainly due to the fact that the bulk of invertebrate trout food abounds in water of this depth and, where the food is, the trout will not be far away. Even in the very deep glacial lakes the food will be found in the upper layers of the loch water and the shallow margins, so, in a way, the trout still feed in shallow water.

Harray is a profoundly fertile and prolific loch and the quantity of indigenous fish is truly astounding, boosted in the mid-summer by the previously mentioned sea-trout. Catches in double-figures are nothing out of the ordinary in the right conditions, and even in the most hopeless weather a fish or two will come along and stretch your string.

As we 'roared' up Harray, I felt like I was in the Tardis, travelling through time. We slipped by the Little Ess Holm, out across the mouth of Esslemont's Bay, and pulled in just under Kirkness Point. The wind, westerly with a hint of north, wasn't perfect for a drift along the shore, but Norman assured us that it was a 'banker' for a fish or two. And so it proved to be, Norm's DI-5 pulled a few where the bottom of the loch disappeared into the depths. My fast intermediate seemed not to be getting the flies deep enough.

Round the corner lay the wide expanses of Merkister Bay, probably the shallowest large tract of water in Harray, a maze of skerries, shallows and narrow deep reaches. In the late springs of my day, this had been a favourite location because the deep trenches and their muddy bottoms held vast quantities of buzzer larvae and pupae and, given the conditions, massive hatches would take place. I wanted to visit my old haunts, but Norm reckoned that such endeavour would be a waste of time, the hatches were – a bit like me – a thing of the past. But he could see by my face that I still wanted to give it a go, so he relented. I did a rapid fly change and stuck a Green Peter Muddler on the top for any shrimp feeders prowling about, with a Sooty Olive variant and a Red Arrow variant for the midge feeders down the cast. The Green Peter Muddler is a fabulous wild brown trout fly for clear water, and always was a go-to fly for Harray, and the other two are classic stillwater patterns for trout feeding on dark and olive midge pupae.

Almost immediately, on the edge of a big skerry I had a pound-plus trout on the muddler which falsely confirmed my expectations that some things never change. But it was a flash in the pan. Norman pulled a couple of smaller fish on his DI-5, but the midge patterns did nothing. I was all for going deeper into the bay, but Norm reckoned he had indulged me enough, and we headed south towards the Ess Holms, the westerly wind whipping across our bow. It was a fine enough day for fishing, but a westerly isn't a good wind for Harray and doesn't suit the best drifts, which are provided by a north-westerly or a south-easterly. Westerlies force the boat angler into short, truncated, drifts across the lines of skerries whereas in a north-westerly or south-easterly one can drift for miles picking up skerries, and trout, all the way.

We visited the mouth of Nistaben Bay, hunted around the Muckle Ess Holm, dipped into the Ballarat Burnmouth, and investigated the tail-end of the Ballarat Reach. The odd offer, and a couple of average trout was all we could manage and the Harray mini-lure selection – black marabou, muddler heads, lots of flash and strong colours – was doing all the work. I rather fancied a trip to the 'Paddling Pool', or Stoneyhill as others call it, but Norm was less than enthused. However, as he set up a drift outside the islands I had an inkling that his resistance was waning.

The Stoneyhill Islands/Paddling Pool is a fascinating feature. It is basically a shallow lagoon, mud and marl bottomed, surrounded by a string of islands which effectively separate it from the main body of the loch, and it tends to fish entirely differently to its parent loch. In my Orkney days I'd regularly fish it in the very early months of the season because it would warm up from the sun's influence much earlier than the rest of Harray, and great midge hatches were a feature of April fishing. Due to its shallowness, and as Orkney's climate doesn't lead to hot summers, it would fish all season through, but it was sensitive to over-fishing. Excessive motoring within its confines would put the fish down, and two boats at a time were about all it could manage.

Due to its early start the average trout weight would be about ¼ pound heavier than in the main loch, and this was a major attraction. Another reason it appealed to me was that very fine techniques were very successful throughout the summer months – dry fly, nymph tactics and small wet flies on low-density lines could earn you a superb basket. Also, because a major spawning burn enters in its eastern corner, top quality pre-spawning browns would gather there in the latter months of the season.

When I was guiding, and if conditions suited, I would always try to get my guests into Stoneyhill for a few drifts, knowing there was a good chance of the best fish of their holiday coming to the boat. And due to its shallowness (its deepest part being about four feet, averaging, at a guess, about two-and-a-half) the fights were always spectacular with long, surging runs being provided by pound-plus fish. Unfortunately, it is considered by many of the locals as a 'duffers' haven' which, in my opinion, is far from the truth. Delicacy of fishing and boat manoeuvre is crucial, a light touch to both essential.

When the main loch is high access is relatively easy, but when the level drops local knowledge is indispensable if the boat isn't going to have to be dragged for a considerable distance through inches of water. I'm not going to provide an access map here because the local ghillies have to keep a few secrets from the proletariat.

Any road up, we slipped in behind the islands, and I rapidly changed my line to a Airflo Fast Glass intermediate, slipped on a small Olive Quill Muddler on the top, a #12 Kate Maclaren in the middle, and a similarly sized Claret Dabbler on the point. A small, palmered black fly is essential in Stoneyhill, and my old favourite was a #12 Palmered Coch, but I couldn't find one in my haste and plumped for the Kate.

Generally speaking, there are two types of aquatic terrain in Stoneyhill – the mud/marl bottom or stony skerries – which hold fish, and one or the other will provide sport. If there is a hatch on the soft bottomed areas will provide the best action, if not then it's best to stick to the stones. As it turned out we got a shot at both.

As the afternoon passed, we noticed that the wind was dropping away and there was a distinct rise in temperature. When we entered Stoneyhill the breeze was still quite fresh and it wasn't long before we were into action. I say 'we' but that would be stretching a point. Norm had stuck to his DI-5 and tried to short-line it in the shallow water which didn't work at all. I, on the other hand, with my intermediate was into a stonking fish in no time at all. I had promised fish to friends, so that gave us a chance to do some spooning. The first fish, around the 1½ pound mark, contained sticklebacks in profusion and took the dabbler. The next, identically sized, slammed into the muddler and showed shrimp and a scattering of midge pupae. This was a hint as to how the afternoon would close.

The breeze was softening, the temperature climbing, and fish were starting to show in ones and twos. The muddler took another two, and now I had enough fish to satisfy my requirements. We headed back up to the western end of the lagoon and I handed my rod to Puck and took the oars whilst Norm changed to an intermediate line. Norm can be a stubborn old bugger, but even he could see the writing on the wall and the DI-5 was headed for the bench.

Midge were hatching everywhere by now and Stoneyhill had come alive and was 'bubbling' with rising trout, but that didn't make them easy. Puck picked up another fish which was instantly returned, and both he and Norm moved a few more. Norm, who is pretty astute as regards targeting rising fish, had plumped for Ian Hutcheon's Midge Hogs, in a variety of colours, as the answer to the problem, but in this instance they failed comprehensively, and the Olive Quill Muddler seemed to tick all the boxes.. For a generation or more, Harray trout have been particularly susceptible to small, finely-dressed muddlers during a midge hatch, a gambit which I have never seen quite so successfully played out anywhere else.

Time was wearing on and hunger was starting to demand attention. Four trout, destined for the dinner table, lay in the bottom of the boat. More had been returned to fight another day. All of them fine fish, in the peak of condition, but the better fish all came from the 'Paddling Pool'. This was late May in a year when winter seemed very loath to loosen its grip on northern Scotland. A degree or two of temperature difference from the main loch to the sheltered confines of the Stoneyhill lagoon had given its trout a boost, which the rest of the loch could not equal.

Successful loch trout fishing hinges on small, easily overlooked, factors such as this. Harray is a collection of micro-environments, each demanding a precise set of influences to perform. As I said earlier, if you wished to create a perfect trout loch, it would end up looking a lot like Harray.

Not the biggest fish in the Durness lochs, but perhaps the prettiest!

− 45 −

Loch Croispol

I SAW THE initial take. I guessed it was a fairly 'run of the mill' Croispol brownie, around about the pound mark. But as the fight progressed I was losing the upper hand, and the bow in the rod was increasing beyond expectation.

I was confused. Had I foul-hooked this fish? The typical fight from a foul-hooked fish is a series of dogged pulls followed by fast, exaggerated runs against the bend of the rod. This fight did not match up at all to that pattern. There was a lot more weight than expected and a large number of arm-shuddering staccato thumps. I looked down into the gin-clear water and there was an amazing sight. Down to about 20 feet I could see not one, not two, but three pound-ish fish all charging about on a two-dropper cast. What was even more surprising was this was happening on a team of buzzers. Multiple hook-ups on wet flies is common enough, but very unusual on buzzer rigs.

Many, many years ago I visited Croispol, a limestone loch in the Durness region, as part of a group of anglers. I also fished Borralaidh (pronounced *Bor-a-lee)* and Caladail in the same area. All were remarkable, particularly because of their (already mentioned) crystal clear waters and very lightly coloured marl substrates.

It was love at first sight with Borralaidh; a little less so with Caladail; and I wasn't much impressed with the individual average size of the trout population of Croispol, to the extent that I have not fished it at all in the intervening years. Big mistake, as I discovered this June.

The aquatic food and fly life of these lochs is phenomenal. In a contained area amongst some of the least productive and barren land and water in the UK, the Durness lochs are pure treasure. You'd have to experience it to believe it. Cow dung fly, oak fly, buzzers, sedges, crane fly, stone fly olives and hordes of terrestrial diptera. And, of course, innumerable shrimp and snails. A literal smorgasbord of invertebrate delicacies. A fly fisherman's paradise.

On the downside, generally speaking the boats on Scottish Highland trout lochs leave a bit to be desired, especially if you are used to the quality craft of the major lowland commercial fisheries. I have become so used to these 'plastic bathtubs' that I take them in my stride and just get on with the fishing, always bearing in mind the precise limitations and restrictions of the particular boat in question. One word of advice, however, is to always take an 'across-the gunnels' boat seat as these boats have typically poor seating arrangements for flyfishing occupants, and also carry a drogue to stabilise a drift.

The quintessential Highland loch boat is one of the Pioner range. After a long trek through the wilds, to discover that the day's fishing has to be out of one of these boats has caused hardened men to burst into tears. They are very low in the gunnel department so that you are continually banging your chin off your knee caps. They have no discernible keel so they don't drift worth a damn, but continually 'crab' all over the shop. They are, though, relatively stable but this doesn't counter-balance the fact that by no stretch of the imagination could you argue that they are designed for flyfishing.

There is a reason for this state of affairs which is not necessarily one of cost. It is that estates may need durable boats that can be dragged to location by off-road vehicles, across distances (sometimes measured in miles) made up of very rough ground indeed. When located at the lochside they will, of necessity, be left to fend for themselves for the duration of the season. I am fairly sure that some may even be simply flipped over come the end of the season and left outside over the winter months.

But don't let this put you off for a moment, because many of these less than satisfactory craft are situated on lochs where the fishing more than compensates. After all, what are a few hours of minor discomfort and frustration compared to memories of fishing that will linger for a lifetime?

When Stan (The Elder) Clementsmith and I arrived at the boat launch site on Croispol, sweating and midge-bitten, encumbered with essential kit, we had to make a decision. Two boats were available – one a high-sided, unstable fibre-glass vessel of no discernible make and lacking a viable keel, or a Pioner, suffering the same lack, with low gunnel height. We plumped for the high-sided job because Stan the Elder felt that the cramped condition of the Pioner would see him needing intensive medical care by the end of the day. This decision was to have embarrassing repercussions later in the day. Read on.

The loch surface was like a mirror and there wasn't much happening to disturb it. As we were tackling up a short shower drifted through and a slight breeze followed. Suddenly, and without warning, flocks of sand martins appeared across the loch surface and fish began to rise as far as the eye could see.

There is an Orcadian-born technique in my armoury which involves putting a floatant-treated Sedgehog on the top dropper and fishing a couple of wets behind it, all fished on a floating, or preferably, a short midge-tip line. The idea is to pull the flies as normal which makes the hog 'pop' – diving below the surface on the pull, and then popping back to the surface between pulls. There are occasions when this drives trout absolutely crazy, most of the takes coming to the hog but also drawing fish to the lower wet patterns. When trout are active in the surface layers and actively 'rising' this is a method I would strongly advise. It has worked for me from Orkney all the way down to Rutland. I reached for this tactic as I created my leader. Claret Sedgehog on the top, Red-Ribbed Sooty Olive variant in the middle, and a small Red Arrow variant on the point.

The winds were light and from a south westerly direction, and as we drifted out from the moorings it was interesting to note that the busy trout activity was positioned in precise bands, located between the extensive weedbeds in the south, west and north, and the very deep waters in the east. Like Borralaidh, Croispol has a deep hole located just beneath the Durness Craft Village, though not as deep as the former. The drop off, the area between the very deep and the very shallow, is quite distinct and is stepped. Areas of trout habitat are designated by colour. The very shallow is a pinkish-brown; the slightly deeper band is yellow, and the area just short of the depths is blue/green. The waters covering the hole are a dark blue. Trout activity was intense in the yellow water, fading out as we progressed into the blue/green.

We needed some trout for dinner, so the first fish, in the 1 to 1½lb range was knocked on the head and spooned. The spoon revealed buzzer pupae, hordes of them. Some minute, others massive. The biggest and most imitable, were a deep brownish orange with distinct wing buds. The medium sized pupae were a dark olive green. No surprise then that it took the Sooty Olive variant wet fly. However, the next fish, needed to complete dinner provisions requirement, contained a few pupae plus a congregation of water mites. The mites were small and quite dark – probably of the Arrenurus family – and I have only ever once before seen mites in a trout gut, in a very similar high pH water in Orkney. Those, however, were red and at least twice the size of the Croispol mites. Sorry, I know I'm being an anorak, but these things fascinate me.

I persevered with the wet fly rig knowing in my heart that the rises I could see were to buzzer pupae trapped in the surface film and I was only witnessing a small proportion of the feeding activity. Most of the ascending buzzer pupae would be being intercepted between substrate and surface. This scenario was screaming out for an epoxy buzzer rig, possibly with a sacrificial Sedgehog on the point to keep the buzzers from diving too quickly into the depths.

A day out is a day to learn. Sometimes you learn a lot by catching nothing; sometimes you learn very little by catching a lot. This day was a mix of the two. I caught a lot and learnt a lot about trout behaviour during a good midge hatch. Fish were active from deep to shallow. Most of the better fish were staying deep and the smaller stuff braved the shallows. The Croispol trout seem largely unimpressed by static buzzer patterns, and were as likely to take a slim wet as an epoxy buzzer. I mixed them up on the cast and saw no great difference in performance.

We headed in at about 2.00 pm for a bite of lunch and a chance to think over our techniques and tactics, to maximise on the positive and eliminate the negative. This is often a dangerous thing to do because in the short time away from the action, things can change dramatically, and if that happens it is very difficult to catch up. There was a change coming that had nothing to do with trout or fishing that I would definitely not welcome.

As we puttered into the boat moorings, I spotted that my cast had slipped its moorings and a dropper fly had lodged in the toe of my waders. As the boat slipped to the shore I leant forward to dislodge this recalcitrant fly... and found myself in the loch. Did I tell you that our chosen craft was unstable? By leaning forward in an exaggerated fashion, the boat took the opportunity to spit me out. I was only in a few feet of water but the boat drifted down over my legs and, try as I might, I could not extract them or get upright. I was forced to turn on my front and crawl out from underneath the craft, soaking myself to the veritable cojones. In 50-plus years of boat fishing this was the first time I had fallen out of a boat. I sincerely hope it proves to be the last.

Too much time would have been wasted in heading back to the digs for a change to dry kit, so I persevered onwards and upwards. It wasn't a particularly cold day but soon I was chilled to the bone. I didn't realise that my dry fly box, which I always keep close to hand, had taken the opportunity to make a bid for freedom and floated away.

Back out on the loch the breeze had died and I falsely thought that this would in no way negatively affect the buzzer fishing. Not so. The good, solid takes of the morning suddenly became tentative, unproductive knocks and jags. I altered retrieve and tried everything possible, from static to relatively fast. The naturals were still hatching and the trout seemed as active as they were before, but nothing was brought to the boat. Then, just as I was seriously thinking of some dry clothes, a very slight breeze returned and we were back in business, getting solid hook-ups.

Croispol trout can't challenge those of Lanlish, Caladail or Borralaidh for size and weight. Fish of two-pounds-plus are reasonably common, and I'm sure there is the odd trophy fish scouring the depths, but it is quantity and beauty that are the hallmark of this strain of trout. Above-average sized trout rarely appear in big catches. In my experience, big trout come to the angler on a day when things are relatively quiet, numbers-wise. And strangely, during a hatch, I expect to see the biggest fish of the day come as the hatch peters out. Big trout seem reluctant to compete with their average-sized brethren, or, perhaps, when the big boys decide to take a place at the table the smaller boys go and make themselves scarce. I really don't know. The evidence points both ways.

The hatch faded away as a big bank of cloud built from the south-west. Weather change was on its way. The loch went dead, and I can't say I was anything but relieved as I was losing feeling in my extremities, those you can and those you can't mention. I badly needed a bath to get the body temperature back up, and I had fish to clean and fillet.

Hey, Croispol! We've got unfinished business. Our brief flirtation has only whetted my appetite. I don't think there is a more attractive aquatic environment in the UK, and your fish are a wonder to behold. But please refrain from intimate contact in future.

When your boat partner turns his back on you, you've got problems!

– 46 –

Heaven and Hell – in a boat!

IF GOOD MARRIAGES come stamped 'Made in Heaven', then good boat partnerships are hand-built in the workshop at the bottom of God's back garden!

I'm no authority on marriages, good or otherwise, but I do have some pretty valid observations on boat partners. The development of a fulfilling and deeply rewarding boat partnership goes something like this:

- The first time you fish together, Jock and you discover a shared a) sense of humour, b) love of compatible fishing styles, and c) loathing for Tony Blair.
- The second outing uncovers other shared passions, such as a) single malt whiskies, b) summer holidays spent hunting wild trout, c) hot curries, and d) girls with big protuberances, and the day is full of chat and laughter.
- After such an auspicious start a) you and Jock fish together as much as possible, b) begin to retell old tales, whilst enjoying them at least as much as the first time told, c) share each other's packed lunches, and d) you pass the 'piss pot' before it's even asked for, and the day is full of comfortable silences.
- By now the pair of you are joined at the hip. You miss wedding anniversaries and wife's birthdays because you've arranged to fish with Jock that day; for Christmas Jock gets an outboard motor from you and your missus gets a paperback book on line-dancing; you have your own armchair in Jock's house; the fishing widows holiday together in Blackpool, while you and Jock are off getting bitten by midges in some gawd-awful wilderness north of Inverness.

Been there, done that, worn the 'jaggy bunnet full of flees'! A good fishing partner is in many ways like a good wife, except that when you've netted his five-pounder for him and you're both exhausted, breathless and satisfied, you don't have to cuddle him for half-an-hour!

If that's the up-side of boat partners, what's the down-side? A bad boat partner is hell on earth, capable of turning the best day's fishing into a nightmare. Sometimes it's simply down to bad chemistry – you hate each other on sight and nothing, repeat ***nothing***, is going to change that. This sort of bad chemistry equation is officially recognised. In many major competitions there exists the ability for a contestant to go to the organisers and request a boat-partner draw change on the grounds of incompatibility. Organisers know that putting two antagonistic anglers together in a boat for a day in the high-pressure atmosphere of competition may end up with accusations of aiding and abetting manslaughter being levelled at them. Bad chemistry is something we learn to live with and rely on mathematical unlikelihood to ensure that we never share a boat with the sod ever again.

And then there is the guy that everybody hates to fish with. He comes in all shapes and sizes, varying from:

- 'The Amiable Buffer', who can't cast without endangering your life and limb or wrapping his leader round your head, rod or anything else sticking out. He apologises every time he lassoes you but keeps on doing it. You can severely strain your kidneys holding back the free flow of urine on such a day. After all, he's stuck a fly in everything else, why should 'John Thomas' escape unscathed?
- 'The Expert', who has a (wrong) opinion on anything and everything and feels it his bounden duty to share all his views on life/politics/fishing/etc., with you. Very little daunts this guy – not reasoned logic, argument, nor silence (which he feels compelled to fill with more inane drivel) – but blunt and to-the-point statements sometimes get through. "For the love of gawd, shut the f*** up!" is my last resort, and it has never failed me yet!
- 'The Natural' – a close relation to Amiable Buffer, this guy was born to catch fish without ever having to learn even the basics of flyfishing. He will catch ten times as many fish as you without the ability to cast, retrieve, or name a fly. ("It's a sort of black and green thing", later turning out to be a Silver Invicta!) while continually repeating the litany "Oh! I think I've got another one!" If you can leave the water after a day with this guy not vowing to take up golf or tearing what remains of your hair out, you're a better man than I am.
- 'Mr Misery' – the sort of bloke who thinks the whole universe is a construct solely designed to piss him off. We've all met this guy – you catch a fish and not only are you 'lucky', you are also an enemy for life. His ability to catch fish is seriously compromised by the waves of negativity that surrounds him like a

cloak. He hates the venue ("I never catch anything here!"); the fish ("They're all bottom feeders/ too hard to catch/ too easy for others to catch/ at the other end of the loch/too few/too deep/etc., etc."), the tactics required ("I hate sinking/ floating lines!" or "I only use sinking/floating lines!")

- And last, but by no means least 'The Smug Competitive B*****d'. This less than charming individual will inevitably, at some time during the day, state that he despises competition fishing and fishermen, whilst proving to be the most competitive person you've ever met. He can recite, at the drop of a hat, how many fish he has caught, moved or 'touched' as long as the totals exceed yours. His memory becomes a bit vague when roles are reversed. It may have been planned as a pleasant day out for you; to him it's a no-holds barred fight to the death. Surprisingly (or perhaps not), he quickly evolves into Mr Misery when his luck is out!

Some years ago I was out on Loch Leven with a guy we shall call Jimmy (for the sake of my front teeth should he ever read this piece). Jimmy was a classic 'Natural'. All his tackle was carried in a small, canvas bag I'd have trouble getting my packed lunch into. His rod had the appearance of a family heirloom, and his net resembled the last thing left unsold at a car-boot sale. This was in the latter days of rainbow trout stockings on the loch, and the fishing was as hard as it had ever been on this less than easy water.

We – well 'I' actually, as Jimmy didn't give a toss – had decided to fish from the Point of St Serf's to the South Deeps. The area had been working and there were both rainbows and good browns to be had, with a bit of luck. The sun was bright and the ripple intermittent, so I rigged up with an intermediate and a long leader bearing a mix of buzzers and nymphs. Jimmy put up a floating line (I suspected that's all he had!) with a mix of traditional wets that Isaac Walton would have considered a bit old fashioned.

Fishing as slowly as I could whilst still imparting the impression of 'life', I started to get the odd knock and abortive take, which came to nothing. Whilst trying to extract success from frustration, I noticed that Jimmy's floating line was lying haphazardly across the surface of the water, with a great bulge in it. He may have thought he was in touch with his flies, but his rate of retrieve was not even keeping up with the boat drift, so you can imagine my surprise to see this great bulge of line start to straighten out in a direction off to Jimmy's right hand side. I realised immediately that a fish had picked up one of Jimmy's flies and set off with malice aforethought. Jimmy, however, was totally oblivious, and continued on with his slow retrieve until everything went as tight as a drum and, with a surprised look on his homely visage, uttered the immortal words "I think I've got one!" 'Who got who?' would have been an interesting topic for debate, but as the fish – a 3½ lb bar of silver rainbow – was inevitably skull-hauled over the side of the boat and dispatched, the honours will have to go to Jimmy.

I shook my head, attempted to close my slack-jawed mouth, and put it all down to experience. This was obviously an aberration, a 'one-off' event unlikely to be repeated given the suspicious and sophisticated nature of Leven trout.

Wrong! Three more times the same thing happened. Slack line, flies hanging dead in the water, fish picking up the same badly over-dressed, lumpy Bibio, and swimming away with it like a small boy gripping a lollypop. And each fish was a beautiful specimen of naturalised, fin-perfect rainbow. Nothing I could do would get more than a pluck from the fish, and even when I switched to a floater, similar patterns and technique, did it work? Did it buggery! I knocked my proverbial 'pan' in and got skunked; Jimmy had a lovely relaxing day. Never changed line or flies, the fish did all the hard work, and he ended up with a cracking bag of rainbows. There's nae justice!

However, the worst boat partner I ever had doesn't fit into any of the above classifications. He was unique, and probably still is. Let's call him Martin, to save embarrassment. We met on a hot summer's morning on Grafham, where we were scheduled to fish an international competition. All things seemed fine; Martin wanted the engine, so I let him have his head. After all, he was local. My practice had indicated dry fly in a specific area of the reservoir, and as we were headed in that direction, I couldn't have been happier.

To set the scene, this was decades ago, and my gear was designed for drift-fishing wild browns. My rod was simply not capable of being accurate up to, and over, thirty yards, had my double taper lines been capable of reaching such a distance. And, in the flat calm conditions, the fish were just too spooky to come close to the boat, and long casting was essential. So, I was badly under-gunned, as became apparent when Martin covered every fish that approached the front of the boat long before they were within my pitiful range. Fish would show away down in front of the boat, outwith even Martin's casting ability. But they would come, sip-sipping their way towards the boat, trackable at all times. As soon as they entered Martin's casting range, he would cover them, either catching the fish or putting it down. I got the odd fish, but I was struggling. However, I was prepared to overlook Martin's greedy need to cover every fish in front and decided that my inabilities had nothing to do with him, and it was my fault if my tackle was letting me down. After all, you wouldn't turn up at a clay pigeon shoot with a bow and arrow.

I was even prepared to overlook the total lack of conversation once the fishing started – he obviously needed to concentrate to be a top-class angler, which he obviously was. But what I couldn't get over or condone was that he was a pig-ignorant rat-bag. Always having been a searcher after knowledge, especially angling knowledge, I thought I could learn a bit about rainbow dry fly technique from watching this guy. When it became apparent that I was watching his retrieve style, and actually had the temerity to ask a few pointed questions on technique, he promptly turned his back to me and faced over the transom of the boat, thereby ensuring that I couldn't see his hands and ruling out any dialogue. It was difficult for him to still cover all the rising fish in front of the boat while sitting this way, but credit where it's due, he managed it.

On the next morning – it was a two-day match, with a new boat-partner – I had the exquisite satisfaction of looking at his stricken face, when upon start-up, his outboard motor jumped about three-feet in the air, before plummeting into about twenty-feet of water. "That'll take about half-an-hour to sort out!" I thought to myself. The next thought that popped, unlooked for, into my head was "There is a God!"

You do meet some real nightmarish personalities when competition boat fishing, but I must say some of the finest guys I know, real gentlemen, are competition anglers. The desire to fish matches doesn't make anyone a bad person; no more than a dislike of competition fishing indicates quality of character. There are good and bad in all walks of life and fishing, and I actually look forward to meeting new boat partners, regardless of my experiences.

Sometime soon I'll tell you about ghillies and boatmen. But before then I'll need to expand my range of invective and cuss-words.

The evenings in the bar when the only conversation topic is 'fish'

– 47 –

A New Wave on the Loch

IN MY LIFETIME vast leaps forward in tactics and techniques have been made in almost all branches of flyfishing. The most noticeable exception being loch fishing for sea-trout and salmon. The majority practising this esoteric sport are using techniques which would be immediately recognisable to their great-grandparents.

There are a variety of reasons for this. The most obvious is that there are increasingly fewer places where it goes on. It can be extremely expensive, necessitating accommodation in lodges and hotels tied to the fishing. Runs of migratory fish are steadily declining due to a myriad of factors, prime amongst them being the activities of multinational aquaculture interests along the west coasts of Scotland and Ireland. And the fact that much of it is carried out by visiting anglers who do little other fishing on a yearly basis and take advice from a small number of ageing ghillies usually means that the percentage game is played, with no time for experimentation.

Another factor which must be taken into consideration is that, to a great extent, modern fishermen demand a return on their investment. From the outside looking in, the concept of spending a string of days catching little or nothing, with only a small chance of a red-letter day, is unappealing. Loch fishing needs conditions within a strict set of factors – low light, substantial breeze, optimum water levels and, to a lesser extent, the right wind direction. River fishing for salmon and sea-trout also require these factors to come together, but not to the same extent. It is also harder to read likely holding areas in a loch than in a river. Let's face it, lochs are daunting to those not used to the wide-open vista of water that holds their desired catch.

The occasional visitor should avail himself of knowledge of the loch in question. A guide/ghillie is the most logical choice, but there are pitfalls in this decision. For example, a few years back my fishing partner and I hired a local ghillie. To be fair, he took us to some good spots where we got fish, but for long periods of the day he had us fishing in what looked an ideal location, but which turned out, after a dip subsurface with the rod tip, to be only two-feet deep. I damned near broke the rod tip off as I was expecting somewhere nearer to five-feet than two. However, I must say, in my experience most ghillies are totally reliable.

An electronic depth finder is standard gear – for modern sea-trout fishers in particular. Sea-trout don't necessarily hog the shorelines or shallows, as salmon almost invariably do, and can be a nightmare to locate. They tend to be found in open water, which may well be featureless. I have caught them in depths ranging from five feet down to twenty feet. Don't be confused by the depths. They don't hog the bottom but freely range high in the water over varying depths. If you start picking up fish sign at a specific depth, search other areas for that designated depth and you won't go far wrong. I have never seen a modern day ghillie use such a device, but if they did a few surprises might emerge.

Given all that, there exist small bands of fishermen dedicated to this form of flyfishing, and I am proud to include myself in this hard-working, hard thinking group. We share experiences; we share fly patterns; we share theories. I like to think of it as the 'Loch Salmon & Sea-trout Think-Tank'. I can't speak for them all, but my governing principle is that there is a helluva lot to learn about sea-trout, and better ways to reduce the number of blanks by searching out the means. I firmly believe that most of the discoveries waiting to be made are right in front of us. My thinking is that sea-trout, and to a lesser extent salmon, are attracted by exactly the same things which lure brown and rainbow trout. An extreme example of this was a rainbow-trouter friend to whom I lent my migratory fly box. Of course, he forgot to take it with him and ended up fishing blobs as top dropper candidates and had a very successful trip. Another friend, faced with bright, flat calm conditions reverted to fishing static wet flies and caught some exceptionally fine sea-trout. Dry fly will catch sea-trout on lochs, and static flies, dying in the water (as previously mentioned), will hook sea-trout and salmon. The standard, centuries old, tactic is to fish wet flies on a floating line – although there are good reasons to believe that the old, greased-up, silk lines of the past may be behaving like intermediates by the end of the day. Many tuned-in sea-trout fishers of the modern era prefer intermediate lines of varying sink rates, particularly on southern waters such as

Loch Lomond, and in difficult conditions of light winds and sunshine I happily endorse this tactic.

A hangover from previous decades when fish were much more numerous is to not change flies. Current thinking amongst the LS&ST T-T is to use pattern choice strategies which work for non-migratory trout. In other words, match fly size and colour to the prevailing conditions. Hardly innovative, Kingsmill-Moore discussed this philosophy when he described his choice of bumbles for migratory fish – blue and silver for fresh fish, and claret and gold for staler fish. We have taken things a stage farther and tend to use orange and yellow for bright conditions.

Pattern size has also been reduced, in keeping with a general change in all disciplines across all the UK and Ireland. In my lifetime I have seen a gradual diminution in pattern size throughout all branches of flyfishing. I think this reflects lowering stock levels and improvements in our tackle and techniques, particularly in monofilament diameter. When I first fished for salmon and sea-trout in lochs, 8s and 6s were prevalent. The standard fly sizes are now 10s and 8s. Hugh Falkus stated that "You can't fish too small for salmon or too big for sea-trout!" I would dispute that conclusion. In my experience, flies for loch salmon should be slightly larger than those for sea-trout, but in fairness I should say that Falkus was, by his own admission, no dedicated loch fisherman and his views tend to reflect river experience. For example, whilst salmon fishers on the river in low water conditions may be using minute flies, loch fishers will, more often than not, be utilising patterns three to four times bigger.

It is my belief that both salmon and sea-trout have some sort of memory of feeding at parr stage, and in their non-feeding state of sexual maturity they respond positively to items which resurrect these memories. We have all experienced the disappointment of seeing something which, in our childhood looked enormous and majestic, and to our adult eyes now looks petty and insignificant. To stimulate latent feeding response in 'silver tourists' we have to present them something which isn't inconsequential.

Now, while we are on the subject of flies, there has been great evolution in preferred patterns and styles flies. Traditional patterns such as Teal, Blue and Silver, Grouse & Claret, Bibio, Kate McLaren, Blue Zulu, etc., are still popular with people who don't tie their own flies. However, all my fishing life I have supported the view that for a wet fly to have maximum efficiency there must be lots of mobility in the dressing. The vast bulk of commercially tied wet flies fail in that department. Exaggeration is the key, and that is why I prefer to finish off my flies with a collar of gamebird hackle. They have great inherent movement, and their individual fibre-bulk suits the bigger hook size better than that of hen or cock hackles.

It is generally accepted that muddlers are indispensable, which is a radical change over the past three decades. If you have salmon in your system you would be crazy not to have a muddler on your top dropper – I frequently fish another on the point as well. Standard shop-bought muddlers tend to lack the inherent mobility required. What I tend to do is add muddler heads to proven patterns. This tactic provides a new pattern, one that you can have total faith in, that can augment your armoury. And it works.

For a time, I was dubious about the effectiveness of muddlers for sea-trout. Whist I was totally convinced about muddlers and salmon, there were doubts in my mind as to whether they were a first line of attack for sea-trout. But in the past few years, having nailed down my most rewarding wet flies and then 'muddlerising' them, all doubts have disappeared.

So, what is my philosophy regarding 21st century loch fishing for migratory fish? We must accept that things have radically changed. No longer are there vast numbers of fish in the loch eagerly awaiting our flies. We must adapt accordingly. The positive side of the argument is that modern gear makes our job easier. However, there is a downside to this state of affairs. Modern rods and lines allow longer casting ranges than those available to those of the past. We regularly throw lines distances that would leave our ancestors gaping with disbelief. But I tend to believe that this is rarely an advantage. Previous generations would 'short-line', casting short-range lines – a couple of pulls, a lift, a bob, and back out again. This ensured that the fish rarely saw or were disturbed by a fly-line landing on the water. There is a belief that flies delivered on a floating line will only attract fish over a distance directly related to the length of leader. In other words, when the tail fly has reached the point at which the end of the fly line hits the water the retrieve has become non-productive. I am not totally convinced by this theory, but I do think that when the going is tough, because of, say, lack of a good wave, a quiet approach is essential and, as most observant anglers would agree, the vast majority of fish taken on a floating line come within the first five pulls. But to overcome any disturbance caused by the approach of the boat I tend to chuck a medium-distance fly line, make five pulls whilst raising the rod to the near-vertical, bring the bob-fly to the surface, then re-launch. I call this 'long distance short-lining', it works for me, and also ensures that a taking fish can turn on a relatively slack line, giving the angler good opportunity to set the hook. A low rod-point often results in missed takes and, in the event of a big fish, a high chance of a break-off.

The use of a floating line is not mandatory, of course. As stated above, many prefer intermediates, but I have my doubts about them for salmon. I am convinced that a floating line is vastly superior for this species, and for sea-trout in a good wave.

There is an area of contention which I would be negligent to avoid. Do salmon and sea-trout feed in freshwater? Whilst almost every one of us would heartily agree that salmon do not feed in freshwater situations, I remember very well sitting on a bridge over the River Thurso watching a salmon sipping down hatching olives as they drifted down over his lie. If salmon do not feed in freshwater what was this chap doing? He was *eating* not *feeding*. What's the difference? We *eat* a mint after *feeding* on steak and chips.

Early in this discourse, I mentioned that there are, I believe, individual memories in migratory fish of feeding in freshwater. This I firmly believe is what encourages a migratory fish to take a fly in fresh water. During my time in Orkney I did a lot of sea-trout fishing in the sea. There were two major 'seasons' – spring and autumn. In the spring we hunted feeding fish; in the autumn, by and large, we sought out fish preparing to run from the salt to the fresh. I loved the spring fishing because the feeding fish were easier to target and lure. The autumn fish could be pernickety to the point that they could drive me crazy.

Migratory fish enter freshwater for one reason – breeding purposes. The onset of sexual maturity will, not coincidentally, see the shut-down of feeding instincts. Sea-trout and salmon will *eat* in lochs and rivers, but they will not actively *feed*. And one only has to look at the flies we find successful for them. No-one in their right mind would call them imitative, whilst most would agree that they suggest food, just like the sparkly paper we wrap around sweets.

Well, that just about covers it. It's esoteric flyfishing, and hopefully it will become less so when governments, the public and the salmon farming multi-nationals get their collective act together and protect, preserve and enhance our invaluable migratory fish populations.

FLY PATTERNS FOR ESOTERIC FLY FISHING

Loch Shrimp

Hook: Fulling Mill, Short Shank Special, #8 & #6, or Competition Heavyweight, #10 & #8
Thread: Black
Tail: Hot yellow over red golden pheasant crest
Rib: Medium red wire
Body: Mayo Flycraft flat gold tinsel
Body hackles: Orange & black cock*
Collar hackles: French partridge hackles, West of Ireland Golden Olive (WOIGO) over crimson

Loch Shrimp Muddler

Hook: Fulling Mill, Competition Heavyweight, #10 & #8
Thread: Black
Tail: Hot yellow over red golden pheasant crest
Rib: Medium red wire
Body: Mayo Flycraft flat gold tinsel
Body hackles: Orange & black cock*
Collar hackles: French partridge hackles, West of Ireland Golden Olive (WOIGO) over crimson
Head: WOIGO deer hair

The Loch Shrimp pattern stems from the previously featured Red Lady (see page 243) but differs so much from the original that I have renamed it.

300

It is a 'nod' to the efficacy of shrimp-style patterns on rivers which is not, currently, being addressed by loch patterns for salmon and sea-trout. It has been so successful that it has become indispensable to me - in bright weather I use the muddled version as a top dropper, backed up by the standard (non-muddled) as a point fly; in dull weather I either fish the standard as a middle fly, but more often the muddler as a point fly.

The Clan Goat

Hook: Fulling Mill, Short Shank Special, #8 & #6, or
                 Competition Heavyweight, #10 & #8
Thread: Black
Tail: Hot yellow golden pheasant crest
Tag: No. 5 GloBrite floss
Rib: Medium flat silver (Lagartun)
Body: Black seal's fur
Body hackles: Red & black cock*
Collar hackles: One turn each of blue guinea fowl over
                 black hen, over red guinea fowl

The Clan Goat Muddler

As above: with black deer hair head, on Fulling Mill,
                 Competition Heavyweight, #10 & #8

A cross between a Clan Chief and a Stone Goat, this pattern has been a revelation and I have no idea why. Perhaps it's the dressing elements, which have the basic ingredients of black, red and silver that are the basis for most sea-trout patterns, and copious amounts of movement. Whatever, it is far and away my best sea-trout pattern that, so far, has yet to prove itself on salmon.

I always have the standard version in the middle position if I am fishing it, as it works miracles in this very unfashionable position.

301

The Stone Goat

Hook:	Fulling Mill, Short Shank Special, #8 & #6, or Competition Heavyweight, #10 & #8
Thread:	Black
Tail:	Hot yellow golden pheasant crest
Rib:	Silver wire
Body:	Claret seal's fur
Body hackles:	Claret, dark magenta & black cock*
Collar hackles:	Blue guinea fowl over black hen (or bottle-green peacock body feather – for more 'kick')

Stone Goat Muddler

As above:	with black deer hair head, on Fulling Mill, Competition Heavyweight, #10 & #8

The Stone Goat is slowly building a reputation for itself as a taker of all species of big salmonids.

Originally devised by Mark Hirst for Lochaber ferox, it has comfortably made the transition to the migratory field where it is fast becoming indispensable. Primarily a dull-day, good wave fly, it rarely fails to get a positive reaction.

I always grease-up the standard dressing and, as such, it has taken quite a few sea-trout for me when static on the surface and an even greater number of both salmon and sea-trout when fished as a 'wet' fly. My best ever salmon day on a loch was using the muddled version on Loch Scourst, Amhuinnsuidhe estate.

The Storm Crow

Hook:	Fulling Mill, Short Shank Special, #8 & #6, or Competition Heavyweight, #10 & #8
Thread:	Black
Tail:	Scarlet cock pheasant fibres
Rib:	Silver wire
Body:	Black seal's fur
Body hackles:	Claret & black cock*
Collar hackle:	Natural French partridge

Storm Crow Muddler

As above:	with black deer hair head, on Fulling Mill, Competition Heavyweight, #10 & #8

An interesting story. I was out in South Uist with a bunch of guys a few autumns ago. One of our party (Neil Patterson) was given a fly to try on the understanding that I never saw it - not an uncommon situation. Neil fished it all day on Fada and caught a 10 lb sea-trout on it. I helpfully netted and unhooked the fish. I have a photographic memory. 'Nuff said.

In my experience, the muddled version is a better salmon fly, but one of my buddies would argue this point, and he rarely has it off his cast.

* In small sizes, strip one side of each palmering hackle. In large sizes tie them full.

PICTURE CREDITS

Thanks are extended to the following for allowing the use of pictures featured in this book:

Stan Clementsmith: Page 282

Peter Gathercole (www.petergathercolephotography.com): All fly images and
        pages 2, 16, 69, 71, 104, 116, 208, 288

Colin 'Puck' Kirkpatrick: Pages 129, 144, 167, 214, 218

Vivien Martin (www.vivienmartin.scot): Page 250

Shane O'Reilly: Pages 182, 185

Colin Riach (www.capnfishy.co.uk): Pages 24, 42, 60, 110, 150, 153, 155, 170, 196,
        199, 201, 220, 230, 236, 239, 241, 256, 260, 262, 264, 269, 276, 294

Glyn Satterley (www.glynsatterley.com): Pages 93 and 95

Paul Young: Page 10

Wikimedia Commons:

Page 19 – Brown Trout: Helge Busch-Paulick (Grand-Duc @ Wikipedia) [CC BY-SA 3.0 de (https://creativecommons.org/licenses/by-sa/3.0/de/deed.en)]

Page 132 – Amhuinnsuidhe Castle: LornaMCampbell [CC BY-SA 4.0 (https://creativecommons.org/licenses/by-sa/4.0)]